Good and Evil

Perspectives

to Know

Religion / Philosophers / Voices

From Caodaism to Hitler

DG Reagle, PhD

First Edition Design Publishing
Sarasota, Florida USA

To the spouses of my children

Thomas and Carolina

Thank you for bringing that extra good into the world

Leo, Mia, Cecilia, Oliver and Cooper

Seek good, and not evil, that ye may live: and so the Lord, the God of hosts, shall be with you, as ye have spoken (Amos 5:14).

In memory of

Tao, Buddha, Bella and Jackson

The unconditional love and smiles you provided
over the years will never be forgotten.

Why might it be important to understand these concepts, or are they constructs?

At what level do you consider evil? Genocide? What level is something good? A new baby? Some might say a broken vase or a fresh cup of coffee.

Is the perception of good and evil universal, or does it vary between people and cultures? If it varies, how do we know what is good and what is evil? Our moral compass?

Can good and evil arise solely from human actions, or could there be a metaphysical dimension? Does science play a role?

Is good and evil based on morals? Whose morals?

Reflecting on these questions can help clarify personal views and encourage a deeper exploration of complex perceptions as you read this book. Understanding others can foster unity. While agreement is not necessary, developing an understanding and tolerance of others' beliefs is beneficial.

Developing understanding and tolerance of others' beliefs is essential as it promotes empathy and fosters a sense of community, even among those who may disagree. When we take the time to understand different perspectives, we often discover shared values or common ground that help bridge divides. Tolerance also creates a respectful space for open dialogue, which can reduce conflicts, broaden our perspectives, and lead to personal growth. This approach doesn't require us to change our own beliefs but encourages a mindset that values diversity of thought as a source of strength and resilience.

It is my hope that you not only enjoy this book, but use it often to help learn and grow. I am sure you will find a few surprising entries; I know I did when I was researching. Also, in the back of the book you will find a great bibliography that I highly recommend if you want to learn more regarding a specific religion or person.

Knowledge requires the hand of time.

G. Reagle

A note from the autho

When I began researching for this book
mind. First, I wanted to create a well-orga
that anyone could use to learn, revisit, or qui
on a more personal level, my own curiosity
and gain new insights. Although I often fin
for, they tend to lead to even more questions
evil is one of those BIG questions. For those v
considered one of the fundamental question

Over the past forty-plus years, I've grappl
questions about God, and my explorations h
globe and through the vast reaches of the un
nature of good and evil has been a long jour
peace with my own insights. My conclusion
everyone, but this book is meant to guide yo
answers that resonate with you. I want to er
and interpretations are personal; there is no
answer. What matters is that you find an unde
peace and aligns with what you believe an
with.

Perspectives on good and evil typically aris
spheres: religion/theology, philosophy, and p
While each perspective contains unique a
certain elements to varying degrees. Some v
others may blend aspects from multiple sou
distinct. Ultimately, each perspective is differe

Here are some questions to consider/p
foundation and deepen your understanding of

1. How do you currently define good and e
    examples of each?

2. Do you associate good with things tha
    and evil with things that bring anguish?

3. Can concepts of good and evil exist inde
    other?

4.

5.

6.

7.

8.

Ref
encou
this bo
isn't n
strong

De
benefi
even
under
goals
for c
persp
requir
values

It i
reflec
I kno
will fi
learn

Kn

D.

Good and Evil Perspectives to Know

Religion

Philosopher

Voices

Religion

Amish

The Amish perspective on good and evil is deeply rooted in their Anabaptist Christian beliefs, emphasizing humility, obedience to God, and separation from the world. Their understanding of morality is guided by the Bible, particularly the teachings of Jesus Christ, and shaped by their desire to live a simple, God-centered life.

Perspective with Key Aspects

Good (Obedience, Humility, and Community)

God as the Source of Good: For the Amish, goodness is defined by obedience to God and living according to His will as revealed in the Bible. They see God as the ultimate source of good and believe that aligning their lives with His teachings is the path to righteousness.

Living a Christ-Like Life: Goodness involves imitating the humility, love, and forgiveness exemplified by Jesus Christ. The Amish emphasize the Sermon on the Mount, which teaches values such as meekness, mercy, peacemaking, and loving one's enemies. Acts of kindness, compassion, and forgiveness are central to their understanding of good.

Community and Mutual Aid: Goodness is also expressed through dedication to the community. The Amish value mutual aid, cooperation, and selflessness, often helping one another in times of need. Supporting the well-being of the community is seen as a way to fulfill God's commandments.

Humility and Simplicity: Humility is a cornerstone of Amish life, and they believe that pride and self-centeredness lead to sin. Goodness involves living a simple life, free from materialism and vanity, which allows them to focus on spiritual matters and serving others.

Separation from the World: The Amish believe in remaining separate from the world to avoid being corrupted by its values. They see modern society as promoting materialism, pride, and immorality, which they associate with evil. By living apart from worldly influences, they seek to maintain a life of goodness aligned with God's principles.

Evil (Sin, Pride, and Worldliness)

Sin as the Root of Evil: The Amish view evil as the result of sin, which is disobedience to God's commandments. They believe that humanity is inherently sinful due to the Fall, but individuals are responsible for their choices and must strive to avoid sin.

Pride and Selfishness: The Amish associate pride with evil because it leads people away from humility and submission to God. Pride is seen as the root of many sins, such as greed, vanity, and rebellion against authority.

Worldliness and Modernity: The Amish consider many aspects of modern society to be evil because they believe these influences promote self-indulgence, materialism, and moral decay. They avoid technology, entertainment, and fashion that they see as distractions from a godly life.

Violence and Retaliation: The Amish reject violence and retaliation, viewing them as evil. They are committed to the principle of nonresistance, which means they refuse to fight in wars or seek revenge, instead trusting in God's justice.

Satan as a Deceiver: Like many Christian groups, the Amish believe that Satan is actively working to lead people away from God. Temptations that encourage disobedience, pride, or worldliness are seen as part of Satan's influence.

The Amish Approach to Good and Evil

Free Will and Responsibility: The Amish believe that individuals have free will and are responsible for their moral choices. They are taught to resist sinful behavior and make decisions that align with God's teachings.

Shunning Sinful Behavior: To maintain moral purity, the Amish practice church discipline, including shunning (Meidung) members who persist in sinful behavior. This practice is not intended to punish but to encourage repentance and restoration within the community.

Forgiveness: While they shun sin, the Amish also emphasize forgiveness, even in extreme cases. Their belief in forgiveness as a moral duty was famously demonstrated after the 2006 Nickel Mines school shooting, when the Amish community forgave the perpetrator and reached out to support his family.

Focus on the Eternal: The Amish prioritize their relationship with God and the salvation of their souls over worldly concerns. They believe that by living a life of goodness and obedience to God, they can achieve eternal life in heaven.

Amish Summary	The Amish define good as living in obedience to God, reflecting Christ's humility and love, and contributing to the well-being of the community. Evil is rooted in sin, pride, and worldliness, which separate individuals from God and lead to moral corruption. The Amish seek to live a life of simplicity, humility, and separation from the world to avoid evil and remain faithful to God. They emphasize forgiveness, community support, and nonresistance as key expressions of goodness, trusting in God's ultimate justice and the hope of eternal life.

Atheism

Atheists, like anyone else, can have a wide range of perspectives on good and evil, as atheism itself does not prescribe a specific moral framework. Instead, atheism is simply the lack of belief in deities or gods. Therefore, atheists often derive their views on morality from secular philosophies, ethical theories, and humanistic principles.

Perspective with Key Aspects

Good as Promoting Well-Being and Reducing Suffering

Many atheists adhere to secular humanism, which emphasizes human well-being and the reduction of suffering as central to defining what is good.

- From this perspective, good is often defined as actions or policies that promote human flourishing, happiness, and well-being. This includes practices that enhance the quality of life for individuals and communities and that contribute to the overall health and progress of society.

- Some atheists use ethical naturalism, which suggests that moral values can be derived from human nature and our understanding of the world. According to this view, what is good is often aligned with what supports human development and social cooperation.

Evil as Actions that Harm or Undermine Human Well-Being

In contrast to good, evil is often understood as actions or behaviors that cause harm, suffering, or undermine human well-being and social harmony.

- From this perspective, evil involves actions that inflict unnecessary suffering, harm, or injustice upon individuals or groups. This includes behaviors that violate ethical principles like fairness, empathy, and respect for others' rights.

- Some atheists might embrace moral relativism, the idea that moral judgments are not absolute but are shaped by cultural, historical, and personal contexts. Under this view, what is considered evil can vary between cultures and societies, but the focus remains on actions that cause harm or suffering.

Good and Evil as Products of Human Experience and Reason

Many atheists rely on reason, empirical evidence, and human experience to determine what is good and evil, rather than divine commandments or religious doctrines.

- Actions or principles that are deemed good are often those that align with rational considerations of fairness, justice, and the well-being of individuals. Ethical decisions are made based on evidence and reasoning about what best supports human flourishing and social justice.

- Actions considered evil are those that contradict rational principles of empathy, justice, and respect for others. This includes behaviors that exploit, oppress, or harm others in ways that are recognized as unjust or detrimental.

Moral Frameworks from Secular Philosophies

Atheists might draw from various secular ethical frameworks to articulate their views on good and evil.

- Utilitarianism: This philosophy evaluates actions based on their outcomes, with the goal of maximizing overall happiness and minimizing suffering. For utilitarians, good actions are those that increase overall well-being, while evil actions are those that cause unnecessary harm.

- Deontological Ethics: This framework focuses on adherence to moral rules or duties. Good is defined by following ethical principles and duties, while evil is associated with the violation of these principles.

- Virtue Ethics: This approach emphasizes the development of virtuous character traits. Good is associated with the cultivation of virtues like kindness, honesty, and integrity, while evil is seen in the lack of these virtues.

Humanistic Values and Ethical Principles

Secular humanism and other human-centered philosophies often guide atheists in their understanding of good and evil.

- Good is seen in actions that align with humanistic values such as compassion, empathy, justice, and respect for all individuals. Evil is identified in actions that violate these values and harm human dignity or rights.

- Atheists might use ethical principles such as reciprocity, fairness, and respect for autonomy to determine what is good or evil. These principles guide behavior in ways that promote a fair and just society.

Atheism
Summary

For atheists, good is typically associated with actions that promote human well-being, happiness, and social harmony, and is often defined by principles derived from secular philosophies, reason, and empirical evidence. Evil, conversely, is seen as actions that cause harm, suffering, or injustice, and that undermine human dignity and societal progress. These perspectives rely on human experience, ethical reasoning, and secular moral frameworks rather than religious doctrines.

Baha'i

The Baha'i Faith is a monotheistic religion founded in the 19th century by Baha'u'llah, which emphasizes the unity of all religious teachings, the oneness of humanity, and the importance of universal peace and justice. The Baha'i perspective on good and evil is deeply rooted in its teachings about the nature of God, the purpose of life, and the development of the human spirit.

Perspective with Key Aspects

The Nature of God and Divine Attributes

In the Baha'i Faith, God is seen as the ultimate source of all goodness and the repository of all divine attributes. God's nature is beyond human comprehension, but God's attributes include qualities like justice, mercy, and love.

- Good is aligned with the divine attributes of God. Actions that reflect qualities such as compassion, justice, truthfulness, and service to others are considered good. These actions are seen as fulfilling the divine purpose and reflecting God's nature.

- Evil is understood as the absence or denial of divine attributes. Actions that reflect qualities such as injustice, falsehood, cruelty, or selfishness are considered evil. These actions are seen as contrary to the divine purpose and God's will.

The Baha'i Faith teaches that humans should strive to embody divine attributes in their lives.

The Purpose of Life

The Baha'i Faith teaches that the purpose of life is to develop one's spiritual qualities and to contribute to the betterment of society. This involves personal growth, service to humanity, and the advancement of civilization.

- Good is any action that contributes to spiritual development, the welfare of others, and the advancement of society. This includes acts of kindness, justice, and efforts to promote unity and peace.

- Evil is seen as actions that hinder personal spiritual growth, cause harm to others, or disrupt social harmony. This includes behaviors that are selfish, unjust, or detrimental to the common good.

The goal of life is to align personal actions with the higher purpose of contributing to the well-being and unity of humanity.

Moral and Ethical Behavior

The Baha'i Faith emphasizes the importance of moral and ethical behavior based on principles such as honesty, integrity, and respect for others.

- Good is characterized by adherence to moral principles, such as honesty, fairness, and respect for the rights of others. These principles are seen as essential for creating a just and harmonious society.

- Evil involves moral failings such as dishonesty, exploitation, and disrespect for others. Such behaviors undermine social harmony and individual spiritual development.

Ethical behavior is seen as a reflection of one's commitment to divine teachings and the betterment of society.

The Concept of Free Will and Responsibility

The Baha'i Faith teaches that humans have free will and are responsible for their choices. This free will allows individuals to choose between good and evil and to shape their own spiritual and moral development.

- Good involves making choices that align with divine principles and contribute positively to oneself and others. It is about exercising free will in a manner that reflects divine guidance and ethical standards.

- Evil involves making choices that deviate from divine principles and result in harm or injustice. Misusing free will to pursue selfish or harmful goals is seen as detrimental to one's spiritual progress and social well-being.

Responsibility for one's actions is a key aspect of moral and spiritual development in the Baha'i Faith.

The Role of Education and Spiritual Growth

Education and spiritual growth are highly valued in the Baha'i Faith. The development of intellectual and spiritual capacities is seen as essential for understanding and practicing divine principles.

- Good is associated with pursuing education and spiritual growth that enhances one's understanding of divine teachings and promotes ethical behavior. This includes lifelong learning and personal development.

- Evil is associated with neglecting education and spiritual growth or using one's knowledge and abilities for harmful purposes. Ignorance or the misuse of one's gifts is seen as a barrier to spiritual and moral progress. Education and spiritual development are seen as means to align more closely with divine attributes and principles.

Unity and Justice

The Baha'i Faith emphasizes the principles of unity and justice as foundational to human progress and societal well-being.

- Good involves actions that promote unity, justice, and peace. This includes working towards social justice, equality, and the elimination of prejudice and conflict.

- Evil involves actions that foster division, injustice, and conflict. This includes behaviors that perpetuate inequality, discrimination, and discord.

Promoting unity and justice is seen as essential for creating a more equitable and harmonious world.

The Spiritual Reality of Good and Evil

The Baha'i Faith teaches that good and evil are not absolute entities but are understood in terms of their alignment with divine will and their impact on spiritual development.

- Good is that which aligns with divine will and contributes to the spiritual and moral upliftment of individuals and society. It is seen as part of the divine plan for human development.

- Evil is that which deviates from divine will and obstructs spiritual and moral growth. It is seen as a result of the misuse of free will and contrary to the divine purpose.

Understanding good and evil is linked to recognizing their effects on spiritual growth and societal progress.

The Impact of Actions on Society

The Baha'i Faith places importance on the impact of actions on both individual and societal levels. Actions are evaluated based on their contributions to personal and collective well-being.

- Good is characterized by actions that have a positive impact on both individuals and society, fostering development, unity, and progress.

- Evil involves actions that cause harm or disrupt societal harmony and development.

The impact of one's actions on society is a measure of their alignment with divine principles and moral standards.

The Role of Prayer and Reflection

Prayer and reflection are integral to the Baha'i practice and are used to seek guidance, strengthen one's connection with the divine, and align one's actions with spiritual principles.

- Good involves engaging in prayer and reflection to seek divine guidance, strengthen moral resolve, and ensure that actions are in accordance with divine will.

- Evil can involve neglecting spiritual practices or using them insincerely, leading to misalignment with divine principles and ethical standards.

Prayer and reflection are seen as tools for spiritual alignment and moral clarity.

The Progressive Revelation of Divine Guidance

The Baha'i Faith teaches that divine guidance is revealed progressively through various religious founders or Manifestations of God. Each Manifestation provides teachings relevant to their time while contributing to the unfolding of a unified spiritual truth.

- Good involves recognizing and following the teachings of the Manifestations of God, which guide humanity towards spiritual and moral development.

- Evil involves ignoring or rejecting divine guidance and the teachings that promote spiritual and ethical growth.

Progressive revelation is seen as a continuous process of divine guidance that helps humanity advance towards a higher understanding of truth.

Baha'i Summary

In the Baha'i Faith, good and evil are understood through the lenses of divine attributes, moral and ethical behavior, free will, and the impact of actions on both individual and societal levels. Good is aligned with divine principles, promotes spiritual growth, and contributes to unity and justice. Evil is characterized by actions that deviate from divine will, cause harm, and hinder spiritual and social development. The Baha'i perspective emphasizes the importance of aligning one's life with divine guidance, pursuing education and spiritual growth, and contributing positively to the well-being of humanity.

Buddhism

In Buddhism, the concepts of good and evil are not framed as absolutes dictated by a divine being, but rather as actions and mental states that lead to either suffering or liberation from suffering. The key focus in Buddhism is on understanding the nature of human existence, ethical conduct, and how one's actions affect oneself and others.

Perspective with Key Aspects

Karma: The Law of Cause and Effect

In Buddhism, good and evil are understood through the concept of karma. Karma refers to intentional actions (mental, verbal, and physical) that create consequences. Good actions lead to positive outcomes, both in this life and future lives, while bad actions lead to suffering. Karma is not punishment or reward from a higher power but simply the natural law of cause and effect, shaping the experiences of individuals over time.

- Good karma (wholesome actions) leads to happiness, peace of mind, and ultimately liberation from suffering, known as nirvana.

- Bad karma (unwholesome actions) leads to suffering, confusion, and continued entrapment in the cycle of rebirth (samsara), prolonging one's spiritual journey.

This means that good and evil are not external forces but are determined by the quality of a person's intentions and actions, emphasizing personal responsibility for one's spiritual development.

The Three Poisons: Roots of Evil

Buddhism identifies three fundamental mental states that are the root causes of all unwholesome actions, often referred to as the "Three Poisons" or "Three Unwholesome Roots":

- Greed (Lobha): The desire for material possessions, wealth, pleasure, or control.

- Hatred (Dosa): Feelings of anger, ill will, or aversion toward others.

- Ignorance (Moha): A misunderstanding or lack of awareness about the true nature of reality, particularly the impermanence of all things and the absence of a permanent self (ego).

These mental states lead to actions that harm oneself and others, causing suffering and perpetuating the cycle of rebirth. Overcoming these poisons through ethical behavior, meditation, and wisdom is key to achieving enlightenment (*nirvana*).

Good and Evil as Skillful and Unskillful Actions

Rather than viewing actions as inherently good or evil, Buddhism often speaks of them in terms of being "skillful" (*kusala*) or "unskillful" (*akusala*):

- Skillful actions: Arise from intentions rooted in generosity, love, and wisdom. These actions promote well-being, peace, and spiritual progress.

- Unskillful actions: Stem from the Three Poisons (greed, hatred, ignorance) and lead to suffering for oneself and others.

This approach emphasizes that ethical behavior is based on wisdom and understanding rather than external rules. A person's intentions and mindfulness determine whether an action is skillful or unskillful.

The Noble Eightfold Path: The Way to Goodness

In Buddhism, the path to overcoming evil and cultivating goodness is the *Noble Eightfold Path*, which is the way to liberation from suffering. The path is divided into three categories:

- Ethical Conduct (Sila): Right speech, right action, and right livelihood.

- Mental Discipline (Samadhi): Right effort, right mindfulness, and right concentration.

- Wisdom (Panna): Right understanding and right intention.

By following this path, individuals cultivate good, reduce suffering, and move closer to enlightenment. The emphasis is on self-discipline and mindfulness, which help prevent unskillful actions driven by ignorance, greed, and hatred.

Samsara: The Cycle of Suffering

In Buddhism, *samsara* refers to the cycle of birth, death, and rebirth in which beings are trapped due to their ignorance and attachment. This cycle is characterized by suffering (*dukkha*), and the aim of Buddhist practice is to break free from samsara by eliminating the causes of suffering (ignorance, desire, and hatred). Evil, in this sense, refers to actions and mental states that keep individuals bound in samsara.

The Concept of No-Self (Anatta)

A key difference between Buddhism and many other traditions is the concept of *anatta*, or "no-self." Buddhism teaches that there is no permanent, unchanging soul or self. What we perceive as "self" is a collection of ever-changing mental and physical processes. Understanding this helps to reduce attachment and ego-driven actions, which are the source of unskillful behavior. When people cling to the illusion of a self, they are more likely to engage in harmful actions driven by greed, anger, or ignorance.

Compassion and Loving-Kindness

Goodness in Buddhism is closely tied to *compassion* (*karuna*) and *loving-kindness* (*metta*). These qualities are actively cultivated through meditation and ethical conduct. Compassion is the desire to alleviate the suffering of all beings, and loving-kindness is the wish for all beings to experience happiness and well-being. Goodness, therefore, involves not only refraining from harmful actions but also actively contributing to the well-being of others.

Evil as Suffering, Not Sin

Unlike the concept of sin in some other religions, in Buddhism, evil is understood more as a manifestation of suffering and ignorance rather than moral transgression against a deity. Unskillful actions are driven by misunderstanding the nature of reality, particularly the impermanence of life and the interconnectedness of all beings. The goal is to eliminate suffering by cultivating wisdom and compassion, rather than to avoid punishment for sin.

Mindfulness and Intentions

In Buddhism, the morality of an action is not judged solely by its external appearance but by the intention behind it. Actions motivated by greed, anger, or delusion lead to negative karma, while actions motivated by generosity, love, and understanding lead to positive karma. *Mindfulness* (*sati*) is crucial in determining whether an action is good or evil, as it helps one become aware of their thoughts, emotions, and actions and make conscious choices based on wisdom and compassion.

Enlightenment and the End of Evil

The ultimate goal in Buddhism is the attainment of *nirvana*, which is the end of suffering, the cessation of the cycle of rebirth, and the extinguishing of the Three Poisons (greed, hatred, ignorance). In this state, a person is no longer bound by the duality of good and evil, having transcended worldly attachments and delusions. Achieving enlightenment is seen as the ultimate good, and it marks the end of all actions that perpetuate suffering.

Buddhism Summary

In Buddhism, good and evil are not viewed as fixed absolutes but are understood in terms of actions and mental states that lead to suffering or liberation from suffering. Good actions arise from compassion, wisdom, and mindfulness, while evil actions are driven by greed, hatred, and ignorance. The ultimate goal is to overcome the causes of suffering and achieve enlightenment through ethical conduct, meditation, and wisdom. The concepts of karma and the Noble Eightfold Path provide guidance for making skillful choices that lead to spiritual liberation.

Caodaism

Caodaism (Đạo Cao Đài - Great Way of the Third Time of Redemption) is a syncretic religion founded in Vietnam in 1926. It draws on elements from major world religions such as Buddhism, Taoism, Confucianism, Christianity, Islam, and local Vietnamese spiritual beliefs. The concepts of good and evil in Caodaism are framed within its teachings of spiritual evolution, karma, and the unity of religious ideals.

Perspective with Key Aspects

The Concept of the Divine and the Purpose of Life

In Caodaism, God (Cao Đài) is the supreme being and creator of the universe. The ultimate purpose of life is to return to God through spiritual evolution and self-cultivation. Humanity is seen as having fallen from grace, and the mission is to transcend the physical world and reunite with the Divine. Good is anything that helps individuals progress toward this divine reunion, while evil is anything that impedes this progress and keeps individuals attached to the material world.

- Good aligns with divine principles and helps the soul advance spiritually.

- Evil represents actions, thoughts, and desires that prevent spiritual growth and entrap the soul in materialism and ego.

Karma and Spiritual Progress

Caodaism teaches that karma plays a significant role in determining the spiritual progress of individuals. Karma refers to the law of cause and effect, where good deeds lead to positive outcomes (both in this life and future lives), and evil deeds result in negative consequences.

- Good actions generate good karma, which helps souls move closer to enlightenment and union with God.

- Evil actions create bad karma, which results in suffering, moral decay, and further entrapment in the cycle of rebirth (samsara).

Thus, the accumulation of good karma through virtuous actions, compassion, and adherence to moral teachings is a key aspect of spiritual practice in Caodaism.

Moral Teachings and Virtue

Caodaism emphasizes the importance of moral conduct and the practice of virtues. Caodaists are encouraged to live by the virtues promoted by various religious traditions, including compassion, honesty, humility, and charity. These virtues help individuals live in harmony with others and with the universe.

- Good is the practice of virtues such as kindness, patience, and humility, which foster harmony and peace.
- Evil is the manifestation of negative traits like greed, pride, hatred, and selfishness, which lead to discord and spiritual degradation.

Good and evil, in this sense, are directly tied to how individuals cultivate their moral character and contribute to the well-being of society and the world.

Spiritual Evolution and Enlightenment

In Caodaism, the journey of the soul is one of spiritual evolution. The goal is to achieve enlightenment, escape the cycle of rebirth, and return to the Divine. Each soul is on a path of progression, from lower states of consciousness to higher states of spiritual awareness.

- Good refers to actions, thoughts, and spiritual practices that elevate the soul and bring it closer to enlightenment.

- Evil refers to actions and attitudes that degrade the soul, lead to ignorance, and keep it trapped in the material realm.

Spiritual practices such as prayer, meditation, and service to others are seen as ways to cultivate good and advance spiritually.

The Role of Religion and Religious Unity

Caodaism is unique in its emphasis on the unity of all religions. The founders of Caodaism believed that all the great religious traditions come from the same divine source and lead humanity toward the same goal: spiritual enlightenment and reunion with God.

- Good is understanding and respecting the common truths found in all religions, and using these truths to guide one's spiritual development.

- Evil includes religious intolerance, divisiveness, or actions that lead to spiritual ignorance and conflict.

By recognizing the shared spiritual teachings of different faiths, Caodaism promotes a sense of global religious unity and harmony, which is seen as essential for the progress of humanity.

Detachment from Materialism

Caodaism teaches that the material world is an illusion (similar to concepts found in Buddhism and Hinduism) and that attachment to material wealth, power, or pleasures leads to spiritual stagnation. To progress spiritually, individuals must cultivate detachment from worldly desires and focus on their inner, spiritual life.

- Good is detaching from materialism and focusing on spiritual growth and service to others.

- Evil is becoming overly attached to material wealth, power, or pleasure, which distracts from the soul's true purpose.

Materialism is seen as a major cause of human suffering, and avoiding it is key to achieving spiritual peace.

Balancing the Physical and Spiritual Worlds

While Caodaism teaches detachment from materialism, it also recognizes the importance of living a balanced life. People are encouraged to live virtuously in the physical world while maintaining a focus on spiritual development. This includes fulfilling responsibilities to family, society, and the world.

- Good is maintaining a balance between the material and spiritual aspects of life, living in harmony with nature, and being a responsible and compassionate member of society.

- Evil is imbalance—focusing too much on either material concerns or neglecting one's spiritual duties.

Achieving this balance is key to creating harmony in one's personal life and in society.

Compassion and Service

Caodaism places a strong emphasis on compassion and service to others. Serving humanity is seen as a way to serve God, and acts of compassion and kindness help individuals advance on their spiritual path.

- Good is selfless service, helping others, and acting with compassion and love.

- Evil is selfishness, indifference to others' suffering, and neglecting one's moral duty to serve.

In Caodaism, selfless love and service to others are central to living a virtuous life and contributing to the overall good of humanity.

The Role of Meditation and Prayer

Meditation and prayer are important practices in Caodaism, used to cultivate spiritual awareness, inner peace, and connection with the Divine. These practices help individuals align themselves with higher spiritual forces and transcend the distractions of the material world.

- Good is engaging in regular spiritual practices like meditation and prayer to purify the mind and soul.

- Evil is neglecting spiritual practice, becoming overly distracted by worldly concerns, and allowing the ego to dominate.

By focusing on spiritual practices, individuals can maintain their connection with the Divine and stay on the path toward enlightenment.

The Role of Prophets and Saints

Caodaism teaches that prophets and saints from various religious traditions serve as spiritual guides for humanity. Figures like Jesus Christ, Buddha, Laozi, and Confucius are all revered in Caodaism as enlightened beings who have come to guide souls toward the path of goodness and spiritual awakening.

- Good is following the teachings and examples of these spiritual guides, using their wisdom to cultivate virtue and compassion.

- Evil is rejecting or ignoring the wisdom of the spiritual masters, which leads to ignorance and spiritual degradation.

Caodaism holds that by honoring and following these figures, individuals can progress on their spiritual journey and contribute to the overall good of society.

**Caodaism
Summary**

In Caodaism, good and evil are closely tied to spiritual evolution, karma, and moral conduct. Good is defined as anything that helps individuals grow spiritually, cultivate virtues, and align with divine principles. It includes practicing compassion, detachment from materialism, and service to others. Evil arises from ignorance, selfishness, material attachment, and actions that hinder spiritual growth. Ultimately, Caodaism seeks to unite all religious teachings and promote harmony, love, and spiritual progress for all souls.

Christianity

In Christianity, the concepts of good and evil are deeply intertwined with the belief in God's nature, human free will, sin, and salvation.

Perspective with Key Aspects

God as the Source of Goodness

In Christian theology, God is the ultimate source of all that is good. His nature is perfectly good, loving, and just. Anything that reflects love, justice, kindness, and righteousness is considered good because it aligns with God's character. Goodness is seen as part of God's creation and His plan for humanity.

The Fall of Humanity and the Introduction of Evil

Christianity teaches that evil entered the world through the disobedience of Adam and Eve, the first humans, in the story of the Fall (Genesis 3). Their decision to eat the forbidden fruit, influenced by the serpent (often identified as Satan), led to the introduction of sin, suffering, and death into the world. This event is often referred to as "original sin," and it explains the existence of evil and brokenness in the world. Humanity's nature was corrupted, making people prone to sin, which separates them from God.

The Role of Free Will

Like in Judaism, Christianity holds that humans have free will. People are capable of choosing between good and evil, but due to the fallen nature of humanity, there is a natural inclination to sin. The choice to do good aligns with God's will, while choosing evil is seen as rejecting God's plan and succumbing to selfish desires or temptation.

Sin as Evil

In Christianity, evil is often understood as sin, which is any action, thought, or behavior that goes against God's commandments. Sin manifests in various ways: pride, greed, envy, violence, and idolatry, among others. Evil, in this sense, is a moral wrong that disrupts the relationship between humans and God, as well as between humans themselves.

- Original Sin: The sin inherited from Adam and Eve that marks human nature with a tendency toward evil.

- Personal Sin: Individual acts of disobedience to God's will.

Satan as the Personification of Evil

In Christian belief, Satan (or the devil) represents the ultimate embodiment of evil. Originally an angel who rebelled against God, Satan is portrayed as a tempter and deceiver who seeks to lead people away from God. He is seen as the source of much of the evil in the world, working to oppose God's kingdom by promoting sin and rebellion among humanity.

Jesus Christ as the Source of Redemption

Central to the Christian view of good and evil is the belief in Jesus Christ as the Savior of humanity. Christians believe that through Jesus' life, death, and resurrection, the power of sin and evil is defeated. Jesus is seen as the embodiment of God's goodness, offering forgiveness and salvation to those who repent and place their faith in Him. This redemption allows people to overcome evil, receive God's grace, and be restored in their relationship with God.

The Role of Grace and Redemption

Grace, in Christian theology, is the unmerited favor of God given to humanity. It is through grace that humans can overcome their sinful nature and grow in goodness. While humans are naturally inclined toward sin due to the Fall, God's grace, made available through Christ, enables them to live righteous and good lives. Christians believe that they are not able to fully overcome evil by their own strength but need divine assistance through grace.

The Battle Between Good and Evil

Christianity often views life as a spiritual battle between good and evil forces. This is seen in passages such as Ephesians 6:12, which speaks of the struggle against "the rulers, the authorities, the powers of this dark world, and the spiritual forces of evil." Christians are called to resist evil and live according to the teachings of Jesus, who represents good and triumphs over evil through His sacrifice on the cross.

The End Times and the Defeat of Evil

Christian eschatology (beliefs about the end times) teaches that evil will ultimately be defeated. The Book of Revelation describes a future where Satan and his forces will be destroyed, and God's kingdom of righteousness and goodness will reign forever. This final defeat of evil and the establishment of eternal good is a central hope in Christian faith.

Heaven and Hell

Christianity teaches that after death, individuals are judged based on their faith and moral choices. Heaven is the ultimate reward for those who have followed God's will, a place of eternal goodness and communion with God. Hell, on the other hand, is often understood as the consequence of choosing evil and rejecting God's grace, a state of separation from God's goodness.

Christianity Summary	In Christianity, good is aligned with God's nature, commands, and kingdom, while evil is understood as rebellion against God, rooted

in sin and the influence of Satan. Humans are endowed with free will, allowing them to choose between good and evil. Although sin leads to separation from God, redemption is available through Jesus Christ, whose life and sacrifice offer a path back to goodness and reconciliation with God. Ultimately, Christianity envisions a future where evil is completely vanquished, and God's goodness reigns eternally.

Confucianism

In Confucianism, the concepts of good and evil are deeply tied to ethics, morality, and social harmony. Confucian thought focuses on human relationships, personal development, and fulfilling one's role in society. Good and evil are understood primarily in terms of how individuals behave toward one another, how they cultivate virtues, and how they contribute to the well-being of society as a whole.

Perspective with Key Aspects

Good as Ethical Virtue (Ren)

In Confucianism, the ultimate form of good is embodied in the concept of Ren (often translated as "benevolence," "humaneness," or "goodness"). Ren refers to the ethical quality of being compassionate, kind, and morally upright in one's interactions with others. It is the highest moral principle and the foundation of a good life in Confucian thought.

- Good is the practice of Ren, which involves empathy, respect, and kindness toward others.

- Evil is the failure to act with Ren, which manifests in selfishness, cruelty, or neglect of one's moral duties.

Confucius emphasized that individuals must cultivate Ren in all aspects of life, from family relationships to interactions with society at large.

The Importance of Righteousness (Yi)

Yi (righteousness or justice) is another key virtue in Confucianism. It refers to the moral disposition to do what is right, not for personal gain, but because it is inherently good. Yi guides people to act with integrity, even when faced with difficult choices.

- Good is acting with a sense of justice and righteousness, following moral principles even at personal cost.

- Evil is acting out of selfishness, greed, or dishonesty, particularly when such actions harm others or disrupt social harmony.

A person who embodies Yi is someone who consistently makes decisions based on what is morally right, regardless of external pressures or temptations.

The Role of Li (Rituals and Social Order)

Li refers to the rules of proper behavior, rituals, and customs that govern society. In Confucianism, Li plays a crucial role in maintaining social harmony and order. By following the proper rituals and respecting societal norms, individuals contribute to a harmonious and well-ordered community.

- Good is respecting and adhering to Li, which helps maintain peace, respect, and order in relationships and society.

- Evil is the violation of Li, leading to disorder, disrespect, and conflict.

Li governs not only formal rituals but also everyday interactions, such as how one shows respect to elders or behaves in social settings. Goodness involves internalizing and practicing these customs, while neglecting or breaking them is considered harmful to the moral fabric of society.

Cultivating Virtue (De)

Confucianism teaches that De (virtue or moral power) is essential for personal and social well-being. De is cultivated through self-discipline, reflection, and the practice of virtuous behavior. A virtuous person exerts a positive influence on those around them and contributes to the greater good of society.

- Good is the continuous cultivation of De through personal effort, education, and moral development.

- Evil arises when individuals neglect the cultivation of virtue, acting out of ignorance, laziness, or selfish motives.

Confucius emphasized education and self-cultivation as means to develop one's virtues and moral character.

The Role of Filial Piety (Xiao)

Xiao (filial piety) is one of the most important virtues in Confucianism, referring to the respect and duty that children owe to their parents and ancestors. Filial piety extends beyond family relationships to include respect for elders, authority, and traditions.

- Good is showing deep respect, care, and loyalty to one's family, particularly to parents and ancestors.

- Evil is disrespecting one's family, neglecting responsibilities, or failing to honor one's parents.

Xiao is seen as the foundation for all other virtues. Confucianism holds that by fulfilling one's family obligations, individuals learn how to behave ethically in society as a whole.

Moral Education and Self-Cultivation

Confucianism places great emphasis on moral education as a means to develop good individuals and a harmonious society. Confucius believed that people are not born inherently good or evil but have the potential for both, depending on their education and upbringing.

- Good is the result of proper moral education and the continuous effort to learn and improve oneself.

- Evil arises from ignorance, poor education, or failure to develop one's moral potential.

Confucius believed that anyone could become a virtuous person through learning, self-reflection, and practice. Moral education involves studying the classics, reflecting on one's behavior, and emulating the virtues of wise and ethical individuals.

Social Harmony and Responsibility

In Confucianism, the well-being of society depends on the proper behavior of each individual. Everyone has a role to play in maintaining social harmony (*He*), and the good of the community is prioritized over individual desires. Confucianism promotes the idea that individuals must act in accordance with their social roles (as parents, children, rulers, or citizens) to maintain balance and order.

- Good is fulfilling one's responsibilities and contributing to the harmony and stability of society.

- Evil occurs when individuals act selfishly, causing discord, conflict, or instability.

Rulers, in particular, are expected to lead with virtue and set a moral example for the people. A just and benevolent ruler will inspire good behavior in society, while a corrupt ruler will lead to chaos and disorder.

The Rectification of Names (Zhengming)

One of Confucius's key teachings is the Rectification of Names (*Zhengming*), which means that words and titles must accurately reflect the true nature of things and roles. For example, a ruler must act like a ruler, a parent must act like a parent, and a child must act like a child. Moral confusion and disorder occur when people fail to live up to the responsibilities implied by their roles.

- Good is when individuals act in accordance with their titles and responsibilities, fulfilling their moral obligations.

- Evil is when individuals fail to fulfill their roles, leading to disorder and moral decay.

The Rectification of Names emphasizes the importance of integrity and honesty in social roles.

The Golden Rule

Confucius taught a version of the Golden Rule: "Do not do to others what you do not want done to yourself." This principle emphasizes empathy and reciprocity in human relationships.

- Good is treating others with the same respect and care that you would want for yourself.

- Evil is treating others poorly, without considering their well-being or feelings.

This rule reflects the interconnectedness of individuals in society and the importance of mutual respect and consideration.

Human Nature and Potential

Confucius believed that human nature is fundamentally good, but it requires cultivation through education, reflection, and proper behavior. People have the capacity for both good and evil, depending on how they are raised and how they choose to act.

- Good is realized through education, self-discipline, and the cultivation of virtues.

- Evil arises when individuals neglect their moral duties or fail to cultivate their potential for goodness.

Confucianism is optimistic about human potential and emphasizes the transformative power of education and moral effort.

Confucianism Summary	In Confucianism, good and evil are understood in terms of moral virtue, social harmony, and ethical behavior. Good is defined by the cultivation of virtues like Ren (benevolence), Yi (righteousness), and Li (proper conduct), and by fulfilling one's responsibilities to family and society. Evil arises from selfishness, neglect of duty, and failure to follow moral principles. The focus in Confucianism is on personal development and the positive influence individuals can have on society through ethical living and respect for social norms.

$\mathcal{D}$ruze

The Druze faith is a unique and esoteric religious tradition that originated in the 11th century in the Middle East, primarily in the Levant region. It incorporates elements from Islam, particularly Isma'ili Shi'a Islam, as well as influences from Gnosticism, Neoplatonism, and other philosophical and religious traditions. The Druze perspective on good and evil is deeply intertwined with their beliefs about the nature of the soul, divine providence, and the quest for spiritual enlightenment.

Perspective with Key Aspects

The Concept of Divine Unity (Tawhid)

The Druze faith is centered around the concept of Tawhid, or the absolute unity of God. This principle asserts that God is singular, transcendent, and beyond human comprehension.

- Good is aligned with the divine will and reflects the unity and harmony of creation. Actions that are in harmony with divine principles and contribute to the greater good are considered good.

- Evil involves actions that contradict the divine will and disrupt the harmony and unity of creation. This can include behavior that is deceitful, harmful, or divisive.

The emphasis on divine unity reinforces the idea that good and evil are understood in terms of their alignment with divine principles.

The Role of the Soul and Reincarnation

The Druze belief system includes the concept of reincarnation and the transmigration of souls. According to Druze teachings, the soul undergoes multiple incarnations to achieve spiritual perfection.

- Good is associated with actions and behaviors that contribute to the soul's progression towards enlightenment and ultimate unity with the divine. This includes living a virtuous life, practicing compassion, and seeking spiritual knowledge.

- Evil is associated with actions that hinder the soul's progress, such as unethical behavior, ignorance, and materialism. These actions can lead to negative karmic consequences in future incarnations.

Reincarnation is seen as a process of spiritual refinement and growth.

The Concept of Divine Providence

The Druze believe in divine providence or the idea that God's will governs all aspects of existence. This includes the belief that events and circumstances are part of a divine plan.

- Good is living in accordance with divine providence, accepting the unfolding of events as part of God's plan, and striving to fulfill one's spiritual and ethical duties.

- Evil involves acting in ways that defy or undermine divine providence, such as resisting the natural flow of events, engaging in wrongful behavior, or failing to recognize the divine order.

Acceptance of divine providence is essential for understanding the nature of good and evil.

Ethical Conduct and Moral Responsibility

The Druze faith places significant emphasis on ethical conduct and moral responsibility. Ethical behavior is considered crucial for spiritual development and the well-being of the community.

- Good is characterized by adherence to ethical principles such as honesty, integrity, justice, and compassion. The Druze value moral behavior that reflects divine virtues and contributes to social harmony.

- Evil involves unethical behavior such as dishonesty, injustice, and harm to others. Such actions are seen as contrary to divine principles and detrimental to spiritual and communal well-being.

Ethical conduct is a reflection of one's alignment with divine will and spiritual growth.

The Importance of Knowledge and Wisdom

Knowledge and wisdom are highly valued in Druze teachings. The pursuit of spiritual and philosophical knowledge is seen as a path to understanding divine truths and achieving spiritual enlightenment.

- Good is associated with the pursuit of knowledge, wisdom, and enlightenment. This includes seeking understanding of divine principles, engaging in intellectual and spiritual study, and applying wisdom in daily life.

- Evil is linked to ignorance, the refusal to seek knowledge, and the rejection of spiritual and intellectual growth. Such attitudes can lead to spiritual stagnation and moral shortcomings.

Knowledge and wisdom are crucial for navigating the complexities of life and understanding the nature of good and evil.

The Role of the Druze Faith and Community

The Druze faith emphasizes the importance of community and the role of the Druze religious leadership in guiding spiritual and ethical practices.

- Good is contributing positively to the community, upholding Druze values, and supporting the spiritual and social cohesion of the group. This includes participating in communal rituals, supporting fellow Druze, and fostering a sense of unity.

- Evil involves actions that disrupt community harmony, undermine Druze principles, or harm fellow members. Such actions are seen as detrimental to both individual and communal spiritual progress.

Community involvement and adherence to religious teachings are key aspects of ethical behavior.

Mysticism and Esoteric Knowledge

Druze beliefs include elements of mysticism and esoteric knowledge, which are central to their understanding of the divine and the nature of reality.

- Good is associated with the pursuit of esoteric knowledge and mystical experiences that lead to a deeper understanding of divine truths and spiritual enlightenment.

- Evil is related to ignorance of or resistance to esoteric teachings, as well as actions that hinder spiritual insight and growth.

Mysticism is seen as a means of connecting with the divine and comprehending the deeper aspects of existence.

The Role of Rituals and Practices

Druze rituals and practices are integral to their spiritual life and moral framework. These include ceremonies, prayers, and communal activities that reinforce their ethical and spiritual values.

- Good is engaging in rituals and practices that uphold Druze principles, strengthen spiritual connections, and foster community cohesion.

- Evil involves neglecting or misusing religious rituals, which can lead to spiritual and ethical decline.

Rituals and practices are important for maintaining spiritual discipline and moral integrity.

Druze Summary	In Druze belief, good and evil are understood through the lenses of divine unity, reincarnation, divine providence, ethical conduct, and the pursuit of knowledge. Good involves living in harmony with divine principles, contributing positively to the community, and pursuing spiritual and intellectual growth. Evil is characterized by actions that disrupt divine harmony, ethical conduct, and spiritual development. The Druze faith emphasizes the importance of understanding divine will, practicing ethical behavior, and seeking spiritual enlightenment as central to navigating the concepts of good and evil.

Eastern Christianity

Eastern Christianity, which encompasses various traditions within the Eastern Orthodox, Oriental Orthodox, and Eastern Catholic churches, has a rich and nuanced understanding of good and evil.

Perspective with Key Aspects

Theological Foundation

Eastern Christianity is deeply rooted in the theological teachings of the early Church Fathers and the doctrines of the First Seven Ecumenical Councils.

- Good is understood as the alignment with God's will and the divine nature. It is rooted in the nature of God, who is seen as the ultimate source of all goodness, truth, and beauty.

- Evil is viewed as a distortion or negation of the divine good. It is often understood as the absence or corruption of good, rather than a force or substance in itself.

Nature of Good

In Eastern Christianity, good is closely associated with:

- Goodness is identified with the nature and essence of God. Everything that aligns with God's will, purpose, and nature is considered good.

- Living a life of holiness, following the teachings of Christ, and practicing virtues such as love, humility, and compassion are expressions of goodness.

Nature of Evil

Evil in Eastern Christianity is often understood in the context of free will and moral choices:

- Evil is considered to be a deprivation or perversion of the good. It is not created by God but is a result of free will choosing to deviate from the divine good.

- Evil is often equated with sin, which represents a separation from God and His divine will. This separation causes spiritual death and suffering.

Free Will and Human Responsibility

Eastern Christianity places significant emphasis on free will and human responsibility:

- Human beings are called to exercise their free will in alignment with God's will. By choosing to love, act justly, and live righteously, individuals participate in the divine good.

- Evil arises from the misuse of free will. When individuals choose actions that are contrary to God's will, they contribute to the existence of evil. Responsibility for evil lies in the misuse of human freedom.

Role of Christ and Redemption

The role of Jesus Christ and the concept of redemption are central in Eastern Christianity:

- Christ is seen as the ultimate good, embodying the fullness of divine goodness. His life, death, and resurrection provide the means for humanity to be restored to the divine image and participate in divine goodness.

- Christ's victory over sin and death through His resurrection offers redemption from the power of evil. Through Christ's sacrifice, the consequences of evil are overcome, and believers are given the opportunity for reconciliation with God.

Theological Anthropology

Eastern Christianity has a particular view of human nature and its relation to good and evil:

- Human beings are created in the image of God and are called to reflect divine goodness in their lives. This involves living according to God's commandments and developing virtues.

- The fall of humanity introduced sin and suffering into the world, but this fall is seen as a corruption rather than a fundamental change in human nature. The restoration of goodness is achieved through Christ and the transformative power of grace.

Theosis and Sanctification

The concept of theosis (deification) and sanctification is significant in Eastern Christianity:

- Theosis refers to the process of becoming one with God's divine nature through grace. Living in accordance with divine goodness leads to sanctification and union with God.

- Sin and evil obstruct the process of theosis. They create barriers to achieving unity with God and participating in divine goodness.

Mystical and Sacramental Life

Eastern Christianity places importance on mystical and sacramental aspects of faith:

- Engaging in the sacraments, such as the Eucharist, confession, and baptism, is seen as participating in the divine life and receiving grace that transforms individuals and communities.

- Neglecting the sacraments or living contrary to the teachings of the Church can lead to spiritual harm and separation from the divine. Sacramental life is seen as a means of healing and overcoming the effects of evil.

Ethics and Virtue

Eastern Christianity emphasizes ethical living and the development of virtues:

- Ethical behavior is guided by the virtues outlined in the Scriptures and Church teachings. Living a virtuous life, characterized by love, patience, humility, and justice, reflects divine goodness.

- Immoral actions, vices, and behaviors that deviate from virtue are considered manifestations of evil. Ethical teachings provide guidance for avoiding such behaviors and cultivating a life of goodness.

Eschatological Perspective

The eschatological view of good and evil also plays a role:

- In the eschatological view, ultimate goodness is realized in the final fulfillment of God's kingdom, where divine justice and peace will prevail.

- Evil is ultimately defeated in the eschaton, where God's justice will rectify all wrongs and bring about the final reconciliation and restoration of creation.

Eastern Christianity Summary

In Eastern Christianity, good and evil are understood through the lens of divine nature, free will, and redemption. Good is identified with God's nature, holiness, and the virtues that reflect divine goodness. Evil is viewed as a distortion of good, arising from the misuse of free will and separation from God. The role of Christ, the process of theosis, and ethical living are central to overcoming evil and achieving unity with divine goodness. The eschatological hope promises the ultimate triumph of good over evil.

$\mathcal{F}olk$

Folk religions, or traditional belief systems, often focus on the practical and communal aspects of spirituality, with a strong emphasis on rituals, ancestors, and the natural world. While these religions vary widely across cultures, some common themes can be identified when discussing good and evil in a folk religion context.

Perspective with Key Aspects

Harmonious Living with Nature

Folk religions frequently emphasize living in harmony with nature and the natural order. Nature is often seen as sacred, and maintaining balance with the environment is crucial.

- Good is living in accordance with natural cycles, respecting the environment, and using resources responsibly. This includes practices such as sustainable agriculture, seasonal rituals, and honoring natural spirits or deities.

- Evil is behavior that disrupts natural balance, such as overexploitation of resources, environmental destruction, or disrespect for natural forces.

Folk religions often include practices and taboos designed to maintain ecological balance and respect for the natural world.

Respect for Ancestors

Many folk religions hold ancestors in high regard, believing that they play a significant role in guiding and protecting the living. Ancestor worship or veneration is common, with rituals and offerings made to honor them.

- Good is showing respect and honoring ancestors through rituals, offerings, and maintaining family traditions. This also involves seeking guidance from ancestors and upholding their values.

- Evil is neglecting ancestral rites, disrespecting ancestors, or breaking family and community traditions. This is often seen as causing disfavor or imbalance in one's life.

Maintaining a connection with ancestors is considered essential for ensuring well-being and community harmony.

Community and Social Harmony

Folk religions often emphasize the importance of community and social relationships. Maintaining harmony and fulfilling communal obligations are central to these belief systems.

- Good is engaging in activities that support community well-being, such as participating in communal rituals, helping neighbors, and upholding social norms.

- Evil is behavior that causes discord, conflicts, or harm to others, such as dishonesty, betrayal, or failure to fulfill communal responsibilities.

Social harmony is seen as integral to the health of the community and is often reinforced through communal rituals and practices.

Rituals and Supernatural Beliefs

Folk religions frequently involve rituals and beliefs in supernatural forces, such as spirits, deities, or magical entities. These beliefs shape the understanding of good and evil.

- Good is engaging in rituals that align with spiritual or supernatural expectations, such as ceremonies for protection, fertility, or prosperity. This also includes seeking the favor of spirits or deities through appropriate offerings and actions.

- Evil is failing to perform necessary rituals, engaging in actions that anger spirits or deities, or practicing harmful magic. This can lead to misfortune or supernatural retribution.

Rituals are seen as a way to maintain favor with supernatural forces and ensure positive outcomes.

Moral and Ethical Norms

While folk religions may not have formalized moral codes like those found in major world religions, they often have ethical norms based on tradition, cultural values, and communal consensus.

- Good is adhering to these ethical norms, which might include honesty, hospitality, loyalty, and respect for elders. These norms are often reinforced through storytelling, proverbs, and communal practices.

- Evil is behavior that contradicts these ethical norms, such as deceit, theft, or betrayal. Violations of these norms can lead to social sanctions or spiritual repercussions.

Ethical behavior is guided by traditional wisdom and the need to maintain social and communal order.

Balance and Reciprocity

Many folk religions emphasize the concept of balance and reciprocity in relationships with the spiritual and natural worlds.

- Good involves maintaining balance in one's actions, such as giving back to nature and spirits in proportion to what one receives. This can include offerings, rituals, and acts of gratitude.

- Evil is imbalance or failure to reciprocate, such as taking from nature or spirits without giving back, which is believed to disrupt harmony and invite misfortune.

Reciprocity is essential for maintaining favorable relationships and ensuring balance in life.

Healing and Protection

Folk religions often have specific practices for healing and protection against harm, which are integral to their understanding of good and evil.

- Good involves using healing practices and protective rituals to ensure health and safety, such as herbal remedies, amulets, or protective charms.

- Evil can involve harmful practices or malicious intent, such as curses, black magic, or acts of witchcraft intended to cause harm.

Healing and protection are seen as ways to safeguard individuals and the community from negative influences.

Spiritual Purity and Impurity

The concepts of purity and impurity are often significant in folk religions, affecting daily practices and rituals.

- Good is maintaining spiritual and ritual purity through proper conduct, cleanliness, and adherence to religious practices.

- Evil involves acts or conditions that lead to spiritual or ritual impurity, such as violating taboos or engaging in prohibited activities.

Purity and impurity are linked to the ability to participate in rituals and maintain spiritual favor.

Traditional Wisdom and Oral Tradition

Folk religions rely heavily on oral traditions and communal wisdom passed down through generations.

- Good is preserving and passing on traditional knowledge, stories, and practices that uphold communal values and beliefs.

- Evil is the loss or distortion of traditional knowledge, which can lead to cultural erosion and disconnection from ancestral wisdom.

Maintaining and respecting traditional wisdom is crucial for the continuity and integrity of folk religious practices.

Cultural and Historical Context

Folk religions are deeply embedded in the cultural and historical contexts of their communities, and their concepts of good and evil are shaped by these contexts.

- Good is behavior and practices that align with the cultural norms, values, and historical experiences of the community.

- Evil involves actions that disrupt or conflict with these cultural and historical contexts.

Understanding good and evil requires an appreciation of the specific cultural and historical background of the folk religion.

**Folk
Summary**

In folk religions, good and evil are often understood through the lenses of natural harmony, ancestor veneration, community well-being, ritual practices, and ethical norms. Good is associated with living in balance with nature, respecting ancestors, fulfilling communal duties, and adhering to traditional wisdom. Evil is linked to disrupting natural balance, neglecting ancestral rites, causing social discord, and violating ethical norms. Folk religions emphasize practical, communal, and spiritual aspects of life, with a strong focus on maintaining harmony and reciprocity with the natural and spiritual worlds.

God

Explaining good and evil from God's perspective involves understanding how different religious and theological traditions conceive of God's nature and how it informs their definitions of moral concepts. While interpretations vary widely across different faiths, there are some common themes that can be addressed.

Perspective with Key Aspects

Good as Divine Will and Nature

In many religious traditions, good is defined as that which aligns with God's will and nature.

- Good is often seen as that which is in accordance with God's divine will and commandments. In Christianity, for example, God's laws and teachings (as revealed in the Bible) are viewed as the ultimate standard for what is good. Goodness is understood as living in accordance with these divine principles and fulfilling God's intentions for humanity.

- In theological terms, good is also understood as that which reflects God's intrinsic nature. For instance, in many traditions, God is characterized by attributes such as love, justice, mercy, and truth. Actions and behaviors that embody these divine attributes are considered good. Thus, good aligns with God's essential qualities and character.

Evil as Rebellion or Separation from God

Evil is often conceptualized as rebellion against God or separation from divine will and goodness.

- In many religious traditions, evil is seen as a form of rebellion or defiance against God's will. This perspective is particularly prominent in Christianity, where sin is understood as disobedience to God's commandments. The story of Adam and Eve's fall in the Garden of Eden is often cited as an example of humanity's rebellion against God.

- Evil is also understood as a separation from or distortion of God's goodness. For example, in some theological frameworks, evil arises when creatures or humans act in ways that deviate from the divine order and harmony established by God. This separation leads to suffering and moral corruption.

Moral Order and Divine Justice

God's perspective on good and evil often includes considerations of moral order and divine justice.

- Many religious traditions believe that God has established a moral order or natural law that defines what is good and evil. Living in accordance with this order is seen as good, while actions that disrupt or violate it are considered evil.

- The concept of divine justice involves the belief that God ensures that good is ultimately rewarded and evil is punished. This may be understood in terms of divine retribution, moral consequences, or the eventual establishment of justice in the afterlife.

Human Free Will and Moral Responsibility

From God's perspective, human free will and moral responsibility play crucial roles in the dynamics of good and evil.

- Many theological traditions hold that God has granted humans free will, allowing them to choose between good and evil. This freedom is essential for moral responsibility, as it enables individuals to make genuine ethical choices and to develop virtues or vices.

- With free will comes the responsibility to act according to moral principles and divine guidance. Individuals are accountable for their choices and actions, which means that their decisions contribute to the unfolding of good and evil in the world.

Redemption and Reconciliation

The concept of redemption and reconciliation is often central to understanding evil from God's perspective.

- Many religious traditions teach that despite the presence of evil, God offers a path to redemption and forgiveness. This often involves repentance, transformation, and a return to alignment with God's will. In Christianity, the life and sacrifice of Jesus Christ are seen as providing the means for redemption and overcoming evil.

- God's perspective may also include the ultimate reconciliation of all things. Some theological views suggest that God's plan involves addressing the problem of evil and restoring harmony and goodness in the end times or through divine intervention.

God Summary	From a theological perspective, good is generally defined as that which aligns with God's will and divine nature, reflecting attributes

such as love, justice, and mercy. Evil is often seen as rebellion against God or separation from divine goodness, resulting in moral corruption and suffering. God's perspective on good and evil involves considerations of moral order, divine justice, human free will, and the possibility of redemption and reconciliation. The specifics of these concepts vary across different religious traditions, but they commonly emphasize the alignment of human actions with divine principles and the ultimate resolution of evil through divine justice and grace.

Hinduism

In Hinduism, the concepts of good and evil are multifaceted and deeply interwoven with its diverse philosophical and theological teachings. Hinduism encompasses a wide range of beliefs and practices, but several core ideas are central to understanding good and evil within this tradition.

Perspective with Key Aspects

Dharma: The Principle of Righteousness

Dharma refers to the moral and ethical duties or laws that govern individual conduct and societal norms. It represents the principle of righteousness and is considered fundamental to living a virtuous life.

- Good is aligned with dharma, which involves fulfilling one's duties and responsibilities according to one's role in society (such as a parent, teacher, or leader) and adhering to ethical conduct.

- Evil occurs when one acts against dharma, engaging in actions that are unjust, unethical, or harmful to others.

Dharma provides a framework for understanding what is right and just in various contexts, emphasizing the importance of balance and duty.

Karma: The Law of Cause and Effect

Karma is the principle of cause and effect, where every action has consequences that affect one's future. Good actions lead to positive outcomes and spiritual progress, while bad actions lead to negative consequences and spiritual regression.

- Good actions generate positive karma, leading to beneficial effects and spiritual growth in this life or future lives.

- Evil actions create negative karma, resulting in suffering and difficulties in this life or future lives.

Karma underscores the interconnectedness of actions and consequences, encouraging ethical behavior and personal responsibility.

Maya: The Concept of Illusion

Maya refers to the illusion or appearance of the material world that distracts individuals from the ultimate reality (Brahman). It represents the veil that obscures the true nature of existence.

- Good involves recognizing and transcending the illusions of maya, seeking spiritual enlightenment, and understanding the true nature of reality.

- Evil is associated with being overly attached to the illusions of the material world, leading to ignorance and suffering.

Understanding maya helps in distinguishing between transient desires and eternal truths, guiding individuals toward spiritual liberation.

The Role of Deities and Divine Principles

Hinduism includes a rich pantheon of deities, each embodying various aspects of the divine. Different deities personify different virtues and moral principles.

- Good can be seen in the qualities represented by deities such as Vishnu (preserver and protector), Lakshmi (goddess of wealth and prosperity), and Saraswati (goddess of wisdom and learning).

- Evil can be associated with demonic figures or asuras, who embody negative qualities such as chaos, deceit, and harm.

Deities serve as models for virtuous behavior and spiritual ideals, while their opposites represent forces that disrupt harmony and order.

Moral and Ethical Teachings

Hindu scriptures, such as the Vedas, Upanishads, Bhagavad Gita, and Mahabharata, provide moral and ethical guidelines for righteous living. These teachings emphasize virtues such as compassion, truthfulness, non-violence, and self-discipline.

- Good is characterized by virtues such as ahimsa (non-violence), satya (truthfulness), and asteya (non-stealing), which contribute to a harmonious and just society.

- Evil involves vices such as violence, dishonesty, greed, and hatred, which create discord and suffering.

These ethical teachings guide individuals in their personal conduct and interactions with others.

Bhakti and Devotion

Bhakti refers to devotion and love toward a personal deity. In Hinduism, devotion to God is considered a path to spiritual liberation and the ultimate realization of divine truth.

- Good is expressed through sincere devotion, love, and worship of the divine, leading to spiritual enlightenment and liberation.

- Evil can be seen in the rejection of divine guidance, neglect of spiritual practice, and pursuit of ego-driven desires.

Devotion fosters a deep connection with the divine and helps individuals align their actions with spiritual principles.

The Cycle of Birth and Rebirth (Samsara)

Hinduism teaches that life is a continuous cycle of birth, death, and rebirth known as samsara. The actions of individuals (karma) determine their future rebirths and experiences.

- Good actions contribute to positive karma, leading to better rebirths and the eventual liberation (moksha) from the cycle of samsara.

- Evil actions lead to negative karma, resulting in more suffering and further cycles of rebirth.

The ultimate goal is to break free from samsara and attain moksha, the liberation from the cycle of birth and rebirth.

Moksha: Liberation from the Cycle

Moksha is the ultimate goal in Hinduism, representing liberation from the cycle of samsara and union with Brahman, the ultimate reality. Achieving moksha involves overcoming ignorance and realizing one's true nature.

- Good is the pursuit of moksha through righteous living, self-realization, and spiritual practice.

- Evil is living in ignorance and attachment to the material world, preventing spiritual progress and perpetuating suffering.

Moksha signifies the ultimate state of spiritual freedom and realization of divine unity.

The Concept of Svadharma

Svadharma refers to one's personal duty or the ethical path suited to an individual's role, nature, and stage in life. Following one's svadharma is considered crucial for living a righteous life.

- Good involves fulfilling one's svadharma with integrity and dedication, contributing to personal and social harmony.

- Evil occurs when individuals neglect or violate their svadharma, leading to moral and social disruption.

Adhering to svadharma helps maintain balance and righteousness in both personal and social contexts.

The Balance of Forces: Dharma and Adharma

Hinduism recognizes the interplay of dharma (righteousness) and adharma (unrighteousness). The universe is seen as being in a dynamic balance between these forces, and maintaining this balance is essential for cosmic order.

- Good is maintaining the balance of dharma, upholding righteousness and justice.

- Evil involves the proliferation of adharma, leading to disorder and suffering.

The balance of dharma and adharma reflects the ongoing struggle between positive and negative forces in the world and the necessity of upholding ethical and moral principles.

Hinduism Summary

In Hinduism, good and evil are understood through a complex interplay of moral principles, cosmic order, and spiritual development. Good is aligned with dharma, ethical virtues, and spiritual practices that lead to karma, enlightenment, and liberation. Evil is associated with actions that disrupt dharma, generate negative karma, and hinder spiritual progress. Hinduism emphasizes personal responsibility, devotion, and adherence to divine principles as pathways to righteousness and spiritual fulfillment.

Islam

In Islam, the concepts of good and evil are foundational to understanding human responsibility, the nature of life, and the relationship between humans and Allah (God).

Perspective with Key Aspects

Allah as the Source of Good

In Islam, Allah is the ultimate source of all goodness. Everything that is morally right, just, compassionate, and beneficial comes from Allah. He is described in the Qur'an as *Ar-Rahman* (The Most Merciful) and *Al-Adl* (The Just), meaning that His actions and decrees are inherently good and just.

Human Free Will and Moral Responsibility

Like in Christianity and Judaism, Islam emphasizes that humans have free will to choose between good and evil. This is a key aspect of Islamic theology. Allah has provided humans with guidance through revelation (the Qur'an) and the example of the Prophet Muhammad (peace be upon him) to help them make the right choices.

Human beings are responsible for their actions and will be judged by Allah based on their choices. This responsibility is seen as a test, with the world serving as a place where humans' moral and spiritual character is developed.

Good and Evil as Defined by Allah's Will

In Islam, good and evil are not arbitrary but are defined by Allah's will. What is good is that which aligns with Allah's commands and pleases Him, while evil is anything that goes against His will. These commands are communicated through the Qur'an and the Sunnah (traditions and practices of the Prophet Muhammad).

Good includes acts like:

- Worshiping Allah alone (*Tawhid* or monotheism)
- Performing righteous deeds (charity, kindness, honesty)
- Observing justice and fairness
- Protecting life and property

Evil includes acts like:

- Associating partners with Allah (*shirk*, which is idolatry or polytheism)
- Engaging in sin (injustice, theft, lying, oppression)
- Transgressing the limits set by Allah

Fitnah: The Test of Life

Islam teaches that life is a test of faith and morality. Allah tests individuals with both good and evil to see how they respond. Surah Al-Mulk (67:2) states: *"He who created death and life to test you as to which of you is best in deed."*

This test is an opportunity for people to choose good over evil, and success in this test determines one's fate in the afterlife.

Nafs (The Self) and the Struggle Between Good and Evil

Islam emphasizes the internal struggle within every person between good and evil, referred to as *jihad an-nafs* (the struggle of the self). The human soul (*nafs*) can incline toward either good or evil, depending on its moral state. There are three types of *nafs* mentioned in Islamic teachings:

- Nafs al-Ammarah: The commanding self, which inclines toward evil and desires sinful actions.

- Nafs al-Lawwama: The reproaching self, which feels guilt and remorse for sinful actions.

- Nafs al-Mutma'innah: The peaceful or satisfied self, which is aligned with righteousness and good deeds.

The purpose of life in Islam is to purify the soul by resisting sinful inclinations and striving to do good.

Shaytan (Satan) and Evil

In Islam, Shaytan (Satan) is the primary instigator of evil and misguidance. He is considered a jinn who refused to bow to Adam and was cast out of paradise. Shaytan's goal is to lead humans astray from the path of Allah by tempting them toward sin and rebellion against God.

However, Shaytan does not have absolute power. He can only suggest or tempt, but humans have the ultimate choice to resist his influence by following Allah's guidance. In Surah Ibrahim (14:22), Shaytan admits that he merely called people to evil, and they followed by their own choice.

Sin (Dhanb) and Repentance (Tawbah)

In Islam, sin is the act of going against Allah's commands, which is seen as evil. Every human being is prone to sin, but Islam emphasizes the importance of repentance (*tawbah*). Allah is described as *At-Tawwab* (The Acceptor of Repentance) and *Al-Ghaffar* (The Forgiving). Sincere repentance, accompanied by a determination not to repeat the sin, can lead to forgiveness from Allah, showing that evil acts do not permanently sever one's relationship with Him.

Justice and Divine Wisdom

Islam teaches that Allah's wisdom encompasses all things, even when humans don't understand why evil or suffering exists. Evil in the world is seen as part of Allah's greater plan, and it serves various purposes, including testing human character, allowing for the development of virtues like patience and resilience, and differentiating between the righteous and the wicked.

Islamic teachings hold that ultimate justice will be meted out in the afterlife. Those who do good will be rewarded with paradise (*Jannah*), while those who persist in evil without repentance may face punishment in hell (*Jahannam*). This concept underscores that, even if justice seems delayed in this life, it will be fully realized in the hereafter.

Commanding Good and Forbidding Evil

One of the duties of a Muslim is to promote good and forbid evil (*Amr bil Ma'ruf wa Nahi anil Munkar*). This means that Muslims are encouraged to create a just society by helping others to follow the path of goodness and preventing wrongs when they see them. This concept is tied to the idea of collective responsibility within the Muslim community (*ummah*).

The Afterlife: Reward and Punishment

Islam teaches that life on earth is temporary, and the ultimate judgment of good and evil will occur in the afterlife. People will be held accountable for their actions on the Day of Judgment (*Yawm al-Qiyamah*). Those who have followed the path of good, worshipped Allah, and done righteous deeds will be rewarded with eternal life in paradise, while those who chose evil and rejected faith will face punishment in hell.

**Islam
Summary**

In Islam, good is defined as that which aligns with Allah's will and guidance, while evil is anything that goes against it. Humans, endowed with free will, are tested in life to see if they will choose good over evil, following the

teachings of the Qur'an and
the Prophet Muhammad. Evil
is often associated with sin,
the influence of Shaytan, and
the desires of the lower self
(nafs), but Islam also
emphasizes repentance and
the mercy of Allah.
Ultimately, Islam envisions a
final judgment where good is
rewarded and evil is
punished in the afterlife.

Jainism

In Jainism, the concepts of good and evil are deeply rooted in the principles of non-violence (ahimsa), non-possessiveness (aparigraha), and the pursuit of spiritual liberation (moksha). Jainism offers a unique perspective on morality and ethics based on its distinctive beliefs about the nature of the soul and the universe.

Perspective with Key Aspects

Ahimsa (Non-Violence)

Ahimsa is the cornerstone of Jain ethics and philosophy. It represents non-violence in thought, word, and action.

- Good is defined as actions, thoughts, and speech that avoid causing harm to any living being. This includes practicing kindness, compassion, and respect towards all forms of life.

- Evil involves causing harm or suffering to others, whether intentionally or unintentionally. This can include physical violence, verbal abuse, and even actions that harm others indirectly.

Ahimsa extends to all living beings, and the principle encourages the reduction of harm to the minimum possible level.

Aparigraha (Non-Possessiveness)

Aparigraha refers to non-attachment and non-possessiveness. It emphasizes limiting desires and material possessions.

- Good is characterized by simplicity, contentment, and the avoidance of excessive attachment to material things. Practicing aparigraha helps in reducing greed and fostering a more harmonious and balanced life.

- Evil is associated with excessive attachment, greed, and the accumulation of possessions. This can lead to exploitation, conflict, and suffering for oneself and others.

Aparigraha promotes detachment from materialistic pursuits and encourages a focus on spiritual and ethical growth.

Karma and Its Effects

In Jainism, karma is seen as a form of spiritual pollution that affects the soul's journey towards liberation. Every action generates karma, which binds the soul to the cycle of birth and rebirth (samsara).

- Good actions are those that generate positive karma by adhering to principles like non-violence, truthfulness, and self-discipline. Such actions help purify the soul and lead towards spiritual liberation.

- Evil actions create negative karma, binding the soul further into samsara. Actions that are violent, deceitful, or greedy contribute to the accumulation of negative karma and hinder spiritual progress.

Understanding and managing karma is essential for achieving spiritual purity and liberation.

The Five Great Vows (Mahavratas)

The Five Great Vows are central to Jain monastic life and include non-violence, truthfulness, non-stealing, celibacy, and non-possessiveness.

- Good is living according to these vows, which guide ethical and moral behavior. These vows help in cultivating virtues and reducing negative karmic influences.

- Evil involves violating these vows, leading to the accumulation of negative karma and spiritual degradation.

Adhering to these vows supports the path to spiritual purity and liberation.

The Concept of Anekantavada (Non-Absolutism)

Anekantavada is the Jain doctrine of non-absolutism, which acknowledges the complexity and multiple perspectives of truth.

- Good is recognizing the diversity of viewpoints and practicing tolerance and understanding. This includes avoiding dogmatism and embracing a more nuanced view of ethical and moral issues.

- Evil is holding rigid, absolutist views that dismiss the complexity of reality and the validity of different perspectives. This can lead to intolerance and conflict.

Anekantavada promotes a balanced and inclusive approach to understanding truth and morality.

Self-Discipline and Spiritual Practice

Jainism places significant emphasis on self-discipline and spiritual practices to overcome desires and attachments.

- Good is engaging in practices such as meditation, fasting, and self-restraint to purify the soul and reduce the influence of karma. These practices help in developing inner peace and ethical behavior.

- Evil is neglecting spiritual practices and indulging in desires and attachments that bind the soul further to samsara.

- Self-discipline and spiritual practices are essential for achieving spiritual progress and liberation.

The Role of Compassion (Karuna)

Karuna refers to compassion and empathy towards all living beings.

- Good is demonstrating compassion and kindness in actions, words, and thoughts. This involves actively seeking to alleviate the suffering of others and practicing empathy.

- Evil is lacking compassion or causing suffering to others, either intentionally or through neglect.

Compassion is integral to living a virtuous life and aligns with the principle of ahimsa.

Avoiding Harmful Actions (Violence and Deceit)

Jainism specifically condemns actions that are harmful or deceitful.

- Good involves avoiding violence and deceit, including being honest and transparent in interactions and refraining from actions that could cause harm to others.

- Evil involves engaging in violent or deceitful actions, which contribute to the accumulation of negative karma and hinder spiritual growth.

Avoiding harm and deceit aligns with Jain ethical principles and supports the path to liberation.

Detachment from Ego and Self

Jainism teaches the importance of transcending the ego and personal identity.

- Good is letting go of ego-driven behaviors and focusing on the welfare of others. This includes practicing humility and reducing self-centeredness.

- Evil is being driven by ego and selfish desires, which lead to conflict and suffering.

Transcending ego is crucial for achieving spiritual purity and understanding the true nature of the self.

The Goal of Liberation (Moksha)

The ultimate goal in Jainism is achieving moksha, or liberation from the cycle of birth and rebirth.

- Good is pursuing actions and practices that lead towards moksha, such as adhering to ethical principles, purifying the soul, and gaining spiritual knowledge.

- Evil is engaging in actions that hinder spiritual progress and perpetuate the cycle of samsara.

The pursuit of moksha involves aligning one's life with Jain ethical principles and spiritual practices.

Jainism Summary	In Jainism, good and evil are understood through the lens of non-violence (ahimsa), non-possessiveness (aparigraha), and the impact of karma. Good involves living ethically according to

Jain principles, practicing compassion, avoiding harm, and pursuing spiritual liberation. Evil involves actions that cause harm, create negative karma, and hinder spiritual progress. Jainism emphasizes the importance of self-discipline, understanding the impermanent nature of life, and striving for spiritual purity and liberation.

Jehovah's Witnesses

The Jehovah's Witness perspective on good and evil is grounded in their interpretation of the Bible and their understanding of God's will. Central to their beliefs are themes of loyalty to Jehovah (God), obedience to His commands, and the role of Satan in bringing evil into the world. Their worldview emphasizes a cosmic struggle between good and evil, with the ultimate triumph of good through God's Kingdom.

Good (Obedience to Jehovah and His Will)

- For Jehovah's Witnesses, good originates from Jehovah, the Creator of the universe. They believe that God embodies absolute goodness, love, justice, wisdom, and power. Anything aligned with His character and purposes is considered good.

- Goodness is demonstrated by obedience to Jehovah's laws and principles as outlined in the Bible. This includes living a morally upright life, showing love and compassion to others, and remaining loyal to Jehovah. Actions that promote harmony, righteousness, and justice are seen as good because they reflect Jehovah's qualities.

- Living According to Bible Principles, Jehovah's Witnesses strive to live according to biblical principles in all aspects of life, including honesty, modesty, chastity, and integrity. For example:

Showing love and forgiveness reflects God's love.

Engaging in evangelism and sharing Bible teachings is considered a good and essential duty.

Practicing self-control and avoiding harmful behaviors, such as substance abuse or greed, aligns with the good.

- Goodness also involves loyalty to God's Kingdom, the heavenly government led by Jesus Christ, which Jehovah's Witnesses believe will soon replace all human governments and bring about a righteous, peaceful world.

Evil (Rebellion Against Jehovah and His Standards)

- Jehovah's Witnesses believe that evil originated with Satan the Devil, a former angel who rebelled against Jehovah. Satan is seen as the primary adversary of God, responsible for introducing sin, suffering, and death into the world. His rebellion began with a lie in the Garden of Eden, leading Adam and Eve to disobey Jehovah.

- Because of Adam and Eve's disobedience, sin and death entered the world, affecting all of humanity. Jehovah's Witnesses view sin as the root cause of evil actions, as it leads people away from Jehovah's standards. Humans are inherently imperfect due to their inherited sinfulness, making them prone to wrong choices and behaviors.

- Evil is also defined as any action or attitude that opposes Jehovah's sovereignty and standards. This includes willful disobedience to His commands, engaging in immoral or harmful behaviors, and supporting worldly systems that are under Satan's influence.

- Jehovah's Witnesses believe that Satan is actively working to mislead humanity through false religion, materialism, immorality, and political systems. They view the world as being largely under Satan's control, making it a place where evil often prevails.

The Cosmic Struggle Between Good and Evil

- Jehovah's Witnesses see the core issue of good and evil as a question of sovereignty: Who has the right to rule—Jehovah or Satan? Satan's rebellion challenged Jehovah's sovereignty, and the current world serves as a test case to demonstrate the consequences of rejecting God's rule.

- God's Allowance of Evil: Jehovah's Witnesses believe that Jehovah has temporarily allowed evil to exist to settle the question of His sovereignty and to allow humans and angels to witness the outcomes of rebellion. However, they emphasize that Jehovah is not the source of evil and that He will ultimately eliminate it.

- Jehovah's Witnesses believe that Jehovah will soon bring about the battle of Armageddon, where He will destroy Satan, his demons, and all human systems under their influence. Afterward, evil will be eradicated, and Jehovah's righteous rule will be established on Earth, bringing eternal peace and goodness.

Moral Responsibility and Free Will

- Free Will and Accountability: Jehovah's Witnesses teach that humans have the gift of free will, allowing them to choose between good and evil. They believe that Jehovah desires individuals to serve Him willingly, out of love rather than compulsion. However, with free will comes accountability, and those who choose evil will face consequences.

- Jehovah's Witnesses emphasize the importance of avoiding evil influences, such as immoral entertainment, bad associations, or practices that go against biblical teachings. They believe that staying spiritually alert and loyal to Jehovah protects them from being misled by Satan.

Hope for the Future

- Jehovah's Witnesses believe that the ultimate expression of good will come through God's Kingdom, which will restore the Earth to its original paradise condition. In this new world, suffering, death, and evil will be eliminated, and humanity will live in perfect harmony with Jehovah's will.

- Jehovah's Witnesses also hold out hope for the resurrection of the dead. Those who have died will have the opportunity to live in a righteous world and to learn Jehovah's ways, further demonstrating His goodness and justice.

Jehovah's Witnesses Summary	From the perspective of Jehovah's Witnesses, good is defined as loyalty to Jehovah, adherence to His commands, and living in harmony with His purpose. Evil originates from Satan, who rebelled against God and brought sin, suffering, and death into the world. Humans, influenced by inherited sin and Satan's systems, are prone to evil,

but they have the free will to
choose good by obeying
Jehovah and following
biblical principles. Jehovah's
Witnesses view the current
world as a temporary
battleground in a cosmic
struggle between good and
evil, with the ultimate victory
of good coming through
God's Kingdom, which will
establish a perfect, righteous
world free from all evil.

Judaism

In Judaism, the concepts of good and evil are deeply rooted in the understanding of *free will* and *moral responsibility*, framed within the relationship between humans and God.

Perspective with Key Aspects

Good and Evil as Choices

In Jewish thought, good and evil are not external forces or beings (like a devil or anti-God figure). Instead, they are seen as *choices* that humans must make. Humans are endowed with free will, meaning they can choose between following God's commandments (good) or rejecting them (evil). This ability to choose is central to human moral responsibility.

Inclination Towards Good and Evil (Yetzer HaTov and Yetzer HaRa)

Judaism teaches that every person has two moral inclinations:

- Yetzer HaTov: The inclination to do good, to act ethically, and to follow God's will.

- Yetzer HaRa: The inclination to do evil or act selfishly. Yetzer HaRa is not seen as inherently bad but as a natural human drive, often associated with self-preservation, material desires, and personal gain.

These inclinations are often in tension with each other, and the purpose of life is to harness Yetzer HaRa for constructive purposes, such as ambition or survival, while allowing Yetzer HaTov to guide moral choices.

Mitzvot (Commandments) as a Path to Goodness

In Judaism, good is closely associated with fulfilling the commandments (*mitzvot*) given by God in the Torah. Observing these commandments leads to a life of righteousness and harmony with God's will. Evil, on the other hand, is understood as straying from these commandments and pursuing selfish or harmful behaviors.

Tikkun Olam (Repairing the World)

Judaism emphasizes *Tikkun Olam*, the concept of "repairing the world," as a key aspect of doing good. It reflects the idea that humanity has a responsibility to improve the world, promote justice, and alleviate suffering. Evil, in contrast, is anything that causes harm or disruption to this ideal state of repair and justice.

Divine Justice and Repentance

Judaism believes in divine justice but also in mercy. When people do evil, they are given opportunities to repent (*teshuvah*) and return to a path of goodness. The focus is on human accountability, yet also on the idea that people can change, learn from their mistakes, and make amends.

Suffering and Evil

Judaism has various explanations for the presence of suffering and evil in the world, one of which is that suffering can serve as a test or a way to bring a person closer to God. Another perspective is that human beings, through their actions, contribute to the presence of evil. God, while omnipotent, allows free will, and thus evil exists as a potential in the human condition.

The Role of Satan in Judaism

In contrast to other traditions where Satan is seen as a rebellious force of evil, in Judaism, Satan is not an independent being who opposes God. Instead, Satan (or *HaSatan*, the adversary) serves as an agent of

God, testing humans and challenging their righteousness to strengthen their moral resolve.

Evil in the Afterlife

Judaism has diverse views about the afterlife, but the focus tends to be more on ethical behavior in this life. Some Jewish teachings hold that the soul is judged after death, with rewards or consequences based on a person's actions. However, the concept of hell (Gehenna) in Judaism is more a place of purification rather than eternal damnation, emphasizing the potential for moral correction even after life.

Judaism Summary

The Jewish perspective on good and evil emphasizes moral choice, responsibility, and the constant struggle between human inclinations. It teaches that people have the power to choose good by following God's commandments, engaging in ethical behavior, and working towards a just and compassionate society. Evil is seen as the result of selfish choices but can be overcome through repentance and the pursuit of righteousness.

Mu-ism

Mu-ism (also known as Mujō-ism or Mujō, meaning "impermanence") is a philosophy that draws from various Eastern spiritual traditions, particularly Zen Buddhism and the Japanese concept of impermanence. It emphasizes the transient nature of life and the importance of understanding and accepting change.

Perspective with Key Aspects

Understanding Impermanence (Mujō)

Mu-ism revolves around the concept of impermanence or transience, which asserts that all things are in a constant state of flux. Nothing is permanent, and this fundamental principle shapes the understanding of good and evil.

- Good is recognizing and accepting the impermanent nature of life, embracing change, and adapting to the flow of existence. This includes living in harmony with the natural cycles and appreciating the transient beauty of life.

- Evil is resisting or denying the reality of impermanence, clinging to transient things, and suffering from attachments or rigid expectations. This resistance can lead to suffering and conflict.

Understanding impermanence encourages a flexible and adaptive approach to life, reducing suffering associated with attachment and resistance.

Non-Duality and the Nature of Good and Evil

In Mu-ism, the concept of non-duality is significant. It suggests that the distinctions between good and evil are not absolute but rather interconnected aspects of the same reality. This view is influenced by Zen Buddhism, which emphasizes the unity of opposites.

- Good and Evil are seen as relative and interdependdent aspects of the same whole. They are not separate entities but are part of the dynamic flow of life. Recognizing this interdependence helps in transcending rigid moral judgments and embracing a more holistic view of existence.

- Evil is understood as an aspect of the same continuum as good, rather than an absolute force. By acknowledging the fluidity and interconnectedness of all phenomena, one can navigate life's challenges with greater wisdom and compassion.

Non-duality encourages seeing beyond binary distinctions and understanding the deeper interconnectedness of all experiences.

Embracing the Present Moment

Mu-ism emphasizes living fully in the present moment and appreciating each experience as it unfolds. This focus on the present moment helps in understanding good and evil as relative to the immediate context.

- Good is being fully present, mindful, and engaged with the current moment, fostering awareness and acceptance. This presence allows for more compassionate and informed responses to situations.

- Evil is being caught up in regrets about the past or anxieties about the future, leading to a lack of awareness and presence. This disconnection can result in unskillful actions and suffering.

By cultivating mindfulness and presence, individuals can respond more skillfully and with greater understanding.

The Role of Compassion and Understanding

In Mu-ism, compassion and understanding are central virtues. Recognizing the impermanence of all things fosters empathy and reduces judgment.

- Good is acting with compassion, understanding others' experiences, and responding with kindness. Compassion arises from the awareness of our shared humanity and the impermanent nature of life.

- Evil is acting out of ignorance, judgment, or a lack of empathy. Harmful actions often stem from misunderstanding or denial of the impermanent nature of life and the interconnectedness of all beings.

Compassion and understanding help bridge gaps between individuals and reduce suffering caused by conflict and misunderstanding.

Self-Transformation and Inner Harmony

Mu-ism encourages self-transformation and the pursuit of inner harmony through practices like meditation and reflection. This inner work is crucial for understanding and integrating the concepts of good and evil.

- Good is engaging in practices that promote inner peace, self-awareness, and transformation. This includes meditation, self-reflection, and efforts to align one's actions with deeper values.

- Evil is resisting personal growth or remaining stuck in destructive patterns of thought and behavior. This resistance leads to inner turmoil and perpetuates suffering.

Inner harmony and self-awareness are essential for navigating the complexities of life and responding to challenges with wisdom and grace.

Ethical Conduct and Relativity

Mu-ism acknowledges that ethical conduct is often relative to the context and the individual's understanding. The emphasis is on acting skillfully and with awareness, rather than adhering to rigid moral codes.

- Good is acting in a way that aligns with the principles of impermanence, non-duality, and compassion. This involves making decisions that consider the well-being of oneself and others and adapting to changing circumstances.

- Evil is acting without awareness or consideration of the context, leading to harm or suffering. This can include acting out of ignorance, selfishness, or denial of impermanence.

Ethical conduct is guided by mindfulness and an understanding of the interconnectedness of all actions.

Acceptance of Life's Dualities

Mu-ism teaches the importance of accepting and embracing the dualities of life, such as joy and sorrow, success and failure. These dualities are seen as natural aspects of existence.

- Good is accepting the full range of life's experiences, understanding that both positive and negative aspects are part of the same reality. This acceptance fosters resilience and equanimity.

- Evil is resisting or rejecting certain aspects of life, leading to a fragmented and less harmonious experience. This resistance can cause internal conflict and suffering.

Acceptance of dualities helps in finding balance and harmony amidst life's fluctuations.

Mu-ism
Summary

In Mu-ism, good and evil are understood through the lenses of impermanence, non-duality, and mindfulness. Good involves recognizing and accepting the transient nature of life, acting with compassion, being present in the moment, and engaging in self-transformation. Evil is associated with denial of impermanence, attachment, ignorance, and resistance to personal growth. Mu-ism emphasizes the importance of understanding the interconnectedness of all experiences and responding to life's challenges with awareness and compassion.

Paganism

Paganism is a broad term that encompasses various polytheistic, nature-based, and folk religious traditions. Since Paganism includes a diverse range of beliefs and practices, the concepts of good and evil can vary significantly depending on the specific tradition. However, some general themes can be identified across many Pagan practices.

Perspective with Key Aspects

Diversity of Beliefs

Paganism is not a single religion but a collection of traditions with differing views on morality and ethics. The diversity of Pagan practices means that the understanding of good and evil can vary widely.

- Good is often associated with living in harmony with nature, respecting the divine and natural world, and maintaining balance in one's life and interactions with others.

- Evil may be understood as actions or behaviors that disrupt harmony, violate natural laws, or cause harm to oneself or others.

The interpretation of good and evil is influenced by the specific beliefs and practices of each Pagan tradition.

The Role of Nature and Natural Order

Many Pagan traditions emphasize the importance of nature and the natural order.

- Good involves living in accordance with the natural cycles and rhythms of the Earth, showing respect for the environment, and fostering balance and sustainability. Actions that support the well-being of the natural world are considered good.

- Evil involves behaviors that harm the environment, disrupt natural processes, or exploit natural resources. Actions that contribute to environmental degradation or imbalance are viewed as contrary to natural order.

Respecting and maintaining harmony with nature is central to understanding good and evil in many Pagan practices.

Polytheism and Deity Worship

In Pagan traditions, polytheism is common, with multiple deities representing various aspects of life and nature.

- Good often involves honoring and aligning with the deities and their respective domains, such as fertility, wisdom, or protection. Acts of reverence, devotion, and alignment with the values of the deities are considered good.

- Evil may be associated with disrespecting the deities, violating sacred traditions, or acting in ways that go against the principles of the deities. Betraying or disregarding the divine aspects represented by the gods can be seen as morally wrong.

The relationship with deities and adherence to their values play a role in defining good and evil.

Personal Responsibility and Ethics

Paganism often emphasizes personal responsibility and individual ethics.

- Good involves making ethical decisions based on personal integrity, respect for others, and the well-being of the community. Personal responsibility and moral choices are central to living a good life.

- Evil involves actions that harm others, betray personal values, or lead to negative consequences for oneself or the community. Personal accountability and ethical behavior are crucial for avoiding evil.

The focus is on individual choices and their impact on oneself and others.

Balance and Duality

Many Pagan traditions recognize the concept of balance and duality.

- Good is often associated with maintaining balance and harmony between various forces, such as light and dark, creation and destruction, or order and chaos. Embracing and understanding duality can be seen as part of a balanced approach to life.

- Evil can be understood as actions or attitudes that disrupt this balance or cause excessive harm. Extremes or imbalances that lead to suffering or chaos may be considered evil.

Balance and harmony are key to navigating the concepts of good and evil.

Ethical Guidelines and Codes

Some Pagan traditions have specific ethical guidelines or codes of conduct.

- Good involves following these guidelines, which often emphasize principles such as respect for life, honesty, and reciprocity. Adhering to ethical codes is seen as aligning with moral and spiritual values.

- Evil involves breaking these ethical codes or engaging in behaviors that violate the principles they represent. Actions that contradict established ethical guidelines are considered morally wrong.

Ethical guidelines provide a framework for understanding good and evil.

Magic and Ritual Practice

In many Pagan traditions, magic and ritual practice are significant.

- Good involves using magic and rituals for positive purposes, such as healing, protection, and personal growth. Rituals that honor the divine and promote well-being are considered good.

- Evil involves using magic or rituals for harmful purposes, such as manipulation, harm, or control. Malicious or unethical use of magical practices is viewed as contrary to the principles of goodness.

The intention behind magical practices is important for determining their moral value.

Community and Social Responsibility

Paganism often places value on community and social responsibility.

- Good involves contributing positively to the community, fostering connections, and supporting the well-being of others. Acts of charity, cooperation, and social justice are emphasized.

- Evil involves actions that harm the community, promote division, or neglect social responsibilities.

Behaviors that undermine communal harmony and support are considered problematic.

Community engagement and social responsibility are integral to understanding good and evil.

Respect for Autonomy and Individuality

Pagan traditions often emphasize respect for autonomy and individuality.

- Good involves honoring individual choices and respecting personal paths while maintaining ethical standards. Personal freedom and self-expression are valued as long as they do not harm others.

- Evil involves infringing on others' autonomy, coercing or manipulating individuals, or engaging in behaviors that restrict freedom and self-expression. Disrespect for individuality and personal choices is viewed as unethical.

Respect for autonomy and individuality plays a role in moral considerations.

Integration of Spiritual Values

Paganism integrates various spiritual values into its understanding of good and evil.

- Good involves living in alignment with spiritual values such as harmony, respect, and reverence for the sacred. These values guide moral decision-making and behavior.

- Evil involves actions that contradict spiritual values or undermine the sacred. Misalignment with spiritual principles is considered harmful and wrong.

Spiritual values guide the interpretation of good and evil.

Paganism
Summary

In Paganism, good and evil are understood through a diverse set of beliefs and practices. Good generally involves living in harmony with nature, honoring deities, following ethical guidelines, and contributing positively to the community. Evil is associated with actions that disrupt balance, harm others, or violate ethical and spiritual principles. Personal responsibility, respect for autonomy, and the integration of spiritual values are key aspects of understanding good and evil in Pagan traditions. The broad and varied nature of Paganism means that interpretations can differ, but common themes include respect for nature, ethical behavior, and balance.

Panentheism

The Panentheistic perspective on good and evil is informed by the belief that God exists both within and beyond the universe, intimately connected to all things while also transcending them. This worldview influences how good and evil are understood, emphasizing the interconnectedness of existence and the dynamic relationship between the divine and the material world.

Good (Alignment with Divine Purpose and Unity)

- In panentheism, good is understood as that which aligns with the divine purpose or fosters the unity and harmony of existence. Since God is seen as present in all things, actions and states of being that reflect divine qualities—such as love, compassion, creativity, and justice—are considered good.

- Goodness is associated with promoting interconnectedness and the flourishing of all creation. Acts that enhance the well-being of individuals, communities, and the environment reflect the divine presence and are seen as good because they contribute to the wholeness and harmony of the cosmos.

- Good is also linked to spiritual growth and the active participation of human beings in realizing divine potential within the world. In a panentheistic view, humans are co-creators with the divine, working to bring about greater unity, love, and justice in alignment with God's overarching purpose.

- Since God is immanent in the world, goodness is experienced as the divine presence within creation. Acts of goodness are those that reveal or magnify the divine within the material world while also respecting the transcendence of God beyond it.

Evil (Disruption of Harmony and Misalignment with the Divine)

- In panentheism, evil is not necessarily an independent force but is understood as a disruption of divine harmony or a state of misalignment with the divine will. Evil arises when individuals or systems act in ways that fragment, harm, or oppose the interconnectedness of creation.

- Many panentheistic traditions emphasize human free will as a factor in the existence of evil. While free will allows humans to co-create with God, it also opens the possibility for choices that harm others, the environment, or oneself. Evil is seen as the result of misusing this agency in ways that contradict the divine purpose.

- Evil can also be understood as arising from ignorance or alienation from the divine presence. When individuals or societies fail to recognize the sacredness of all life and their connection to God, they may act in ways that cause harm or perpetuate injustice.

- Some panentheistic perspectives see evil as part of the imperfection inherent in the process of becoming. Since the universe is in a state of ongoing growth and transformation, moments of conflict, suffering, and disorder may be viewed as necessary elements of this process. Evil, in this sense, is not eternal but is a temporary aspect of the evolving relationship between God and creation.

The Nature of Good and Evil

- Good and evil are not seen as absolute, static categories but as relational concepts within the dynamic interplay between God and the universe. Goodness reflects actions, intentions, and states of being that deepen the relationship between God and creation, while evil disrupts or diminishes this relationship.

- Some panentheistic traditions reject a strict dualism between good and evil, emphasizing that both may serve a larger divine purpose. Even apparent evils can lead to greater understanding, transformation, or the eventual realization of good.

- In process theology, a form of panentheism, good is linked to the promotion of creativity, novelty, and the flourishing of all entities. Evil, by contrast, represents the stagnation or diminishment of potential. God is seen as working within creation to maximize good outcomes while minimizing evil, though not coercively.

The Role of Humans in Addressing Evil

- Humans, as part of creation, are seen as partners with God in bringing about good. They have the responsibility to act ethically, promote justice, care for the environment, and build relationships that reflect divine unity.

- The response to evil involves efforts to heal divisions, restore harmony, and work toward the flourishing of all beings. In panentheism, evil is not just something to be opposed but a condition to be understood and transformed through divine-human cooperation.

- Cultivating an awareness of God's immanence in all things helps individuals align their actions with the divine will and resist contributing to the fragmentation that causes evil.

Hope and the Ultimate Triumph of Good

- Many panentheistic perspectives include the belief that good will ultimately prevail, as God works to bring creation into fuller harmony with the divine purpose. This vision provides hope that evil and suffering are temporary and will be overcome through the ongoing relationship between God and the universe.

- While evil and suffering are acknowledged, they are often seen as opportunities for growth, deeper understanding, and the realization of good. In this way, even negative experiences contribute to the unfolding of God's plan.

Panentheism
Summary

From a panentheistic perspective, good is defined as alignment with the divine purpose, fostering interconnectedness, and promoting the flourishing of all creation. Evil is seen as a disruption of harmony, a misalignment with God's will, or the result of ignorance and misuse of free will. Good and evil are relational and dynamic, reflecting the evolving relationship between God and the universe. Humans play a vital role in co-creating good, addressing evil, and working toward the ultimate unity and harmony of all things with the divine.

Quaker

The Quaker perspective on good and evil is rooted in their Christian beliefs, emphasizing the Inner Light—the presence of God within each person—and the importance of living in accordance with divine guidance. Quakers (also known as the Religious Society of Friends) focus on the transformative power of God's presence, nonviolence, and personal integrity in navigating moral questions.

Good (Alignment with the Divine and Living the Truth)

- Quakers believe that every person has an Inner Light, which is the presence of God within them. Good is defined as actions and attitudes that align with this divine guidance. Living in harmony with the Inner Light allows individuals to discern God's will and act accordingly.

- Goodness involves listening to and following God's guidance in all areas of life. Quakers emphasize the importance of direct experience with God over rigid doctrines or rituals. Acts that promote peace, justice, and love are seen as expressions of goodness because they reflect God's nature.

- Quakers highly value truth and integrity. Living a truthful life, being honest in all dealings, and staying true to one's convictions are central aspects of goodness. This is reflected in their testimonies, such as the Testimony of Integrity.

- Goodness also involves promoting peace and resolving conflicts without violence. The Quaker Peace Testimony emphasizes that war and violence are contrary to God's will. Acts of reconciliation, understanding, and compassion are seen as embodiments of goodness.

- Quakers believe that living a good life means serving others and working to alleviate suffering. Acts of kindness, charity, and advocacy for justice reflect the divine presence and are central to their understanding of good.

Evil (Separation from the Divine and Harmful Actions)

- Evil, in the Quaker perspective, is seen as a disconnection from God's guidance and the Inner Light. When individuals ignore or suppress the divine presence within themselves and others, they are more likely to act in ways that cause harm or perpetuate injustice.

- Quakers understand sin as any action or attitude that goes against God's will or diminishes the dignity and worth of others. Sin is not seen as a fixed or inherited condition but as a failure to live in harmony with divine love and truth.

- Evil is often associated with actions that cause harm, oppression, or injustice. Quakers reject violence, exploitation, and systems of inequality, viewing these as manifestations of evil that arise when people prioritize selfishness, greed, or power over love and community.

- Beyond individual actions, Quakers recognize the presence of systemic evil, such as slavery, war, environmental degradation, and economic inequality. They actively work to challenge and dismantle these systems as part of their moral responsibility.

The Nature of Good and Evil

- Quakers tend to avoid a rigid dualism between good and evil. Instead, they focus on the potential for transformation and redemption within every individual. They believe that all people, no matter how misguided or harmful their actions, possess the Inner Light and can return to goodness through reflection and spiritual growth.

- Evil is not an independent force but a result of misalignment with God's will and a failure to recognize the divine presence in oneself and others. Quakers emphasize that evil arises from choices and actions, not from an inherently evil nature.

- Quakers believe that everyone is capable of being transformed by God's love. Through spiritual reflection, repentance, and a willingness to listen to the Inner Light, individuals can move away from evil and toward goodness.

Responding to Good and Evil

- Quakers are committed to responding to evil with nonviolence and forgiveness, rather than retaliation. They believe in breaking cycles of harm by addressing the root causes of conflict and injustice with compassion and understanding.

- Quakers emphasize the importance of corporate discernment, where the community gathers in silence to seek God's guidance on moral issues. This practice helps individuals and the group discern how to respond to evil and act for good.

- Quakers are known for their work in social justice, advocating for peace, racial and gender equality, prison reform, and environmental stewardship. They see activism as a way to align with God's will and combat systemic evil.

- Quakers practice silent worship as a way to connect with the Inner Light and seek guidance on living a good life. This discipline helps them remain spiritually grounded and attuned to God's will, even in the face of challenges.

Testimonies as Guides to Goodness

Quakers are guided by core testimonies, which shape their understanding of good and evil and provide practical principles for living:

1. Peace: Rejecting violence and working for reconciliation.
2. Integrity: Living truthfully and consistently with one's values.
3. Simplicity: Avoiding material excess and focusing on what truly matters.
4. Equality: Affirming the worth of all people and opposing discrimination.
5. Stewardship: Caring for the environment and using resources responsibly.

These testimonies help Quakers discern what is good and how to resist evil in their personal lives and the broader world.

Quaker Summary

For Quakers, good is living in alignment with the Inner Light—God's presence within everyone—and acting in ways that promote love, peace, justice, and truth. Evil is seen as separation from God's guidance, leading to harm, injustice, and disconnection from the divine and others. Quakers focus on nonviolence, forgiveness, and social justice as ways to resist evil and foster goodness. They believe in the transformative power of God's love, emphasizing the potential for redemption and the ability of individuals and communities to align with divine will through reflection and action.

Rastafari

In the Rastafari worldview, the concepts of good and evil are understood primarily through the lens of spiritual and socio-political struggles, reflecting their African roots, Christian influences, and anti-colonial resistance.

Perspective with Key Aspects

Good (Righteousness)

- Jah (God): Goodness in Rastafari is synonymous with living in alignment with Jah, the supreme being. Jah is seen as the Christian God, often identified with Haile Selassie I, the former Emperor of Ethiopia, who is revered as a divine figure. Living righteously means embodying the principles of love, unity, justice, truth, and respect for nature.

- Ital Living: Adhering to Ital, a way of life focused on purity, natural living, and spiritual balance, is considered good. This includes a plant-based diet, rejecting processed and artificial foods, and maintaining a deep connection to the earth.

- African Identity and Repatriation: Goodness also involves embracing African heritage and identity. Rastafari view Africa, especially Ethiopia, as their spiritual homeland. Many believe in repatriation, either physically or spiritually, to Africa, which symbolizes a return to their roots and liberation from oppression.

Evil (Babylon)

- Babylon as Evil: The term "Babylon" represents evil in Rastafari. It symbolizes the oppressive, corrupt, and materialistic system that perpetuates injustice, exploitation, and inequality. This is often associated with Western colonial powers and their legacies of slavery and oppression.

- Materialism and Exploitation: Babylon is characterized by greed, materialism, and environmental degradation. It promotes a lifestyle that is disconnected from Jah and is centered on consumerism and worldly pursuits, leading to moral decay.

- Mental Enslavement: Rastafari teach that Babylon enslaves not just the body, but the mind and spirit as well. Evil, in this sense, includes the false ideologies and systems that keep people mentally and spiritually oppressed. Rastafari emphasize the need to free the mind from Babylon's influence, embracing truth and spiritual liberation.

The Struggle Between Good and Evil

Rastafari see life as a constant struggle between good and evil, or Jah's kingdom and Babylon. They view themselves as warriors fighting to establish a righteous world, resisting Babylon's influence, and promoting justice and equality. Rastafari spirituality emphasizes this fight as both personal and global, with the ultimate goal being the fall of Babylon and the rise of Jah's kingdom of peace and righteousness.

Redemption and Hope

Many Rastafari believe that redemption will come through the eventual collapse of Babylon and the establishment of Jah's divine order on Earth. This is symbolized by the return to Africa and the restoration of African dignity, both in a physical and spiritual sense.

Rastafari Summary	In Rastafari philosophy, good is defined by living in harmony with Jah, embracing

an Ital lifestyle, reconnecting with African identity, and resisting the materialism and corruption of Babylon. Evil, represented by Babylon, is seen as an oppressive system that promotes materialism, exploitation, and mental enslavement. Life is a constant struggle between these forces, with the hope of eventual redemption through the fall of Babylon and the establishment of divine justice and peace.

Seventh-day Adventist

The Seventh-day Adventist (SDA) perspective on good and evil is rooted in the Bible and the denomination's emphasis on the Great Controversy theme, which describes a cosmic struggle between Christ (good) and Satan (evil). Their beliefs focus on God's character, human free will, and the ultimate restoration of a perfect world through Jesus Christ.

Good (God, Obedience, and Love)

- Seventh-day Adventists believe that God is the ultimate source of all that is good. His character is defined by love, justice, mercy, and holiness. Goodness is anything that reflects God's character and aligns with His will as revealed in the Bible.

- Central to SDA theology is the idea of the Great Controversy, a cosmic battle between good and evil that began in heaven when Lucifer (Satan) rebelled against God. Goodness is represented by Jesus Christ, who embodies God's love and truth. The plan of salvation through Christ is God's ultimate act of goodness in restoring humanity and the universe to harmony with His will.

- The Ten Commandments and Biblical Principles: Goodness is expressed through obedience to God's Ten Commandments and the teachings of the Bible. These commandments provide a moral framework for living a righteous life. Adventists believe that keeping the commandments, including the Sabbath (the seventh day), is an essential part of demonstrating loyalty to God.

- Adventists also connect goodness to principles of health, stewardship, and care for others. They emphasize healthy living, including dietary practices and abstinence from harmful substances, as a way to honor God. Acts of kindness, service, and compassion reflect God's goodness and are encouraged as part of Christian life.

- True goodness is ultimately made possible through faith in Jesus Christ. Adventists believe that human efforts alone cannot achieve goodness, but through God's grace, believers can live in harmony with His will.

Evil (Satan, Sin, and Rebellion)

- Satan as the Source of Evil: Seventh-day Adventists believe that evil originated with Lucifer, a high-ranking angel who rebelled against God. Lucifer's rebellion was fueled by pride and a desire for power, leading to his transformation into Satan, the adversary. He was cast out of heaven along with the angels who joined him in his rebellion.

- The Fall of Humanity: Evil entered the human world through Adam and Eve's disobedience in the Garden of Eden, influenced by Satan's deception. This act of sin resulted in the fall of humanity and brought sin, suffering, and death into the world.

- Sin as Separation from God: For Adventists, sin is the root of all evil and is defined as separation from God's will. Sin disrupts the harmony of God's creation and results in broken relationships, suffering, and death. Sinful behavior arises when humans choose to rebel against God's laws and follow their own desires.

- The Role of Free Will: Adventists emphasize that God created humans with free will, allowing them to choose between good and evil. While free will is a gift that enables love and meaningful relationships, it also allows for the possibility of evil when individuals misuse their freedom to rebel against God.

- Satan's Influence in the World: Adventists believe that Satan continues to work to deceive humanity and lead people away from God. He uses temptation, false teachings, and worldly distractions to promote evil. The suffering and moral corruption in the world are seen as results of Satan's influence and humanity's sinfulness.

The Cosmic Struggle Between Good and Evil

- The conflict between good and evil is viewed as a central theme of human history. Adventists believe this cosmic struggle involves every individual, and the choices people make determine their alignment with either Christ or Satan.

- Adventists emphasize that God is just, but He has allowed evil to continue temporarily to fully demonstrate the consequences of sin and rebellion. This process vindicates God's character and His justice before the entire universe.

- Jesus Christ is the central figure in the victory over evil. His life, death, and resurrection are seen as the ultimate demonstration of God's love and the decisive defeat of Satan. Through Christ's sacrifice, believers can be forgiven of sin and empowered to live righteous lives.

Hope and the End of Evil

- Second Coming of Christ: Seventh-day Adventists believe in the literal Second Coming of Christ, when He will return to Earth to bring an end to sin, evil, and suffering. At this time, God's people will be resurrected or transformed to live eternally in His presence.

- The Millennium and Final Judgment: After Christ's return, there will be a millennium (a thousand-year period) during which Satan is bound, and the righteous will participate in reviewing God's judgments. At the end of the millennium, Satan, his followers, and all evil will be destroyed in the lake of fire, a final act of justice known as the second death.

- New Earth: Following the eradication of evil, God will create a new heaven and new earth where righteousness dwells. This perfect world will be free from sin, suffering, and death, fulfilling God's original purpose for creation.

Moral Responsibility and the Path to Goodness

- Adventists believe that goodness is achieved through a combination of faith in Jesus Christ and obedience to God's commandments. While human efforts alone are insufficient, God provides grace and strength to help believers overcome sin and live according to His will.

- The process of sanctification—becoming more like Christ—is a key aspect of the Adventist view of goodness. Through prayer, Bible study, and reliance on the Holy Spirit, believers grow in their ability to resist evil and reflect God's character.

- Part of living a good life includes sharing the gospel with others and helping them understand God's plan of salvation. Adventists see evangelism as a moral duty and a way to align with God's will.

Seventh-day Adventist Summary	In the Seventh-day Adventist perspective, good is rooted in God's character, obedience to His will, and faith in Jesus Christ. It involves living in harmony with God's commandments, reflecting His love, and contributing to the well-being of others. Evil originates from Satan's rebellion and humanity's sin, which cause suffering, separation from God, and moral corruption. The world is seen as the stage of a cosmic struggle between good and evil, with God's ultimate

victory assured through Christ's sacrifice and the Second Coming. Adventists look forward to a future free of sin and evil, where God's perfect goodness will prevail in a restored creation.

Shinto

In Shinto, the indigenous spiritual tradition of Japan, the concepts of good and evil are distinct from those in many other religions, as they are not tied to a dualistic, moral opposition or strict rules about right and wrong. Instead, Shinto emphasizes harmony with nature, purity, and the well-being of the community.

Perspective with Key Aspects

Harmony and Purity as the Foundation of Goodness

In Shinto, good is understood primarily as maintaining harmony (*wa*) with nature, the community, and the *kami* (spiritual beings or deities). Purity (*kiyome*) is central to Shinto's conception of goodness. Anything that promotes peace, balance, cleanliness, and well-being is considered good. This includes respect for nature, proper conduct in rituals, and actions that benefit the community.

- Goodness is seen as living in harmony with others, following traditions, and respecting the natural world and the *kami*.

Kami: Spirits and Deities

The *kami* are spiritual beings or deities that inhabit natural phenomena, objects, and sacred places. They are not moral arbiters in the way that deities in other religions might be. Instead, they represent forces of nature, ancestors, or protectors of particular areas. Goodness is often associated with actions that please the *kami*, such as showing reverence through rituals, offerings, and festivals (*matsuri*). Living in harmony with the *kami* is essential for ensuring prosperity and avoiding misfortune.

Evil as Impurity or Disruption

In Shinto, evil is not seen as an absolute force opposed to good, but rather as something that disrupts the natural harmony of life. This disruption is often conceptualized as *kegare* (impurity or pollution), which can result from physical, spiritual, or moral contamination. Impurities are believed to offend the *kami* and disrupt the natural balance, leading to misfortune, illness, or disaster.

- Evil can come from negative emotions like hatred or envy, natural disasters, death, or contact with things considered spiritually unclean. These are seen as disturbances to the natural order, rather than moral failings.

Tsumi: Offenses and Pollution

The concept of *tsumi* refers to actions or conditions that create impurity or offense. *Tsumi* can be caused by:

- Wrongful actions, such as dishonesty or disrespect.

- Natural events like death, illness, or natural disasters.

- Contact with things considered unclean, like blood or death, which create spiritual impurity.

While *tsumi* can lead to negative consequences for individuals or communities, it is not regarded as "sin" in the sense of a permanent moral stain. Instead, it is seen as a disruption that requires purification.

Purification Rituals: Restoring Goodness

Purification (*harae* or *misogi*) is central to Shinto practice and is how people restore purity and harmony after they experience or cause impurity. These rituals cleanse both physical and spiritual pollution, ensuring that individuals and communities can reconnect with the *kami* and return to a state of harmony.

- Harae rituals involve offerings, prayers, and symbolic acts like washing in water or waving a purification wand (*haraigushi*).

- Misogi involves ritual bathing in natural water sources, such as rivers or waterfalls, to cleanse the body and spirit.

Through purification, the effects of *tsumi* are removed, restoring goodness and the natural order.

No Absolute Concept of Evil

Unlike in religions that posit a clear divide between good and evil, Shinto does not conceptualize evil as a distinct force or an inherently evil being (like Satan in Christianity). There is no eternal evil or devil figure in Shinto. Instead, *evil* is temporary, related to pollution, misfortune, or imbalance, and can be corrected through appropriate rituals and respect for the natural world.

Human Nature

In Shinto, human nature is not viewed as inherently sinful or corrupt. Humans are born pure, and impurity arises from interactions with the world. Evil actions are generally considered to be the result of ignorance, failure to follow proper rituals, or external misfortune, rather than moral depravity. Therefore, people are not inherently evil, and through purification and right action, they can always return to a state of harmony.

Respect for Tradition and Community

Goodness in Shinto is also associated with respecting traditions, ancestors, and community values. Proper conduct during rituals, festivals, and in daily life is a form of goodness, as it promotes social harmony. Acts of evil, or *tsumi*, are often those that disrupt community harmony or show disrespect to others or the environment.

- Good actions promote communal well-being, cooperation, and reverence for tradition.

- Bad actions involve selfishness, causing harm to others or to the environment, or ignoring traditional values.

Matsuri: Festivals as Goodness

Shinto places great emphasis on *matsuri* (festivals), which are celebratory events held to honor the *kami* and foster harmony within the community. These festivals promote joy, togetherness, and a reaffirmation of the connection between humans, the *kami*, and nature. Participating in these events is considered good, as it strengthens the bonds between people, their environment, and the spiritual realm.

Living in Harmony with Nature

Nature is sacred in Shinto, and reverence for natural elements like mountains, rivers, trees, and animals is central to the concept of goodness. Goodness involves living in a way that respects and protects nature, as the natural world is seen as a reflection of the *kami*. Environmental destruction or neglect is viewed as a form of evil because it disrupts the balance between humans and the *kami*.

Shinto Summary	In Shinto, good is associated with maintaining harmony, purity, and respect for nature, the kami, and the community. Evil is viewed as disruption or impurity (kegare), which can be caused by wrongful actions, natural misfortunes, or contact with things deemed spiritually unclean. There is

no strict moral dualism between good and evil, nor is there a concept of inherent sinfulness. Instead, purification rituals restore harmony and purity after periods of imbalance or pollution. Goodness is found in acts that foster connection with the kami, honor tradition, and protect the natural world.

Sikhism

In Sikhism, the concepts of good and evil are closely tied to one's relationship with God (*Waheguru*), ethical living, and the pursuit of spiritual truth. Good and evil are understood in terms of actions that bring one closer to God or lead one away from God. The ultimate goal in Sikhism is to live a life of righteousness, selflessness, and devotion to God, which brings harmony to both the individual and society.

Perspective with Key Aspects

God as the Source of All Goodness

In Sikhism, *Waheguru* (God) is the ultimate source of all goodness. God is described as the creator, sustainer, and protector, embodying virtues like truth, compassion, justice, and love. Goodness in Sikhism is defined as aligning oneself with God's will (*Hukam*) and living in harmony with the divine order of the universe.

- Good is anything that brings one closer to God, promotes righteousness, compassion, and truth.

- Evil is anything that distances a person from God and leads to ignorance, selfishness, and attachment to worldly desires.

Ego (Haumai): The Root of Evil

In Sikh teachings, the primary cause of evil is the ego, known as *haumai*. This is the false sense of individuality or self-centeredness that causes humans to forget God and pursue their own desires, leading to negative actions. The ego creates a sense of separation from God and fosters greed, anger, pride, attachment, and lust—often referred to as the "Five Thieves" (*Panj Chor*).

The Five Thieves are:

- Lust (Kaam)
- Anger (Krodh)
- Greed (Lobh)
- Attachment (Moh)
- Pride (Ahankar)

These vices lead to suffering and prevent spiritual growth, causing individuals to act in ways that harm themselves and others. Overcoming these vices is essential for living a good life in Sikhism.

Goodness as Living in Harmony with God's Will (Hukam)

Goodness in Sikhism is seen as living in accordance with God's will (*Hukam*). This means recognizing the divine presence in all things, acting with humility, and leading a life of service, honesty, and devotion. Those who understand and accept God's will are considered to live in a state of *Gurmukh*, which means being God-oriented.

- A *Gurmukh* is someone who follows the Guru's teachings, controls the ego, and performs righteous actions.

- A *Manmukh* is someone who is self-centered, driven by ego and worldly desires, and therefore disconnected from God's will.

The Importance of Karma

Sikhism also teaches the concept of *karma*—the law of cause and effect, where a person's actions determine their future. Good actions bring positive consequences, while evil actions lead to suffering. However, unlike some other traditions, Sikhism places a strong emphasis on *God's grace* (*Nadar*) in overcoming the effects of past actions and attaining liberation. Through sincere devotion, prayer, and righteous living, one can rise above the effects of karma.

- Good actions include charity, honesty, compassion, humility, and selfless service (*seva*).

- Evil actions arise from selfishness, greed, and actions that harm others or go against God's will.

Seva (Selfless Service): A Key Expression of Goodness

In Sikhism, *seva* (selfless service) is one of the highest forms of goodness. Serving others without any expectation of reward or recognition is considered a way to suppress the ego and connect with God. *Seva* can take many forms, including feeding the hungry, helping those in need, and contributing to the well-being of the community.

- Langar (community kitchen) is a key practice in Sikhism where food is prepared and shared freely with everyone, regardless of caste, religion, or social status, as an expression of *seva*.

Equality and Justice as Goodness

Sikhism emphasizes the equality of all human beings, teaching that all people are created by God and deserve equal respect and dignity. Discrimination based on caste, religion, gender, or social status is seen as evil because it is rooted in ignorance and ego. Living a good life means promoting justice, fairness, and the well-being of all people.

The Sikh Gurus, especially Guru Nanak, spoke out against social inequalities and injustices, advocating for a society where everyone is treated fairly and compassionately. Guru Gobind Singh, the tenth Sikh Guru, emphasized standing up against oppression and injustice as part of living a righteous life.

Meditation on God's Name (Naam Simran)

Goodness in Sikhism also comes from constant remembrance of God through meditation on God's name (*Naam Simran*). By focusing the mind on God and engaging in devotional practices like reciting the *Guru*

Granth Sahib (Sikh scriptures), Sikhs seek to purify their hearts and minds. This practice helps to overcome the ego and vices and leads to spiritual enlightenment.

Meditation on God's name is considered one of the highest forms of worship and a way to align one's soul with divine truth and goodness.

Maya: The Illusion of the World

Sikhism teaches that much of the evil in the world arises from attachment to *maya*—the illusion of the material world. *Maya* distracts people from their true spiritual nature and leads to selfishness, greed, and desire for wealth, power, and worldly pleasures. The pursuit of *maya* strengthens the ego and creates suffering.

A good life in Sikhism involves recognizing the impermanence of worldly things and detaching oneself from material desires in order to focus on spiritual growth and the service of others.

Forgiveness and Compassion

Sikhism emphasizes forgiveness and compassion as essential qualities of goodness. Holding grudges or seeking revenge is seen as a manifestation of ego and anger, which leads to negative karma and suffering. Sikhs are encouraged to forgive others, even when wronged, and to show compassion to all living beings.

Guru Nanak, the founder of Sikhism, taught that one should "conquer the mind" and "be kind to all" as a way of living a good and spiritual life.

Evil as Separation from God

In Sikhism, evil is essentially the state of being separated from God due to ignorance, ego, and attachment to worldly things. When people forget God and become attached to their own desires, they act in selfish ways that cause harm to themselves and others. Evil is not an external force but a result of one's own actions and mindsets.

The way to overcome evil is to remember God, engage in *Naam Simran*, practice *seva*, and live a life aligned with *Hukam*.

Sikhism Summary

In Sikhism, good is defined by living in accordance with God's will, overcoming the ego, and practicing virtues like compassion, humility, and selflessness. Evil arises from the ego (haumai), which leads to selfishness, greed, and attachment to worldly desires. Sikhs are encouraged to live a life of service (seva), meditation on God's name (Naam Simran), and devotion to God. Through righteous actions, equality, justice, and spiritual practice, individuals can purify themselves and achieve union with God, which is the ultimate form of goodness. Evil, in contrast, is seen as a state of ignorance and separation from God that can be overcome through spiritual practice and God's grace.

Spiritualism

Spiritualism is a religious movement that emphasizes direct communication with spirits through mediums. It emerged in the 19th century and encompasses a range of beliefs and practices related to the afterlife and the spiritual world. Spiritualism generally promotes the idea that spirits of the deceased can provide guidance and that spiritual development continues beyond physical death.

Perspective with Key Aspects

The Nature of Spiritual Evolution

In Spiritualism, spiritual evolution is central to understanding good and evil. It is believed that souls continue to grow and evolve after death.

- Good is associated with actions and behaviors that promote spiritual growth, ethical living, and harmony with spiritual principles. This includes acts of kindness, compassion, and personal integrity, which are seen as advancing the soul's development and alignment with higher spiritual truths.

- Evil involves actions that hinder spiritual growth, such as selfishness, deceit, and harm to others. These actions are seen as obstacles to spiritual progress and can result in negative consequences for the soul's evolution.

Spiritual evolution is a key aspect of determining the moral value of actions.

The Role of Spirits

Spirits play a significant role in Spiritualism, providing guidance and insight into moral and ethical issues.

- Good involves seeking guidance from benevolent and enlightened spirits, who can provide wisdom and support for making ethical decisions. Communicating with positive spirits is believed to help individuals align with spiritual truths and moral principles.

- Evil can be associated with misleading or malevolent spirits that may attempt to deceive or harm individuals. Engaging with such spirits or being influenced by their negativity can lead to actions that are considered morally wrong.

The quality of spiritual guidance is important in discerning good and evil.

Moral Responsibility and Free Will

Spiritualism teaches that individuals have moral responsibility and free will in their actions and decisions.

- Good is characterized by the exercise of free will in making choices that align with ethical principles, personal integrity, and spiritual growth. Individuals are responsible for their actions and their impact on others.

- Evil involves the misuse of free will to engage in harmful, unethical, or deceitful behavior. Such choices are seen as detrimental to spiritual development and social harmony.

Moral responsibility and the consequences of free will are central to understanding good and evil.

The Impact of Actions on Spiritual Development

In Spiritualism, the impact of actions on spiritual development is crucial.

- Good actions are those that contribute positively to spiritual growth, enhance one's understanding of higher spiritual truths, and foster a sense of connection with others and the divine. Such actions are believed to bring about positive spiritual and personal transformations.

- Evil actions are those that obstruct spiritual progress, cause harm to others, or create spiritual imbalance. These actions are seen as hindrances to achieving higher states of spiritual awareness and harmony.

The impact on spiritual development helps to determine the moral nature of actions.

The Concept of Karma and Reincarnation

Many Spiritualists incorporate beliefs in karma and reincarnation, which suggest that actions have consequences that affect future lives.

- Good involves actions that create positive karma and contribute to spiritual advancement in this life and future ones. Ethical behavior, compassion, and personal growth are seen as ways to accumulate favorable karma.

- Evil involves actions that generate negative karma and result in spiritual setbacks or difficulties in future lives. Harmful or unethical behavior is believed to have repercussions that affect the soul's future experiences.

Karma and reincarnation are important for understanding the long-term effects of actions.

Personal Experience and Intuition

In Spiritualism, personal experience and intuition are important for understanding and discerning good and evil.

- Good is often recognized through personal experiences of harmony, insight, and spiritual confirmation. Intuitive feelings and inner guidance are used to assess the moral quality of actions and decisions.

- Evil can be discerned through feelings of discomfort, inner conflict, or negative spiritual experiences. Personal intuition and spiritual discernment are used to identify actions that are misaligned with ethical and spiritual principles.

Personal experience and intuition play a role in navigating moral decisions.

The Role of Mediumship and Spiritual Communication

Mediumship and spiritual communication are central practices in Spiritualism.

- Good is associated with authentic and uplifting spiritual communication that provides guidance, support, and insight into ethical living. Positive mediumship experiences are believed to align with higher spiritual truths and principles.

- Evil involves deceptive or harmful spiritual communication that misleads or manipulates individuals. Negative experiences with mediumship can indicate misalignment with genuine spiritual guidance.

The nature of spiritual communication affects one's understanding of good and evil.

The Pursuit of Truth and Enlightenment

Spiritualism emphasizes the pursuit of truth and enlightenment.

- Good involves the active pursuit of spiritual truth, personal enlightenment, and ethical understanding. This pursuit is seen as essential for achieving spiritual growth and contributing to the well-being of others.

- Evil involves the rejection of truth or the pursuit of falsehood, which can lead to spiritual confusion and moral compromise.

The pursuit of truth and enlightenment is central to navigating moral choices.

Ethical Living and Social Responsibility

Ethical living and social responsibility are emphasized in Spiritualism as ways to contribute positively to the world.

- Good involves living ethically and contributing to social harmony, justice, and the well-being of others. This includes actions that reflect compassion, fairness, and responsibility toward others and society.

- Evil involves neglecting social responsibility or engaging in actions that harm others or disrupt social harmony. Ethical and social considerations are key to determining the moral value of actions.

Ethical living and social responsibility are crucial for spiritual and moral alignment.

Integration of Spiritual Principles

Spiritualists often integrate various spiritual principles and teachings into their understanding of good and evil.

- Good is seen as aligning with universal spiritual principles, such as love, compassion, and integrity. Integration of these principles helps individuals live in accordance with higher spiritual values.

- Evil involves actions that are inconsistent with or contrary to these spiritual principles. Misalignment with core spiritual values is viewed as detrimental to personal and spiritual well-being.

Integration of spiritual principles guides moral understanding and behavior.

Spiritualism Summary

In Spiritualism, good and evil are understood through the lenses of spiritual evolution, the role of spirits, moral responsibility, and the impact of actions on spiritual development. Good involves actions that promote spiritual growth, ethical living, and alignment with divine principles, while evil involves behaviors that hinder spiritual progress and cause harm. The pursuit of truth, ethical living, and personal intuition play significant roles in discerning moral choices. Spiritualists emphasize the importance of authentic spiritual communication and the integration of spiritual principles in navigating the concepts of good and evil.

$Sufism$

Sufism, the mystical dimension of Islam, offers a unique and profound perspective on the concepts of good and evil.

Perspective with Key Aspects

Divine Unity and Goodness

Sufism emphasizes the Unity of God (Tawhid) and the divine attributes associated with this unity.

- In Sufism, all true goodness is ultimately derived from God, who is the source of all divine attributes such as mercy, compassion, and love. Goodness is understood as aligning with the divine will and reflecting the nature of God. It involves living in a way that seeks to embody divine qualities and recognize the presence of God in all things.

- Evil is seen as a manifestation of separation from God's essence and will. It arises from ignorance (Jahiliyyah) or deviation from divine love and guidance. Evil is often viewed as an illusion or absence of the divine light and goodness rather than a separate force.

Inner Purity and Spiritual Growth

Sufism focuses on inner purification and spiritual development.

- Goodness involves the purification of the heart (Qalb) and the cultivation of virtues such as sincerity (Ikhlas), humility (Tawadu), and love (Mahabbah). This inner transformation aligns the self with divine attributes and fosters a deep connection with God.

- Evil is associated with the impurities and negative traits of the soul, such as pride (Kibr), greed (Hirz), and hatred (Bughz). These traits obstruct spiritual growth and distance the individual from divine love and understanding.

Love and Devotion

The concept of love (Ishq) is central to Sufi thought.

- True goodness is manifested through divine love and devotion. Sufis believe that loving God and expressing this love through acts of kindness, compassion, and selflessness reflect divine goodness. Devotion to God leads to the realization of goodness in one's actions and character.

- Evil is seen as the absence of divine love and the result of turning away from God's presence. Actions motivated by selfish desires or separation from divine love are considered evil.

The Role of the Self (Nafs)

Sufism addresses the concept of the self (Nafs) and its role in spiritual development.

- The process of overcoming the lower self (Nafs al-Ammarah) and aligning with the higher self (Nafs al-Mutmainnah) involves striving for goodness. This includes overcoming base desires and aligning oneself with divine will and virtues.

- The lower self, with its egotism, desires, and negative traits, represents the source of evil in Sufi teachings. Addressing and transforming these aspects of the self is crucial for overcoming evil and attaining spiritual purity.

Illumination and Enlightenment

The concept of illumination (Ishraq) is important in Sufism.

- Spiritual illumination involves gaining insight into the divine truths and aligning one's life with these truths. Goodness is associated with the clarity and light that come from divine enlightenment, which guides individuals toward righteous actions and decisions.

- Darkness and ignorance are seen as the opposite of illumination. Evil arises from a lack of spiritual awareness and understanding of divine truth. Ignorance of the divine presence leads to actions that are contrary to divine goodness.

Cosmic Order and Divine Will

Sufism emphasizes the concept of divine will and cosmic order.

- Goodness is viewed as living in accordance with the divine will and recognizing the order of the universe as created by God. This involves aligning one's actions with the cosmic harmony and divine purpose.

- Evil is associated with actions that disrupt or disregard the divine order and cosmic harmony. Disobedience to divine will and failure to recognize the interconnectedness of creation lead to moral and spiritual disorder.

Unity and Duality

Sufism explores the concept of unity and the interplay of dualities.

- In the Sufi view, true goodness transcends dualities and is rooted in the unity of God. Living in harmony with the divine unity means transcending personal dualities and embracing the oneness of existence.

- Dualistic thinking and separation from the divine unity contribute to the perception of evil. Evil is seen as a manifestation of dualistic conflicts and separation from the oneness of God.

Transformation and Grace

The concept of transformation (Tazkiyah) and divine grace (Barakah) are central in Sufism.

- Spiritual transformation through divine grace involves overcoming evil and achieving a state of purity and alignment with divine will. Grace enables individuals to transcend their shortcomings and live in accordance with divine goodness.

- Evil is overcome through the transformative power of divine grace. It represents the process of moving from imperfection and ignorance to spiritual enlightenment and alignment with divine goodness.

Ethical Living and Compassion

Sufi teachings emphasize ethical living and compassion.

- Ethical behavior, compassion, and service to others are seen as expressions of divine love and goodness. Sufis strive to live out these virtues in their interactions with others and in their daily lives.

- Actions that cause harm, injustice, or suffering to others are viewed as contrary to divine compassion and goodness. Ethical lapses and lack of compassion reflect a departure from the divine attributes.

Mystical Experience and Direct Knowledge

Sufism values mystical experience and direct knowledge of God.

- Mystical experiences that bring individuals closer to God and reveal divine truths are considered a source of goodness. Direct knowledge of God enhances one's ability to live in accordance with divine will.

- Ignorance of the divine and lack of mystical insight lead to misunderstanding and misalignment with divine goodness. Evil can be seen as the result of failing to recognize and experience the divine truth.

Sufi Summary	In Sufism, good is associated with divine love, inner purity, spiritual growth, and alignment with the divine will and cosmic order. Evil is seen as separation from divine goodness, arising from ignorance, the lower self, and actions that disrupt divine harmony. Sufism emphasizes the transformative power of divine grace, the pursuit of mystical experiences, and ethical living as means to overcome evil and achieve spiritual enlightenment. The concepts of love, illumination, and unity play a central role in understanding and addressing good and evil from a Sufi perspective

Sunni

In Sunni Islam, the concepts of good and evil are central to understanding the moral and spiritual framework that guides human actions. These concepts are rooted in the belief in Allah (God) as the ultimate source of all morality and the teachings of the Qur'an and the Sunnah (traditions and sayings of Prophet Muhammad). The distinction between good and evil is crucial for achieving success in this life and the hereafter.

Perspective with Key Aspects

Good (Khayr)

- Obedience to Allah's Commands: In Sunni Islam, good is defined by actions and beliefs that align with the will and commands of Allah as revealed in the Qur'an and through the Prophet Muhammad's life and teachings. Following Sharia (Islamic law) and observing the five pillars of Islam—faith, prayer, fasting, charity, and pilgrimage—are considered acts of goodness.

- Intention (Niyyah): An essential element of goodness in Islam is intention. Even mundane actions can be transformed into acts of worship if performed with the sincere intention to please Allah. The purity of one's heart and the intention behind actions are crucial in determining their moral value.

- Morality and Ethics: Good actions are those that reflect justice, kindness, honesty, generosity, and respect for others. The Prophet Muhammad said, "The best among you are those who have the best manners and character." Acts such as helping the poor, treating others with kindness, and fulfilling one's duties to family and society are emphasized as moral virtues.

- Worship and Piety: Living a life of piety and regular worship is seen as essential to being good. Acts of worship, like praying five times a day, reciting the Qur'an, and making du'a (supplications), help purify the soul and keep a person on the path of righteousness.

Evil (Sharr)

- Disobedience to Allah: Evil is defined as any action, belief, or intention that goes against Allah's commands. Sin, whether minor or major, constitutes an act of evil. This includes ignoring the teachings of the Qur'an, failing to observe obligatory practices, or engaging in prohibited activities.

- Shirk (Associating Partners with Allah): The greatest sin in Islam is shirk, which means associating partners with Allah or denying His oneness. Shirk is viewed as the ultimate form of evil and is unforgivable if one dies without repenting.

- Satan (Shaytan) and Temptation: Evil is often associated with the influence of Shaytan (Satan), who seeks to lead people astray from the path of righteousness. Sunni belief holds that Shaytan whispers temptations and tries to encourage sinful behavior, but humans have the free will to resist these temptations.

- Injustice and Oppression: Acts of evil also include injustice, oppression, lying, cheating, harming others, and causing corruption on earth. Sunni teachings emphasize that justice is a core principle in Islam, and those who commit injustice, whether at a personal or societal level, are seen as committing evil.

- Neglecting Moral Responsibility: Sunni Islam teaches that humans are entrusted with the responsibility to use their free will wisely. Neglecting this responsibility, whether by engaging in sinful behavior or failing to promote good, is seen as contributing to evil.

The Struggle Between Good and Evil

- Free Will and Accountability: Sunni Islam believes that humans have been given free will to choose between good and evil, but they are accountable for their choices. On the Day of Judgment, individuals will be judged according to their deeds, and their eternal fate—paradise or hell—will depend on whether they followed the path of goodness or gave in to evil.

- Jihad al-Nafs (Struggle Against the Self): One of the most important forms of jihad (struggle) in Sunni Islam is the jihad al-nafs, or the struggle against one's own lower desires and inclinations towards sin. This internal struggle is considered a lifelong battle between good and evil within oneself.

- Tawba (Repentance): Islam offers a path for redemption through tawba (repentance). Even those who commit evil can seek Allah's forgiveness if they repent sincerely and turn back to the path of righteousness.

Sunni
Summary

In Sunni Islam, good is defined by obedience to Allah's will, following Islamic law, performing acts of worship, and living a moral life with good character. Evil encompasses disobedience to Allah, sinful behavior, and causing harm or injustice to others. Humans have free will and are responsible for choosing between good and evil, and they will be judged by Allah in the hereafter based on their deeds. The struggle between good and evil is both external, in resisting evil influences, and internal, in battling one's own desires and weaknesses. Islam offers a path to redemption through repentance, encouraging believers to constantly strive for goodness and avoid evil.

Taoism

In Taoism, the concepts of good and evil are seen differently from many other religious and philosophical systems. Taoism emphasizes harmony with the *Tao* (also spelled *Dao*), which is the fundamental principle that underlies the natural order of the universe. Good and evil are not rigid, opposing forces but are instead viewed in the context of balance, flow, and the natural order.

Perspective with Key Aspects

The Tao: The Way of Nature

In Taoism, *Tao* is the ultimate reality, the source, and the guiding principle of everything in the universe. It is often described as "the Way" or the "path" and is beyond human comprehension. Living in harmony with the Tao is the ultimate good. The Tao is not a moral force that dictates right and wrong but rather the natural way of things—the flow of life, nature, and the universe.

- Good is aligning oneself with the Tao, living naturally and in balance with the world.

- Evil is anything that disrupts this harmony or goes against the natural flow of the Tao.

Balance and Harmony: Yin and Yang

Central to Taoist thought is the concept of *Yin* and *Yang*, the complementary forces that make up the universe. Yin and Yang are not opposites in conflict but interdependent, each containing the seed of the other. Together, they represent balance and the cyclical nature of life. Neither force is inherently good or evil; instead, goodness arises from maintaining the proper balance between the two.

- Yin represents qualities like darkness, passivity, femininity, and receptiveness.

- Yang represents qualities like light, activity, masculinity, and assertiveness.

Goodness comes from maintaining a harmonious balance between Yin and Yang. When one force becomes dominant and disrupts the balance, this leads to disharmony, which can be perceived as evil.

Wu Wei: Non-Action or Effortless Action

One of the key principles in Taoism is *Wu Wei*, which translates as "non-action" or "effortless action." This doesn't mean doing nothing, but rather acting in a way that is in harmony with the natural flow of the Tao. Actions taken in accordance with the Tao are spontaneous, natural, and without force or excessive effort.

- Good actions are those that align with the Tao, are done effortlessly, and reflect the natural order.

- Evil actions, in Taoism, are those that stem from forcing, striving, or interfering with the natural flow of life. These actions are unnatural and disrupt the balance of the Tao.

No Absolute Good and Evil

In Taoism, there is no rigid or absolute concept of good and evil as fixed categories. Instead, good and evil are seen as relative and dynamic. What is "good" in one situation might not be in another, and the same goes for what is "bad." Because life and nature are in constant flux, Taoism emphasizes flexibility and adaptability rather than adherence to rigid moral codes.

- Good is not a moral absolute but a relative concept based on harmony and balance.

- Evil is a state of imbalance or disharmony, often arising from human desires, attachments, or actions that go against the natural way.

Human Nature and Simplicity

Taoism teaches that humans, like all things, are naturally in harmony with the Tao. Problems arise when people become too attached to desires, materialism, or ego, which pulls them away from their natural state. A return to simplicity, humility, and modesty is seen as a way to restore goodness.

- Good is living simply, with humility and modesty, free from excessive desires.

- Evil is the result of excess, greed, ambition, and striving for things that are unnatural or unnecessary.

Taoism encourages individuals to reduce their desires and ambitions, which are seen as sources of imbalance and suffering.

The Role of Desire

Desires, particularly selfish or materialistic desires, are seen as a major cause of imbalance and disharmony in Taoism. Desires pull individuals away from their natural state of being and lead to actions that disrupt harmony with the Tao.

- Goodness involves being content with simplicity, appreciating the natural world, and avoiding unnecessary desires.

- Evil arises when desires lead to excessive action, conflict, or harm, either to oneself or to others.

Flexibility and Spontaneity

Goodness in Taoism is often associated with flexibility and spontaneity. Rather than following rigid rules or principles, a good person adapts to changing circumstances in a natural and effortless way, just as water flows around obstacles.

- Good behavior is like water: it adapts to the environment, nourishes life, and does not seek dominance.

- Evil behavior is rigid, forceful, and resistant to the natural flow, leading to conflict and imbalance.

Naturalness (Ziran)

A key value in Taoism is *Ziran*, which means "naturalness" or "being so of itself." It refers to the quality of acting in accordance with one's true nature and the nature of the world. Goodness is living in accordance with *Ziran*, without artifice, pretension, or manipulation.

- Goodness is found in authenticity, being true to one's nature and the nature of things.

- Evil occurs when people act unnaturally, trying to control or manipulate situations for their own benefit.

Sagehood: The Ideal Person

In Taoism, the ideal person is the sage, someone who lives in perfect harmony with the Tao. The sage does not strive, force, or impose but instead flows effortlessly with life, making decisions based on intuition and alignment with the Tao. The sage embodies virtues like humility, compassion, and simplicity.

- Goodness is the wisdom and peacefulness of the sage, who acts without ego or attachment.

- Evil, in contrast, is ignorance or attachment to desires, which leads to conflict, stress, and imbalance.

Compassion and Humility

While Taoism does not focus on moral codes, it values qualities like compassion, humility, and non-contention as pathways to living in harmony with the Tao. These virtues reflect an understanding of the interconnectedness of all things and help maintain balance.

- Goodness includes compassion, acting kindly toward others without seeking reward or recognition.

- Evil can manifest as selfishness, pride, and the desire to dominate or harm others, which disrupts the natural order.

Taoism Summary	In Taoism, good and evil are seen as relative concepts, not fixed moral absolutes. Goodness is living in harmony with the Tao, the natural way of the universe, by embracing balance, simplicity, and humility. Evil, in contrast, is any action or mindset that disrupts this harmony, typically caused by ego, desire, or forceful behavior. Rather than seeing good and evil as opposing forces, Taoism views them as part of the natural cycle of life, with balance and flexibility being key to a life of goodness.

Unitarian Universalist

The Unitarian Universalist (UU) perspective on good and evil is grounded in its commitment to inclusivity, individual spiritual exploration, and ethical living. Unlike many religious traditions, UUs do not adhere to a single creed or dogma, and their understanding of good and evil is shaped by a variety of philosophical, religious, and humanistic traditions.

Good (Ethical Living, Compassion, and Justice)

- At the heart of UU thought is the belief in the inherent worth and dignity of every person. Actions that affirm and promote this dignity are considered good. UUs see goodness as rooted in compassion, respect, and the recognition of the interdependence of all life.

- Goodness is expressed through actions that promote justice, equity, and compassion in human relationships. This includes working to alleviate suffering, protect human rights, and create a more equitable and peaceful world.

- UUs emphasize the interconnected web of existence, viewing good as anything that nurtures and strengthens this connection. This includes care for the environment, fostering community, and promoting global well-being.

- Goodness involves personal responsibility for one's actions and striving to live according to ethical principles. UUs encourage individuals to explore their own moral frameworks, guided by reason, experience, and a commitment to the greater good.

Evil (Harm, Injustice, and Disconnection)

- UUs typically define evil as anything that causes harm, suffering, or injustice. This could include actions that diminish the dignity of others, exploit the vulnerable, or perpetuate systemic inequalities.

- Evil is also understood as a disconnection or disruption of the interconnected web of existence. Actions or systems that damage relationships, harm the environment, or foster alienation and division are seen as forms of evil.

- UUs recognize the existence of systemic evils, such as racism, sexism, environmental degradation, and economic inequality. These are not just individual failings but structural issues that require collective action to address.

- UUs often attribute evil to ignorance, fear, or a lack of empathy. They focus on addressing the root causes of harm, such as misunderstanding or systemic oppression, rather than labeling individuals as inherently evil.

The Nature of Good and Evil

- UUs generally reject a strict dualism between good and evil, emphasizing that morality is complex and contextual. They avoid simplistic or absolutist definitions of good and evil, recognizing that individuals and systems often contain elements of both.

- Morality is seen as relative and subject to change based on new insights, experiences, and contexts. UUs believe that understanding of good and evil evolves as humanity gains greater knowledge and wisdom.

- UUs emphasize the potential for good in all people and encourage practices that nurture empathy, understanding, and ethical action. They focus on restorative justice and reconciliation rather than punishment or condemnation.

Sources of Moral Guidance

UUs draw moral and ethical insights from many sources, including:

- World religions (e.g., Christianity, Buddhism, Hinduism, and Judaism).
- Humanism, which emphasizes reason, ethics, and the potential of human beings.
- Science and reason, which inform their understanding of the natural world and human behavior.
- Personal experience and individual spiritual exploration.

UUs are guided by seven core principles, which shape their understanding of good and evil. These include affirming the worth of every person, promoting justice and compassion, and respecting the interconnected web of existence.

Addressing Evil and Promoting Good

- UUs are committed to addressing systemic evils through social justice work, such as advocating for racial equality, LGBTQ+ rights, environmental sustainability, and economic justice. They view activism as a way to promote good and combat harm.

- UUs emphasize the importance of education, dialogue, and understanding in reducing harm and preventing evil. They believe that ignorance and fear often underlie harmful actions and that these can be addressed through open communication and shared learning.

- UUs focus on restorative justice, which seeks to heal and repair relationships rather than simply punishing wrongdoers. This approach emphasizes accountability, empathy, and reconciliation.

Hope and Human Responsibility

- UUs hold an optimistic view of human nature, believing in the potential for growth, transformation, and the creation of a better world. They emphasize human responsibility to act for good rather than relying on divine intervention.

- Goodness is seen as something that can be cultivated through collective effort, compassion, and dedication to justice. Evil, while real, is not viewed as insurmountable but as something that can be overcome through understanding, cooperation, and action.

Unitarian Universalist Summary	From a Unitarian Universalist perspective, good is defined as actions and principles that affirm the dignity of all people, promote justice and compassion, and nurture the interconnected web of existence. Evil is seen as harm, injustice, or disconnection from others and the world. UUs reject strict dualism, focusing instead on addressing the root causes of harm and fostering human potential for good. Guided by their seven principles and a commitment to inclusivity, education, and activism, UUs seek to create a world where goodness can thrive and evil can be minimized through collective human effort and moral growth

Voodoo

Voodoo (or Vodou) is a syncretic religion practiced primarily in Haiti, but also in other parts of the Caribbean and the Americas. It blends elements of African traditional religions, particularly from the Yoruba and Fon peoples, with Catholicism and other influences. Voodoo encompasses a rich tapestry of beliefs and practices involving spirits (Loa or Lwa), ancestors, and rituals.

Perspective with Key Aspects

Understanding the Nature of Spirits (Loa or Lwa)

In Voodoo, the Loa (also spelled Lwa) are spirits or deities that interact with the human world. They are central to Voodoo practice and are divided into various families or groups, each with its own characteristics and domains.

- Good is associated with working in harmony with the Loa, showing respect, and adhering to the proper rituals and offerings. Engaging positively with these spirits can bring blessings, protection, and guidance.

- Evil involves actions that disrupt the relationship with the Loa, such as failing to respect their rituals, neglecting offerings, or engaging in practices that anger or disrespect them. This can lead to misfortune or spiritual discord.

Maintaining a positive and respectful relationship with the Loa is crucial for well-being and spiritual harmony.

The Role of Ancestors

Ancestor veneration is a significant aspect of Voodoo. Ancestors are believed to watch over their descendants and can influence their lives positively or negatively.

- Good involves honoring and remembering ancestors through rituals, offerings, and prayers. This respect strengthens the connection between the living and the dead and helps ensure guidance and protection from the ancestral spirits.

- Evil is neglecting or disrespecting ancestors, which can lead to spiritual imbalance or misfortune. Failing to uphold ancestral traditions may result in disfavor or difficulties.

Respect for ancestors is essential for maintaining spiritual harmony and family continuity.

Moral and Ethical Behavior

Voodoo incorporates a strong ethical framework, often influenced by the broader cultural and societal norms of its practitioners.

- Good is reflected in behaviors that align with ethical and moral values, such as honesty, integrity, and kindness. These behaviors foster positive relationships with both the Loa and the community.

- Evil is associated with actions that violate ethical norms, such as deceit, betrayal, or harm to others. Such actions disrupt social and spiritual harmony and can lead to negative consequences.

Ethical behavior is integral to maintaining spiritual and social balance.

The Concept of Balance and Harmony

In Voodoo, maintaining balance and harmony is crucial. This extends to interactions with spirits, ancestors, and the natural world.

- Good involves actions that contribute to balance and harmony, such as proper ritual practices, maintaining positive relationships, and respecting the natural order.

- Evil involves actions that create imbalance or discord, such as disruptive rituals, harmful intentions, or disrespect towards spirits and traditions.

Balancing spiritual, social, and environmental factors is key to achieving and maintaining harmony.

Healing and Protection

Voodoo includes practices for healing and protection, utilizing the power of the Loa, rituals, and herbal remedies.

- Good is engaging in healing practices, seeking protection from negative influences, and using spiritual knowledge to promote well-being and safety.

- Evil can involve the misuse of magical practices for harmful purposes, such as curses or malevolent spells. This can lead to harm and spiritual disturbance.

Healing and protection practices are meant to enhance well-being and safeguard against negative influences.

The Role of Rituals and Offerings

Rituals and offerings are central to Voodoo practice and play a significant role in maintaining good relationships with the Loa and ancestors.

- Good involves performing rituals and offerings correctly, with sincerity and respect. This includes following traditional practices, making appropriate offerings, and participating in communal ceremonies.

- Evil is neglecting or performing rituals improperly, which can offend spirits or ancestors and disrupt spiritual connections.

Proper ritual practices are essential for maintaining spiritual favor and harmony.

The Influence of Personal Intentions

Personal intentions and motives are important in Voodoo. The intention behind actions and rituals can influence their outcomes.

- Good intentions involve acting with integrity, compassion, and respect for others and the spiritual world. Positive intentions lead to favorable outcomes and spiritual alignment.

- Evil intentions involve malevolence, manipulation, or self-serving motives. Such intentions can lead to negative consequences and spiritual repercussions.

The intention behind actions plays a critical role in determining their moral and spiritual impact.

Community and Social Responsibility

Voodoo places importance on community and social responsibility, with communal rituals and practices playing a key role.

- Good is contributing positively to the community, participating in communal rituals, and supporting social and spiritual well-being. This fosters a sense of unity and shared responsibility.

- Evil is engaging in behavior that harms the community or disrupts social cohesion. This includes actions that create conflict or division.

Community involvement and social responsibility are integral to maintaining harmony and support within the Voodoo community.

Mystical and Esoteric Knowledge

Voodoo includes elements of mystical and esoteric knowledge, which are often passed down through oral traditions and initiation.

- Good is seeking and utilizing mystical knowledge for spiritual growth and understanding. This includes proper use of esoteric practices for positive outcomes and personal development.

- Evil is the misuse of esoteric knowledge for harmful purposes, such as dark magic or manipulation. Misuse of mystical practices can lead to spiritual and moral issues.

Mystical knowledge is meant to be used responsibly and ethically.

Syncretism and Adaptation

Voodoo's syncretic nature involves blending various religious and cultural elements, adapting to different contexts and traditions.

- Good is embracing the syncretic nature of Voodoo in a way that respects and harmonizes diverse elements and practices. This includes integrating different traditions while maintaining core principles.

- Evil is using syncretism to misrepresent or distort core teachings and practices for personal gain or to deceive others.

Respectful and authentic adaptation is important for preserving the integrity of Voodoo practices.

Voodoo Summary	In Voodoo, good and evil are understood through the lenses of spiritual relationships, balance, ethical behavior, and mystical knowledge. Good involves aligning with divine principles, maintaining harmonious relationships with the Loa and ancestors, practicing ethical conduct, and contributing positively to the community. Evil involves actions that disrupt spiritual and social harmony, disrespect spirits or ancestors, and misuse spiritual knowledge. Voodoo emphasizes the importance of intention, respect for traditions, and maintaining balance and harmony in both spiritual and everyday life.

Yingyangjia

Yingyangjia (also known as Yin-Yang School) is a Chinese philosophical tradition that is often associated with the broader context of Chinese cosmology and thought. This school of thought is closely related to the concepts of Yin and Yang, which are fundamental to Chinese philosophy and religion.

Perspective with Key Aspects

Concept of Yin and Yang

The Yingyangjia perspective revolves around the Yin-Yang cosmology, which describes the universe in terms of two complementary and interdependent forces.

- Good is often associated with the balance and harmonious interaction between Yin and Yang. In this view, good is not merely a set of moral actions but is seen as the state of equilibrium and proper functioning of these cosmic forces.

- Evil arises when there is an imbalance or disharmony between Yin and Yang. Actions or states that disrupt this balance are considered problematic and may lead to suffering or disorder.

The harmony and balance of Yin and Yang are crucial to understanding good and evil in this framework.

Interdependence and Transformation

In Yingyangjia thought, Yin and Yang are not static but constantly transform into each other.

- Good is linked to the natural flow and transformation of Yin and Yang, promoting a state where these forces are in dynamic equilibrium. Actions and behaviors that align with the natural order and support this balance are considered good.

- Evil is associated with actions or states that disrupt this natural flow and lead to imbalance or stagnation. Interference with the natural processes or forcing an unnatural state can be seen as contributing to evil.

The interdependence and continuous transformation of Yin and Yang are key to understanding moral and ethical behavior.

Natural Order and Harmony

The concept of natural order and harmony is central to the Yingyangjia perspective.

- Good involves aligning oneself with the natural order and promoting harmony in both personal conduct and interactions with the world. This includes respecting natural cycles, maintaining balance, and supporting the well-being of oneself and others.

- Evil involves actions or attitudes that disrupt harmony and natural order. Disregard for natural principles, such as causing harm or creating disorder, is considered evil.

Living in harmony with the natural order is essential for moral behavior.

Relativity and Context

Yingyangjia philosophy recognizes the relativity of good and evil.

- Good and evil are seen as relative concepts that depend on the context and the balance of Yin and Yang. What might be considered good in one situation may have negative consequences in another if it leads to imbalance.

- Evil is not viewed as an absolute state but as a condition that results from improper balance or misalignment with natural principles. The relativity of these concepts emphasizes the importance of context and the dynamic nature of moral judgments.

The relativity of good and evil is highlighted by the need to consider context and balance.

Holistic Approach

Yingyangjia promotes a holistic approach to understanding the universe and morality.

- Good is associated with a holistic view that considers the interconnectedness of all things. Actions that support the overall harmony and integration of various aspects of life and nature are seen as good.

- Evil involves actions that disregard the interconnectedness and contribute to fragmentation or disunity. Disrupting the holistic balance and failing to consider the broader implications of one's actions can be viewed as evil.

A holistic approach underscores the interconnectedness and balance of all aspects of existence.

Ethical Conduct and Balance

Ethical conduct in Yingyangjia is closely linked to the principles of balance and moderation.

- Good behavior involves practicing moderation and maintaining balance in all aspects of life. This includes ethical decision-making that supports harmony and avoids extremes.

- Evil behavior involves excesses or deficiencies that lead to imbalance and disorder. Acting in ways that are extreme or out of harmony with natural principles can be considered evil.

Moderation and balance are key principles for ethical conduct.

Integration with Other Philosophies

The Yingyangjia perspective often integrates with other Chinese philosophical traditions, such as Daoism and Confucianism.

- Good is frequently understood in relation to Daoist principles of aligning with the Dao (the Way) and promoting natural harmony. Confucian values of righteousness and propriety also inform the understanding of good.

- Evil can be seen as contrary to both Daoist and Confucian principles, involving actions that disrupt natural harmony or social order.

Integration with other philosophies provides a broader context for understanding good and evil.

The Role of Personal Conduct

Personal conduct and intentions are important in determining good and evil.

- Good involves actions that reflect a genuine effort to maintain balance, harmony, and ethical integrity. Intentions that align with the principles of

Yin and Yang and contribute positively to oneself and others are considered good.

- Evil involves actions that stem from selfishness, disregard for balance, or harm to others. Intentions and behaviors that disrupt harmony and contribute to imbalance are viewed as evil.

Personal conduct and intentions play a significant role in moral evaluation.

Practical Application

In practice, the Yingyangjia perspective emphasizes practical application of its principles.

- Good involves applying the principles of Yin and Yang in daily life to achieve balance and harmony. This includes making decisions that support well-being, respect natural processes, and foster positive relationships.

- Evil involves failing to apply these principles, leading to actions that cause imbalance or harm. Neglecting the practical implications of harmony and balance can result in undesirable outcomes.

Practical application of balance and harmony is essential for moral living.

Spiritual and Moral Development

The Yingyangjia perspective also considers spiritual and moral development.

- Good is associated with spiritual growth and the development of qualities that promote balance, wisdom, and harmony. This includes cultivating virtues that support the natural order and contribute to personal and collective well-being.

154

- Evil involves behaviors that hinder spiritual and moral development, leading to imbalance and negative consequences. Actions that obstruct personal growth and disrupt harmony are seen as detrimental.

Spiritual and moral development is linked to the principles of balance and harmony.

Yingyangjia Summary	In the Yingyangjia perspective, good and evil are understood through the lens of Yin-Yang cosmology. Good is associated with balance, harmony, and alignment with natural order, while evil is linked to imbalance, disharmony, and disruption of natural processes. The relativity of good and evil, personal responsibility, and the practical application of balance are key aspects of this perspective. Integrating with other Chinese philosophical traditions and emphasizing holistic and ethical conduct, Yingyangjia provides a comprehensive framework for understanding moral behavior and spiritual development.

Zoroastrianism

Zoroastrianism is one of the world's oldest known religions, founded by the prophet Zoroaster (or Zarathustra) in ancient Persia. It centers on the dualistic struggle between the forces of good and evil, embodied by the deities Ahura Mazda and Angra Mainyu.

Perspective with Key Aspects

Dualism and Cosmic Struggle

Zoroastrianism is fundamentally dualistic, emphasizing the cosmic struggle between good and evil.

- Good is represented by Ahura Mazda, the supreme god who embodies truth, order, and righteousness. Goodness in Zoroastrianism involves aligning oneself with the divine attributes of Ahura Mazda, such as wisdom, justice, and compassion.

- Evil is represented by Angra Mainyu (or Ahriman), the evil spirit who embodies chaos, falsehood, and destruction. Evil actions and intentions are those that align with Angra Mainyu's attributes and disrupt the divine order established by Ahura Mazda.

The dualistic nature of Zoroastrianism frames the moral universe as a battleground between these opposing forces.

The Role of Free Will

Free will is a crucial concept in Zoroastrianism. Individuals are seen as having the ability to choose between good and evil.

- Good involves making choices that align with the divine will of Ahura Mazda, such as truthfulness, justice, and benevolence. Humans are encouraged to actively choose and promote good in their lives.

-

- Evil involves choices that align with Angra Mainyu, such as deceit, injustice, and malevolence. The misuse of free will to engage in harmful or dishonest behavior is considered to contribute to the spread of evil.

-

Free will allows individuals to participate in the cosmic struggle and shape their spiritual destiny.

The Concept of Asha (Truth and Order)

Asha is a central concept in Zoroastrianism, representing truth, order, and the divine principle of righteousness.

- Good is associated with living in accordance with Asha, which involves promoting truth, justice, and harmony in both personal conduct and social interactions. Adherence to Asha is seen as aligning with the divine will of Ahura Mazda.

- Evil is associated with Druj (falsehood or chaos), which represents actions and behaviors that contradict Asha. These include dishonesty, injustice, and disorder, which contribute to the influence of Angra Mainyu.

Living according to Asha is essential for maintaining spiritual and cosmic order.

Moral and Ethical Behavior

Zoroastrianism emphasizes moral and ethical behavior as a reflection of one's alignment with good or evil.

- Good behavior includes virtues such as honesty, charity, and respect for others. Ethical actions that promote justice, order, and the well-being of others are considered manifestations of aligning with divine principles.

- Evil behavior involves actions such as deceit, cruelty, and exploitation. Such actions are seen as contributing to the disruption of divine order and the influence of evil forces.

Ethical behavior is integral to participating in the divine struggle against evil.

The Influence of Actions on Spiritual Progress

In Zoroastrianism, actions have significant implications for spiritual progress and the cosmic balance.

- Good actions contribute to spiritual growth and the triumph of good over evil. Acts of kindness, justice, and devotion to Ahura Mazda are seen as enhancing one's spiritual standing and contributing to the cosmic order.

- Evil actions hinder spiritual progress and perpetuate the influence of Angra Mainyu. Harmful actions, dishonesty, and cruelty are believed to affect one's spiritual development negatively and contribute to the chaos of the cosmic struggle.

Actions have a direct impact on the spiritual and cosmic balance.

The Role of Rituals and Devotion

Rituals and devotion play an important role in Zoroastrian practice.

- Good involves engaging in rituals and prayers that honor Ahura Mazda, uphold Asha, and support the divine order. Rituals such as fire worship and offerings are means of aligning oneself with divine principles.

- Evil involves neglecting rituals or engaging in practices that dishonor Ahura Mazda or disrupt divine order. This includes actions that are disrespectful to the sacred elements and rituals of Zoroastrianism.

Rituals and devotion are means of reinforcing one's alignment with good.

The Concept of Saoshyant (Future Savior)

Saoshyant is a prophetic figure in Zoroastrianism who is believed to come in the future to defeat evil and bring about the final triumph of good.

- Good involves supporting the principles and values that the Saoshyant will ultimately uphold, such as truth, justice, and righteousness. Working towards the realization of these principles is seen as contributing to the ultimate victory of good.

- Evil involves opposing or undermining these principles and contributing to the forces of Angra Mainyu. Actions that work against the anticipated triumph of good are considered contrary to divine will.

Belief in the Saoshyant provides hope and motivation for working towards a future of ultimate justice and harmony.

The Role of Individual Responsibility

Individual responsibility is emphasized in Zoroastrianism as each person's actions contribute to the cosmic struggle.

- Good involves taking personal responsibility for one's actions, making ethical choices, and striving to uphold divine principles in daily life. Each individual's efforts contribute to the overall struggle between good and evil.

- Evil involves shirking responsibility or engaging in actions that perpetuate evil. Neglecting one's duty to uphold Asha and contribute positively to the world is seen as failing to support the divine struggle against chaos.

Individual responsibility is central to participating in the cosmic struggle and supporting the divine order.

The Importance of Truth (Rast)

Truth (Rast) is a fundamental value in Zoroastrianism.

- Good is associated with truthfulness and honesty, reflecting the divine nature of Ahura Mazda. Speaking and acting in accordance with truth is considered essential for maintaining spiritual and cosmic order.

- Evil is associated with falsehood and deceit, which align with the disruptive forces of Angra Mainyu. Dishonesty and deception are seen as contributing to spiritual and cosmic disorder.

Truthfulness is a key aspect of ethical and moral behavior.

The Concept of Afterlife and Final Judgment

Zoroastrianism teaches about the afterlife and final judgment where souls are judged based on their actions.

- Good involves leading a life that aligns with the principles of Ahura Mazda and contributing to the triumph of good. Those who have lived righteously are believed to be rewarded in the afterlife and support the final cosmic victory over evil.

- Evil involves actions that contradict divine principles and contribute to the influence of Angra Mainyu. Souls that have lived in opposition to divine order may face judgment and consequences in the afterlife.

The afterlife and final judgment reinforce the moral framework of Zoroastrianism.

Zoroastrianism Summary

In Zoroastrianism, good and evil are understood through the dualistic struggle between Ahura Mazda and Angra Mainyu. Good is associated with truth, order, and alignment with divine principles, while evil is associated with falsehood, chaos, and opposition to divine will. The exercise of free will, ethical behavior, and individual responsibility are central to participating in this cosmic struggle. Rituals, devotion, and adherence to the principle of Asha (truth and order) are important for aligning with the divine and contributing to the ultimate triumph of good over evil.

Philosopher

Aristotle

Aristotle's perspective on good and evil is rooted in his ethical theory, particularly as outlined in his work *Nicomachean Ethics* (the science of the good for human life). His approach is grounded in the idea of virtue ethics, which focuses on the development of good character traits (virtues) and achieving a balanced, flourishing life (eudaimonia).

Good (Virtue and Eudaimonia)

- Eudaimonia (Flourishing or Happiness): For Aristotle, the highest good for human beings is eudaimonia, often translated as "flourishing" or "happiness." It is not merely a feeling but an objective state of living a fulfilled and meaningful life. Eudaimonia is achieved by living in accordance with reason and cultivating virtues over time. It is the ultimate goal that all human actions aim to achieve.

- Virtue (Arete): Goodness is characterized by the development of virtue. For Aristotle, a virtue is a habitual and rational disposition to act in accordance with reason. Virtues represent the mean between two extremes of behavior—excess and deficiency. For example, courage is the mean between recklessness (excess) and cowardice (deficiency). By finding the right balance in different aspects of life, one becomes virtuous.

- The Doctrine of the Mean: Central to Aristotle's understanding of virtue is his Doctrine of the Mean, which asserts that good action lies between two extremes (vices). The "mean" is relative to each individual and situation, and achieving it requires practical wisdom (phronesis). For example, in the context of giving, generosity is a virtue that lies between wastefulness and stinginess.

- Practical Wisdom (Phronesis): Achieving goodness involves not just understanding the virtues but also applying them in real life. Practical wisdom is the ability to make sound judgments and decisions based on reason and experience. It guides one in determining what the right action is in various circumstances, leading to virtuous behavior.

Evil (Vice and Imbalance)

- Vice (Excess or Deficiency): For Aristotle, evil arises from vice, which is the opposite of virtue. Vices represent extremes—either excess or deficiency—in behavior. For example, cowardice is the lack of courage, and recklessness is the excess of it. Both vices are forms of moral failure because they deviate from the rational mean and prevent the individual from achieving eudaimonia.

- Irrationality and Lack of Self-Control: Evil, or immoral behavior, occurs when a person's actions are not guided by reason. Aristotle believed that humans have a rational soul, and living in accordance with reason is essential for achieving the good. When people are overcome by irrational desires or emotions (akrasia, or lack of self-control), they fall into vice and do evil.

- Injustice and Imbalance: Injustice, or acting unjustly, is considered a form of evil. Injustice occurs when someone takes more than their fair share or treats others unfairly. This disrupts the balance necessary for the good life. Aristotle also believed that extreme inequalities and imbalances in society can contribute to evil, as they prevent individuals and communities from flourishing.

The Role of Reason and Choice

- Rationality as the Key to Goodness: Aristotle emphasized that humans are unique in their ability to reason, and living a good life means living a life of rational deliberation. It is through the proper use of reason that one can discern the virtuous mean in various situations. For Aristotle, virtue is a habit formed through deliberate and rational action, and it requires practice.

- Voluntary Action and Responsibility: Aristotle argued that people are responsible for their actions, especially when those actions are voluntary. Since individuals have the capacity for rational choice, they are capable of choosing between good (virtue) and evil (vice). Deliberate choices that lead to vice are considered morally wrong because they reflect a failure to act according to reason.

The Struggle Between Good and Evil

- Moral Development and Habit: Aristotle believed that becoming virtuous is a process that requires moral education and the formation of good habits. People are not born virtuous, but they develop virtue through practice, guided by reason. The struggle between good and evil in Aristotle's philosophy is not about external forces, but about the internal process of cultivating virtues and overcoming vices.

- Character and Responsibility: Aristotle emphasized that one's character is formed by repeated actions. If someone habitually makes poor choices, they develop a vicious character, and if they habitually make good choices, they cultivate a virtuous character. In this sense, good and evil are the result of the patterns of behavior that individuals choose to adopt over time.

Aristotle Summary

From Aristotle's perspective, good is defined by the cultivation of virtue and living in accordance with reason to achieve eudaimonia (flourishing). Goodness is found in acting with practical wisdom, choosing the mean between excess and deficiency in behavior, and striving for moral balance. Evil arises from vice, which is characterized by either excess or deficiency, irrational behavior, and the failure to live in accordance with reason. Humans are responsible for their choices, and through rational deliberation and practice, they can cultivate virtues and avoid vices, leading to a fulfilled and balanced life.

Augustine

St. Augustine of Hippo, a prominent early Christian theologian and philosopher, developed a profound and influential perspective on good and evil. His views are primarily articulated in works such as *"Confessions"* and *"City of God."* Augustine's ideas are rooted in his Christian faith and his interpretations of Scripture.

The Nature of Good and Evil

- Good as a Reflection of God: For Augustine, good is fundamentally linked to the nature of God. God is the ultimate source of all goodness, and anything that aligns with God's will and divine nature is considered good. Goodness is a reflection of God's perfect, unchanging, and eternal nature. As a result, true goodness is derived from and measured against God's absolute standard of goodness.

- Evil as a Privation of Good: Augustine's most famous contribution to the understanding of evil is his concept of evil as a *privation of good* (privatio boni). According to Augustine, evil is not a substance or a force in itself but rather a lack or distortion of the good. This idea stems from the notion that God created everything good, and evil arises when created beings misuse their free will and turn away from God's goodness. In this sense, evil does not exist independently but is a corruption or perversion of the good.

The Problem of Free Will

- Free Will and Moral Responsibility: Augustine placed significant emphasis on human free will as central to understanding the existence of evil. He believed that God granted human beings free will, which allows them to choose between good and evil. The misuse of this freedom leads to moral evil. Augustine argued that true goodness requires the possibility of choosing evil, and free will is necessary for genuine moral responsibility.

- Original Sin: Augustine's doctrine of original sin is integral to his understanding of evil. He taught that the first humans, Adam and Eve, abused their free will by disobeying God, which introduced sin and moral corruption into the human condition. This original sin has consequences for all of humanity, affecting human nature and leading to a propensity for sin.

The Role of Grace and Redemption

- Divine Grace: Augustine believed that human beings, due to original sin, are incapable of achieving goodness on their own. Divine grace is essential for salvation and for the ability to do good. Grace, according to Augustine, is an unearned gift from God that enables individuals to overcome sin and live in accordance with divine will. It is through grace that humans can be redeemed and restored to a state of goodness.

- Redemption through Christ: Augustine's theology emphasizes the role of Jesus Christ in overcoming evil and restoring humanity to a state of righteousness. Christ's sacrifice and resurrection provide the means for redemption and the forgiveness of sins. For Augustine, Christ is the embodiment of divine goodness and the path to overcoming the corruption brought about by evil.

Theological Implications

- Theodicy and Divine Providence: Augustine addressed the problem of evil in the context of theodicy, seeking to reconcile the existence of evil with the belief in a good and all-powerful God. He argued that God allows evil to exist in order to preserve human free will and to ultimately bring about greater good. In Augustine's view, divine providence works through even the presence of evil to achieve a greater purpose and ultimate good.

- The Two Cities: In *"City of God,"* Augustine contrasts the City of God (a spiritual realm where God's will is upheld) with the Earthly City (a secular realm characterized by self-love and moral corruption). This distinction illustrates his belief that goodness is aligned with the divine order and that evil is associated with human pride and rebellion against God's sovereignty.

Augustine Summary

St. Augustine's perspective on good and evil is deeply rooted in his Christian theology. He posits that good is a reflection of God's nature and that evil is a privation or corruption of the good. Augustine emphasizes the importance of free will in the existence of evil, arguing that moral evil arises from the misuse of human freedom. Divine grace is crucial for overcoming sin and achieving goodness, with Christ's redemption playing a central role in restoring humanity to righteousness. Augustine's views integrate the concepts of original sin, divine providence, and the distinction between the City of God and the Earthly City to provide a comprehensive theological framework for understanding good and evil.

Buber

Martin Buber, a Jewish philosopher known for his work in existentialism and philosophy of dialogue, offers a unique perspective on good and evil that is deeply rooted in his concept of relationship and dialogue. His ideas are primarily articulated through his influential work, *I and Thou* (or *I and You*), where he explores the nature of human relationships and the ethical implications of these interactions.

Good as Authentic Relationships and Mutual Recognition

In Buber's philosophy, the concept of good is closely tied to the idea of authentic relationships and the genuine mutual recognition of the other as a unique individual.

- For Buber, good is found in the context of authentic, I-Thou relationships. These relationships are characterized by mutual recognition, respect, and engagement. In an I-Thou relationship, individuals encounter each other as whole beings, valuing each other's intrinsic worth and engaging in a dialogue that is genuine and open. This kind of relationship fosters an environment where individuals can realize their potential and contribute to the well-being of one another.

- Mutual Recognition: Good is also associated with recognizing and affirming the other as an equal and unique individual. This involves seeing others not merely as objects or means to an end (I-It relationships) but as partners in a shared human experience. This mutual recognition creates a space for ethical behavior and genuine connection.

Evil as Objectification and Disregard for the Other

In contrast, evil is associated with the objectification of others and the lack of genuine engagement and recognition in relationships.

- From Buber's perspective, evil occurs when individuals engage in I-It relationships, where others are treated merely as objects or means to an end, rather than as subjects with their own intrinsic value. This objectification leads to a disregard for the dignity and worth of others, resulting in harm, exploitation, and alienation.

- Disregard for the Other: Evil is also reflected in actions and attitudes that ignore or dismiss the needs and humanity of others. This includes behaviors that perpetuate inequality, oppression, and dehumanization. When individuals fail to engage with others in a way that acknowledges their inherent value, it leads to a breakdown in ethical relations and moral responsibility.

Good and Evil in the Context of Dialogical Ethics

Buber's ethics are deeply rooted in the philosophy of dialogue, which emphasizes the importance of genuine communication and shared understanding.

- Good is characterized by a commitment to dialogue that fosters mutual understanding and respect. In dialogical ethics, the focus is on engaging with others in a way that is open, empathetic, and responsive. This approach to ethics values the process of communication as a means to build authentic relationships and address moral issues collaboratively.

- In the context of dialogical ethics, individuals have a moral responsibility to engage with others in ways that reflect respect and empathy. This involves listening to and understanding others' perspectives, as well as recognizing and addressing the impact of one's actions on others.

Good and Evil in the Context of Community and Society

Buber also explores the implications of his philosophy for broader social and communal contexts.

- In a societal context, good involves creating and nurturing communities where authentic relationships and mutual recognition are prioritized. This includes fostering environments where people can engage with each other as equals and work together to address common goals and challenges.

- Evil, on the other hand, is manifested in societal structures and systems that perpetuate alienation, exploitation, and inequality. When societal norms and institutions fail to recognize the inherent dignity of individuals and promote objectification, they contribute to moral harm and social injustice.

Good and Evil in Spiritual and Existential Terms

Buber's philosophy also touches on the spiritual and existential dimensions of good and evil.

- For Buber, authentic I-Thou relationships are not only ethical but also have a spiritual dimension. They represent a deeper connection to the divine and the sacred in everyday life. Good is thus associated with living in a way that is spiritually fulfilling and aligned with a sense of higher purpose and connection.

- Existential Responsibility: Existentially, Buber emphasizes the importance of personal responsibility and the role of individual choices in shaping ethical behavior. Good involves actively choosing to engage in authentic relationships and to act with integrity and respect, while evil involves failing to uphold these values and allowing objectification and dehumanization to persist.

Buber Summary

Martin Buber's perspective on good and evil is centered around the nature of human relationships and the ethical implications of how we engage with others. Good is defined by authentic I-Thou relationships characterized by mutual recognition, respect, and genuine dialogue. Evil is associated with objectification, dehumanization, and the failure to engage with others in meaningful and respectful ways. Buber's philosophy emphasizes the importance of ethical communication, communal responsibility, and the spiritual dimensions of human interactions in understanding and addressing moral issues.

$\mathcal{D}$escartes

René Descartes' view of good and evil is shaped by his rationalist philosophy, his ideas about free will, and his belief in God as the source of all goodness. Descartes saw morality as rooted in the application of reason and the proper use of free will, with error and evil arising from the misuse of these faculties.

Good (God, Reason, and Free Will)

- Descartes was a devout Christian, and his concept of good is closely tied to his belief in God. For Descartes, God is the supreme being, infinitely perfect, and the source of all that is good. Anything that exists and is real has its origin in God, who is the ultimate cause of all that is true and good. In this sense, goodness is aligned with truth and reality, and acting in accordance with the good means acting in accordance with God's will and the natural order.

- Descartes believed that reason is the key to discerning what is good. Humans, created in the image of God, possess free will and intellect. Through the proper use of reason, one can discover the truths of the universe, which align with what is good. Therefore, the good life is one guided by reason, where individuals make decisions based on clear and distinct knowledge of what is true and good.

- Descartes emphasized that humans have free will, which allows them to choose between good and evil. This free will is, according to Descartes, a gift from God, and it reflects the infinite nature of God's goodness. When exercised properly, free will enables individuals to act morally and in line with the good.

Evil (Error and Misuse of Free Will)

- Descartes did not believe that evil exists as a positive, independent force. Rather, he viewed evil as a lack of perfection, a privation of good. In this way, evil is similar to error—it arises not from an active principle of evil but from a deficiency in knowledge or judgment. In Descartes' view, errors occur when the human will extends beyond what is clearly understood by reason. When people act based on ignorance or incomplete knowledge, they make mistakes, leading to actions that can be considered evil or harmful.

- Descartes argued that error (and by extension, moral evil) comes from the misuse of free will. The human will is limitless in its scope—it can choose to affirm or deny anything—but the human intellect is limited, meaning that we often do not have full knowledge of what we are considering. When people make decisions without sufficient knowledge or without applying reason, they are prone to error and can commit acts that are morally wrong.

    For instance, if a person makes a judgment or decision without full understanding or certainty, they are likely to make a mistake. This misuse of free will results in evil because it leads to actions that deviate from the good or the truth.

- Given that Descartes believed God is perfect and all-good, he had to address the question of why evil exists. He argued that while God is not the source of evil, God allows free will to exist, which inevitably leads to the possibility of error and evil. God does not directly cause evil, but he allows human beings to exercise free will, even though this sometimes results in mistakes and moral failings.

    Imperfection in the World: Descartes acknowledged that the world contains imperfections, which can cause suffering and evil. However, he believed that these imperfections are necessary for the overall goodness and balance of the universe. Just as in a painting, contrasts (even between light and dark) contribute to the overall beauty of the work, so too the imperfections in the world serve a greater purpose that humans may not fully understand.

The Role of Knowledge in Avoiding Evil

- Descartes believed that the best way to avoid error and evil is through the pursuit of knowledge. By applying one's reason and exercising free will carefully, a person can align themselves with the good. Descartes' famous method of systematic doubt—doubting all things until what remains is clearly true—was designed to ensure that only true knowledge guides one's will and actions.

- For Descartes, clear and distinct ideas represent the hallmark of truth. If a person makes judgments only based on ideas that are clear and distinct (meaning they are certain and beyond doubt), they will not fall into error. Hence, the way to avoid evil is to refrain from making decisions or judgments when knowledge is unclear or incomplete.

Descartes Summary

For Descartes, good is associated with God, truth, and acting in accordance with reason and knowledge. Humans possess free will, a divine gift, which allows them to choose between good and evil. However, evil arises not from an active force of malevolence, but from error, ignorance, and the misuse of free will. When individuals make judgments without sufficient understanding or allow their will to extend beyond the limits of their intellect, they are prone to mistakes, which result in evil actions. To live a good and moral life, one must pursue knowledge, use reason properly, and align one's actions with truth, avoiding error and aligning with the divine good.

Dewey

John Dewey, an influential American philosopher and educator, is known for his work in pragmatism and progressive education. Dewey's perspective on good and evil is shaped by his pragmatic philosophy, which emphasizes the practical consequences of beliefs and actions rather than adherence to fixed moral absolutes.

Pragmatism and Moral Philosophy

- Dewey's pragmatism focuses on the practical implications of ideas and actions. For Dewey, good is understood in terms of its practical effects and contributions to human well-being. Good actions and decisions are those that lead to positive outcomes and solve real problems effectively. Conversely, evil is viewed as those actions or beliefs that produce harmful consequences or fail to address important issues effectively.

- Dewey believed that moral judgments should be based on ongoing inquiry and problem-solving rather than fixed principles or absolute standards. Goodness is determined through a process of experimentation, reflection, and evaluation, with an emphasis on the results of actions and their impact on individuals and society.

Ethical Development and Social Context

- Dewey's view of ethics is dynamic and developmental. He saw moral understanding as a process that evolves over time through experience and social interaction. Goodness is associated with the ability to adapt, grow, and improve one's moral reasoning based on new experiences and changing social conditions.

- Dewey emphasized the role of social context in shaping moral values. He argued that ethical principles are not static but are shaped by the needs and challenges of society. Goodness is therefore linked to the ability to respond effectively to social and environmental contexts, and evil arises from actions or beliefs that fail to address or exacerbate social problems.

Education and Moral Values

- Dewey's educational philosophy underscores the role of education in moral development. He believed that education should promote critical thinking, problem-solving, and active engagement with real-world issues. Through education, individuals learn to evaluate and act on moral questions in a thoughtful and practical manner.

- Dewey's concept of learning by doing highlights the importance of experiential learning in developing moral understanding. Goodness is achieved through reflective and informed actions based on direct experience, while evil results from ignorance or inadequate engagement with practical realities.

Ethics and Democracy

- Dewey saw democracy as a fundamental aspect of ethical development. He believed that democratic practices promote moral values by encouraging participation, dialogue, and cooperation. Goodness, in this context, is associated with the promotion of democratic principles and the fostering of a society where individuals can contribute to and benefit from collective decision-making.

- Dewey's emphasis on democratic values also involves the concept of moral agency. Individuals are seen as active participants in shaping their moral lives and society. Goodness is linked to exercising moral agency in ways that contribute to the common good and address societal challenges.

Critique of Absolute Morality

- Dewey rejected the idea of absolute moral truths or fixed moral principles. Instead, he advocated for a flexible and context-sensitive approach to ethics. For Dewey, moral values are not universal absolutes but are contingent on their practical application and effectiveness in addressing specific situations and problems.

- Dewey's approach can be seen as a form of moral relativism, where ethical judgments are based on their contextual relevance and practical outcomes rather than adherence to absolute moral norms. Goodness and evil are therefore understood in relation to their practical consequences and the ongoing process of moral inquiry.

Dewey Summary

John Dewey's perspective on good and evil is grounded in his pragmatic philosophy, which emphasizes the practical implications of actions and beliefs. For Dewey, good is associated with actions that produce positive outcomes and effectively address real problems, while evil involves harmful consequences or inadequate responses to issues. He views morality as a dynamic process of inquiry and growth, influenced by social context and democratic values. Dewey's rejection of absolute morality in favor of a context-sensitive approach highlights his belief in the importance of practical effectiveness and ongoing moral development in understanding good and evil.

Hume

David Hume's perspective on good and evil is grounded in his empiricist and sentimentalist approach to moral philosophy. Rather than basing moral distinctions on reason, Hume believed that moral judgments stem from human emotions and feelings. For him, good and evil are not objective properties in the world but are instead based on how things affect us emotionally.

Empiricism and Morality

- Hume was an empiricist, meaning he believed that all knowledge comes from sensory experience. This also applies to moral knowledge. Hume argued that we do not discover good and evil through reason alone, but rather through our experiences and the emotions those experiences evoke in us.

- According to Hume, moral sentiments—such as approval, disapproval, pleasure, or pain—are the basis of our moral judgments. When we call something "good," we do so because it elicits feelings of pleasure or approval in us or benefits society. Conversely, we label something "evil" or "bad" when it produces pain or disapproval or harms others.

- For instance, when we see an act of kindness, we feel a sense of approval and associate it with goodness. When we witness cruelty or injustice, we feel disapproval and call it evil. These feelings are universal, but Hume emphasizes that they come from our emotional responses, not from reason.

Good and Evil as Matters of Feeling

- For Hume, good and evil are not inherent qualities in objects or actions. Instead, they are determined by the emotional reactions they provoke in us. This means that morality is subjective—good and evil depend on the feelings of individuals or the collective sentiments of society.

  > Good is what brings pleasure, satisfaction, or benefit to individuals and society.

  > Evil is what causes pain, suffering, or harm to individuals and society.

- Hume believed that moral judgments are often grounded in the usefulness (or utility) of actions and traits to society. For example, benevolence and justice are considered good because they contribute to the well-being and stability of society. Acts of cruelty or injustice are considered evil because they cause harm and disrupt social harmony.

  > Hume argued that the virtues we admire, like kindness or fairness, are those that promote social cooperation and benefit others. On the other hand, vices like selfishness or cruelty are condemned because they create discord and suffering.

Reason's Role in Morality

- Hume famously stated that "reason is, and ought only to be the slave of the passions." By this, he meant that reason alone cannot tell us what is good or evil. Reason is useful in helping us determine the facts of a situation and understand cause and effect, but it is ultimately our emotions that lead us to moral judgments.

  > For example, reason can tell us that stealing leads to harm for the victim, but it is our feelings of empathy or disgust at the harm caused by stealing that make us consider it morally wrong. Therefore, moral distinctions between good and evil are based

on how actions make us feel, not on cold, rational calculations.

Sympathy as the Basis for Moral Judgments

- One of the key concepts in Hume's moral theory is sympathy. He believed that humans are naturally sympathetic beings, capable of sharing in the feelings of others. This capacity for sympathy allows us to make moral judgments that consider the well-being of others, not just ourselves.

- When we witness someone suffering, we feel sympathy for them, and this leads us to judge actions that cause suffering as evil. Similarly, when we see someone performing a kind or altruistic act, we feel pleasure in response to their goodness, which leads us to consider it morally good.

- Sympathy also forms the basis for moral standards in society. As we interact with others, we learn to align our feelings with those of our community, and shared feelings of sympathy lead to common moral norms.

The Role of Society in Defining Good and Evil

- Conventional Nature of Morality: Hume argued that while moral feelings are natural, the specific rules of what is considered good or evil are often shaped by social conventions. Morality emerges from human beings living together in society and developing norms that promote cooperation and well-being. Thus, what is seen as morally good or evil can vary across different societies and historical periods, depending on social needs and circumstances.

- The Importance of Utility in Society: Hume believed that utility, or the benefit something provides to society, plays a crucial role in determining what is considered morally good. Traits and actions that contribute to the happiness and functioning of society are regarded as virtuous, while those that disrupt social harmony are considered vices. For example, justice is good because it promotes social order, and injustice is evil because it leads to chaos and harm.

Moral Relativism and Universality

- Since moral judgments are based on feelings and the utility of actions to society, Hume acknowledged that what is considered good or evil can differ between cultures and individuals. There is no absolute standard of morality that applies to all people at all times. Instead, moral norms are shaped by the particular needs and circumstances of a society.

- However, Hume also believed that certain moral sentiments, like sympathy and the tendency to seek the happiness of others, are universal. While the specific rules of morality might change from society to society, the fundamental feelings of approval and disapproval based on how actions affect others are shared by all humans.

Hume Summary

David Hume's approach to good and evil emphasizes that these moral distinctions are based on human emotions and sentiments, rather than objective facts or divine commands. For Hume, moral judgments arise from feelings of approval or disapproval toward actions, based on how they affect individuals and society. Good is what brings pleasure, benefit, or utility to society, while evil is what causes harm, pain, or suffering. Hume argued that while reason helps us understand facts, it is ultimately our emotions and capacity for sympathy that guide our moral decisions. Morality is therefore both subjective and shaped by social conventions, but some basic moral sentiments, such as sympathy, are universal across humanity.

Jung

Carl Jung, a Swiss psychiatrist and psychoanalyst, offers a distinctive perspective on good and evil through his theories of psychology and individual development. His views are informed by concepts such as the collective unconscious, archetypes, and shadow.

Good and Evil as Psychological Archetypes

Jung's approach to good and evil is deeply rooted in his concept of archetypes, which are universal symbols and themes that arise from the collective unconscious.

- Jung believed that archetypes such as the Hero, the Shadow, and the Self shape human experiences and moral understanding. The Hero represents positive qualities such as courage and virtue, while the Shadow embodies the darker, repressed aspects of the psyche, including aspects of evil.

- Good, from a Jungian perspective, is often associated with the integration and expression of positive archetypes, such as the Hero or the Wise Old Man. These archetypes guide individuals toward self-realization, wholeness, and ethical behavior.

- Evil is associated with the darker aspects of the Shadow, which includes the repressed, unconscious elements of the psyche that are often projected onto others. Evil emerges when individuals fail to confront and integrate these shadow aspects, leading to destructive or harmful behavior.

The Shadow and Moral Ambiguity

Jung's concept of the Shadow is central to understanding his view on good and evil. The Shadow represents the unconscious, repressed parts of the self that are often projected onto others.

- Jung argued that confronting and integrating the Shadow is crucial for personal development. Good involves acknowledging and integrating these darker aspects of the self rather than projecting them onto others. This process leads to greater self-awareness and ethical behavior.

- Jung believed that when individuals fail to recognize their own Shadow, they are more likely to project these negative traits onto others, resulting in conflicts and moral judgments. This projection can perpetuate cycles of evil and misunderstanding.

Good and Evil in the Context of Individuation

Jung's concept of individuation—the process of becoming a whole and integrated individual—plays a significant role in his understanding of good and evil.

- Good is associated with the progress of individuation, where individuals work toward integrating all aspects of their personality, including the Shadow. This process involves reconciling opposing forces within the self and achieving a balanced, authentic expression of one's true nature.

- Through individuation, individuals develop a greater understanding of their own moral values and the complexities of good and evil. This self-awareness allows for more nuanced and compassionate ethical decisions.

Collective Unconscious and Moral Values

Jung's idea of the collective unconscious contains universal themes and symbols shared across humanity. This concept influences his understanding of moral values.

- Jung believed that certain moral values and ethical principles are embedded in the collective unconscious and manifest through cultural myths, religious symbols, and archetypes. These shared values contribute to a common understanding of good and evil across different societies.

- Jung also recognized that moral values are influenced by cultural and historical contexts. While there are universal archetypes, the interpretation of good and evil can vary depending on cultural narratives and individual experiences.

Good and Evil in Personal and Societal Contexts

Jung's perspective extends to both personal and societal dimensions of good and evil.

- On a personal level, good involves engaging in self-reflection, confronting one's own Shadow, and striving for psychological wholeness. Evil arises from the failure to address one's inner conflicts and the projection of personal issues onto others.

- In societal contexts, Jung saw the potential for collective shadow dynamics, where societal groups project their repressed fears and conflicts onto others. This can lead to large-scale conflicts and moral issues, such as prejudice, discrimination, and war.

Jung Summary

Carl Jung's perspective on good and evil is rooted in his psychological theories, including the collective unconscious, archetypes, and the Shadow. Good is associated with the integration of positive archetypes, the process of individuation, and the acknowledgment of the Shadow. Evil is linked to the projection of repressed aspects of the self and the failure to confront and integrate these darker elements. Jung's approach emphasizes the importance of self-awareness, personal development, and the impact of collective unconscious factors on moral values and ethical behavior.

Kant

Immanuel Kant, a central figure in Enlightenment philosophy, provides a rigorous and systematic approach to understanding good and evil through his ethical theories. His perspective is rooted in the concept of duty, moral law, and rationality.

Good as Acting According to Duty and the Moral Law

Kant's concept of good is closely tied to the idea of acting according to duty and adherence to the moral law.

- For Kant, the good will is the only thing that is good without qualification. A good will is defined by its commitment to act according to moral principles and duty, rather than personal desires or consequences. The moral worth of an action lies in the intention behind it, not in its outcomes.

- Kant argues that the moral law is expressed through the categorical imperative, a principle that requires individuals to act only according to maxims that they would want to become universal laws. Good actions are those that align with this universal moral law, which is determined through rational deliberation and adherence to duty.

Evil as Acting Against Duty and the Moral Law

In Kantian ethics, evil is associated with actions that violate the moral law and fail to act according to duty.

- Evil, in Kant's view, involves actions that are driven by maxims that cannot be universalized or that disregard the intrinsic dignity of others. For instance, if an action is performed based on a principle that one would not want everyone to follow (e.g., lying to get out of trouble), it is considered morally wrong.

- Actions are evil if they demonstrate a lack of respect for the moral law and the rational capacity of individuals. This includes behaviors that exploit, deceive, or harm others in ways that undermine their inherent worth and dignity.

The Categorical Imperative and Moral Law

Kant's moral philosophy is based on the categorical imperative, a foundational principle that guides ethical decision-making.

- One formulation of the categorical imperative is the principle of universalizability, which states that one should act only according to maxims that can be consistently willed as a universal law. If an action cannot be universalized without contradiction, it is morally impermissible.

- Respect for Persons is another formulation of the categorical imperative. It requires treating others as ends in themselves and never merely as means to an end. This means recognizing and respecting the inherent worth and rational autonomy of individuals.

Moral Autonomy and Rationality

Kant emphasizes the role of moral autonomy and rationality in defining good and evil.

- Kantian ethics holds that individuals are morally autonomous agents capable of making rational decisions based on the moral law. Good actions arise from the exercise of this autonomy in accordance with duty and moral principles.

- Rationality is central to Kant's ethical framework. Actions are considered good if they stem from rational deliberation and adherence to moral principles, rather than being motivated by personal inclinations or external consequences.

Good and Evil in Practical Terms

Kant's ethical theory has practical implications for understanding and evaluating moral behavior.

- Practically, good actions are those that follow the dictates of the moral law and are performed out of a sense of duty. This includes actions that respect the rights and dignity of others and adhere to universal moral principles.

- Evil actions are those that violate the moral law, fail to respect the inherent dignity of individuals, or involve acting on maxims that cannot be universalized. Such actions are characterized by a disregard for moral duty and the rational principles that underpin ethical behavior.

Kant Summary

Immanuel Kant's perspective on good and evil is grounded in the concepts of duty, moral law, and rationality. Good is defined by acting according to the categorical imperative, which requires individuals to follow maxims that can be universalized and to treat others with respect and dignity. Evil, conversely, involves actions that violate the moral law, fail to adhere to duty, or exploit others. Kantian ethics emphasizes the importance of rational deliberation and moral autonomy in determining the ethical value of actions.

Leonardo

Leonardo di ser Piero da Vinci, more commonly Leonardo, the Renaissance polymath known for his contributions to art, science, and engineering, did not explicitly develop a systematic philosophy of good and evil in the way that philosophers or theologians might. However, insights into his views on these concepts can be gleaned from his writings, observations, and artistic works.

Human Nature and Morality

Leonardo da Vinci's views on good and evil can be inferred from his observations on human nature and behavior.

- Leonardo had a keen interest in human anatomy and psychology, studying the intricacies of human behavior and emotions. He often depicted human nature in his art with a focus on both its beauty and its flaws. His detailed observations suggest that he saw human nature as complex and capable of both virtuous and immoral actions. This complexity implies that good and evil are deeply intertwined with human intent and behavior.

- Leonardo valued reason and intellectual inquiry, which can be connected to his understanding of morality. Goodness, in his view, might be associated with the pursuit of knowledge, rationality, and the application of these virtues in one's actions and creations. Conversely, evil could be seen as stemming from ignorance, irrationality, or the misuse of knowledge.

Ethics in Art and Innovation

Leonardo's ethical views can also be interpreted through his approach to art and innovation.

- Leonardo's approach to art was grounded in a desire for truth and authenticity. His commitment to capturing the essence of his subjects with precision and depth reflects an ethical concern for representing reality faithfully. This emphasis on integrity and truthfulness in art aligns with a conception of good as honesty and authenticity.

- As an inventor and scientist, Leonardo's work aimed at advancing human knowledge and capabilities. His innovations, which ranged from engineering marvels to anatomical studies, suggest a belief in the positive potential of human creativity and intellect. Good, in this context, can be seen as using one's talents and innovations for the betterment of humanity, while evil might involve the exploitation or harmful application of such knowledge.

Influence of Renaissance Humanism

Leonardo was deeply influenced by the Renaissance humanism of his time, which emphasized the value of human potential and individual achievement.

- Renaissance humanism focused on the dignity and worth of the individual and the importance of personal development. Goodness, therefore, was associated with the pursuit of personal excellence, moral integrity, and the enrichment of human life through learning and creativity.

- Leonardo's works often explore themes of moral ambiguity and complexity. For instance, his portraits and studies of human emotions reflect the nuanced and multifaceted nature of human morality. This suggests that Leonardo may have seen good and evil not as absolute categories but as aspects of the broader human experience.

Philosophical Reflections

Leonardo's notebooks contain philosophical reflections that provide insight into his views on morality.

- Leonardo's writings sometimes touch on themes of virtue and ethical behavior. His reflections on the nature of virtue and vice suggest an appreciation for the moral dimensions of human actions and the importance of aligning one's conduct with principles of goodness and integrity.

- Leonardo's pragmatic approach to solving problems and his emphasis on practical knowledge reflect an ethical stance that values effectiveness and utility. Good, from this perspective, could be seen as achieving practical and beneficial outcomes, while evil might involve failing to address problems effectively or causing harm through ineffectiveness.

Leonardo Summary

Leonardo da Vinci's perspective on good and evil can be understood through his emphasis on human nature, intellectual integrity, and the ethical implications of art and innovation. Goodness is associated with truthfulness, rationality, and the constructive use of knowledge, while evil might be linked to ignorance, dishonesty, and the misuse of one's abilities. Influenced by Renaissance humanism, Leonardo valued personal development and moral integrity, and his reflections suggest a nuanced understanding of morality as deeply intertwined with human intent and behavior.

Locke

John Locke's perspective on good and evil is deeply rooted in his empiricist philosophy and moral theory. For Locke, the concepts of good and evil are not innate, fixed qualities but are largely determined by human experience, reason, and utility.

Good and Evil as Pleasure and Pain

Locke defines good and evil in terms of pleasure and pain. In his *Essay Concerning Human Understanding*, he explains that we come to understand what is good as that which causes pleasure, and evil as that which causes pain. Human beings seek pleasure and avoid pain, and thus, actions or things that lead to pleasure are regarded as good, while those that lead to pain are seen as evil.

Moral Relativism and Utility

Locke emphasizes that what is considered good or evil can vary from person to person and culture to culture, depending on how certain actions or things contribute to pleasure or pain. This makes his moral theory somewhat relativistic, as good and evil are not absolute but depend on the utility of things in promoting happiness or avoiding suffering.

Natural Law and Divine Will

While Locke believes that good and evil are determined through human experience, he also links them to natural law, which is a law given by God. For Locke, God created humans with the ability to reason, and through reason, we can discern what is morally good or evil according to the natural law. Moral good and evil, therefore, align with God's will and what reason tells us will lead to the flourishing of human beings in society.

Moral Obligations

Locke believes that moral good and evil are also about obligations, especially in a social context. Human beings have certain duties, such as the duty to preserve their own life and the lives of others. Actions that fulfill these obligations are morally good, while those that violate them are morally evil.

Freedom and Responsibility

Locke's theory of free will also plays a role in understanding good and evil. He argues that humans have the ability to choose their actions based on reason, and with this freedom comes responsibility. Therefore, individuals are accountable for their choices, and it is this capacity for free choice that underpins moral judgments of good and evil.

Locke Summary

In Locke's philosophy, good and evil are not objective, unchanging absolutes but are understood in terms of their relation to pleasure, pain, and utility. They are guided by natural law and reason, and human beings have the freedom and responsibility to act in ways that contribute to the common good or harm.

Luther

Martin Luther, the 16th-century theologian and key figure in the Protestant Reformation, had a distinctive perspective on good and evil that is deeply rooted in his theological beliefs and his interpretation of Christian doctrine. His views are primarily expressed through his writings on theology, ethics, and biblical interpretation.

Good as Acting in Faith and Following God's Will

Luther's concept of good is fundamentally tied to faith and the will of God. He emphasized that true goodness is defined by one's relationship with God and adherence to His will as revealed in the Scriptures.

- Faith Alone (Sola Fide): Luther's doctrine of justification by faith alone asserts that individuals are justified before God not by their own merits or good works but by faith in Jesus Christ. For Luther, true goodness is realized through faith, which aligns with God's will and grace.

- Following God's Will: Good actions are those that align with God's commands and moral teachings as found in the Bible. This involves living a life that reflects the teachings of Christ and the ethical standards set forth in Scripture.

Evil as Sin and Rebellion Against God

In Luther's view, evil is primarily understood as sin and rebellion against God. Sin is seen as a fundamental separation from God's will and a violation of divine commandments.

- Sin: Luther viewed sin as a fundamental condition of human nature, resulting from the fall of Adam and Eve. Sin is not just individual acts of wrongdoing but a deeper, pervasive corruption of human nature that alienates individuals from God.

- Rebellion Against God: Evil is also understood as an active rebellion against God's will. This rebellion manifests in actions that defy God's commandments and disrupt the order He has established. For Luther, acts of evil are expressions of this deeper rebellion and alienation from God.

The Role of Grace and Redemption

Luther emphasized the importance of grace and redemption in understanding good and evil. He believed that humans cannot achieve goodness on their own but rely on divine grace for salvation.

- According to Luther, divine grace is the only means through which individuals can be reconciled with God. Grace is unearned and freely given by God, and it enables believers to live in accordance with God's will despite their inherent sinfulness.

- Luther's theology centers on the belief that Jesus Christ's sacrifice provides redemption and forgiveness of sins. Through faith in Christ, individuals are redeemed and empowered to live a life that aligns with God's moral standards.

Good and Evil in the Context of the Law and Gospel

Luther distinguished between the Law and the Gospel in his understanding of good and evil.

- The Law (as found in the Old Testament) serves to reveal human sinfulness and the standards of righteousness required by God. It shows individuals their need for redemption but does not provide the means to achieve it.

- The Gospel (as found in the New Testament) offers the message of salvation through faith in Jesus Christ. It provides the good news of redemption and the power to live in accordance with God's will.

Ethical Implications and Christian Life

Luther's views on good and evil also have practical implications for the Christian life and ethical behavior.

- For Luther, living out one's faith involves following God's commandments and reflecting His love and justice in daily life. Good actions are those that manifest faith and align with the ethical teachings of the Bible.

- Luther introduced the concept of the two kingdoms: the spiritual kingdom (governed by the Gospel) and the earthly kingdom (governed by secular authority and the Law). He believed that Christians should navigate these realms by living according to faith in their spiritual lives while also engaging responsibly in secular matters.

Luthur Summary

Martin Luther's perspective on good and evil is deeply rooted in his theological beliefs about faith, grace, and redemption. Good is defined by faith in God, adherence to His will as revealed in Scripture, and the transformative power of divine grace. Evil is understood as sin and rebellion against God, reflecting a deeper separation from divine commandments. Luther's theology emphasizes the importance of grace and redemption through Jesus Christ, distinguishing between the Law and the Gospel, and applying faith to both spiritual and earthly aspects of life.

Maimonides

Maimonides (Rabbi Moses ben Maimon), a medieval Jewish philosopher, rabbi, and physician, developed a nuanced perspective on good and evil, deeply rooted in Jewish thought and influenced by Aristotelian philosophy. His ideas are primarily presented in his major works, including *The Guide for the Perplexed* and *Mishneh Torah*. Maimonides approaches good and evil through the lenses of divine wisdom, human intellect, and moral responsibility.

Good and Evil as Intellectual and Moral Perfection

For Maimonides, good and evil are closely related to the intellectual and moral development of individuals. He believes that human beings are created with the potential for intellectual and moral perfection, and their actions are judged based on how well they fulfill this potential.

- Maimonides equates good with the pursuit of wisdom, knowledge of God, and moral virtues. The highest form of good is intellectual perfection—understanding the universe and God's nature through reason. Along with this, acting ethically in accordance with divine commandments is part of living a good life.

- Evil, for Maimonides, is primarily a result of ignorance, moral failure, and separation from divine wisdom. He does not view evil as an independent force but as the absence of good, much like darkness is the absence of light. People do evil when they fail to act rationally and ethically, turning away from the path of intellectual and moral perfection.

Human Free Will and Responsibility

Maimonides strongly believes in human free will, which plays a central role in understanding good and evil. He argues that humans have the ability to choose between right and wrong, and they are morally responsible for their actions.

- Good results from choosing to live according to reason and divine commandments. When individuals use their free will to pursue wisdom, knowledge of God, and virtuous behavior, they contribute to the good in the world.

- Evil arises when individuals misuse their free will, choosing ignorance, selfishness, or unethical behavior. Maimonides insists that people cannot blame external forces for their moral failings—evil is a consequence of personal choice and neglect of moral responsibility.

The Problem of Evil and Divine Providence

Maimonides addresses the problem of evil in light of God's justice and goodness. One of the main challenges he discusses is how evil can exist in a world created by a perfect and benevolent God. He offers several insights into this issue:

- Maimonides distinguishes between two types of evil: natural and moral. Natural evils—such as earthquakes, disease, and death—are part of the physical world and follow natural laws. These occurrences, while often seen as harmful, are not "evil" in themselves; they are part of the world's necessary structure. Human suffering from natural disasters or illness is a consequence of the material nature of the universe, not a direct punishment from God. Maimonides emphasizes that the physical world is not perfect in the sense that everything is comfortable for humans, but it is perfect in terms of fulfilling its natural purpose. Humans experience suffering from these events because of their attachment to the material world, which is inherently subject to change, decay, and destruction.

- Moral evil is a result of human free will. When people act unjustly or immorally, they create evil in the world. This type of evil is within human control and can be avoided through ethical behavior and adherence to divine law.

- Maimonides reconciles the existence of evil with God's justice by emphasizing the role of divine providence. He argues that God's providence primarily concerns those who seek wisdom and live righteously. People who align themselves with divine wisdom are under the care of providence, while those who live in ignorance or moral failure may experience greater exposure to the natural evils of the world. However, Maimonides stresses that not all suffering is divine punishment— sometimes it is simply a consequence of living in a material world.

Good and Evil in Relation to the Commandments

Maimonides also sees the concepts of good and evil through the framework of the Torah's commandments (mitzvot). For him, the commandments provide a clear guide for living a morally good life. By observing the commandments, individuals align themselves with God's will and bring good into the world.

- Observing the commandments is inherently good because it brings people closer to God and ensures moral and social order. The commandments are designed to promote both individual and communal well-being.

- Disregarding or violating the commandments is considered evil because it leads to disorder, both in the individual's life and within society. Failing to follow the commandments results in moral corruption and distance from God.

The Role of Intellect in Understanding Good and Evil

Maimonides places a great emphasis on the role of intellect in discerning good and evil. He believes that humans have the capacity to understand divine wisdom through reason, and this understanding is essential to achieving moral and intellectual perfection.

- Good is achieved when humans use their intellect to understand the world and God. This pursuit of knowledge brings them closer to the divine and enables them to live virtuous lives. Intellectual and moral development go hand in hand for Maimonides.

- Evil arises from ignorance and the failure to use one's intellect properly. People who do not engage in intellectual growth or fail to seek wisdom are more likely to act immorally and bring harm to themselves and others. For Maimonides, ignorance is a primary cause of moral evil.

The Absence of Evil in God

Maimonides is also clear that God is the source of all good and cannot be the source of evil. In *The Guide for the Perplexed*, he argues that evil does not come from God directly but from the imperfection of the material world or human actions. God, as a perfect and benevolent being, only wills good, and any evil that exists is either a necessary part of the material world or the result of human choices.

Maimonides Summary

For Maimonides, good is the pursuit of intellectual and moral perfection, living in accordance with reason, divine commandments, and the knowledge of God. It is achieved by using free will to make ethical choices and aligning oneself with divine wisdom. Evil arises from ignorance, misuse of free will, and moral failure. It is not an independent force but the absence of good—often caused by human actions or the limitations of the material world. Maimonides views human beings as responsible for their moral development, with the capacity to achieve goodness through the pursuit of wisdom and ethical living.

Marx

Karl Marx's perspective on good and evil is deeply rooted in his critique of capitalism, his theory of historical materialism, and his vision of a classless society. Rather than defining good and evil in traditional moral or religious terms, Marx viewed these concepts through the lens of class struggle, economics, and the material conditions that shape human life. For Marx, morality is not absolute but shaped by the economic system and the relations of production.

Good and Evil as Products of Material Conditions

- Marx believed that human history is driven by material conditions and the means of production. In this view, good and evil are not fixed moral categories, but are shaped by the economic base of society. What is considered good or evil depends on the interests of the ruling class and the specific mode of production in a given historical period. In a capitalist society, moral ideas, including those of good and evil, are shaped by the bourgeoisie, the ruling capitalist class that controls the means of production. The proletariat, or working class, is subjected to exploitation, and their moral worldview is often shaped by this oppression.

- For Marx, morality is often part of the ideology created by the ruling class to maintain its dominance. Bourgeois morality defines good as behaviors and systems that protect private property, individualism, and capitalist profit-making. Evil, in this framework, is anything that threatens the capitalist order, such as rebellion, revolution, or the pursuit of collective ownership. Marx argues that this morality serves the interests of the ruling class and is imposed on the working class to justify their exploitation and keep them in their subordinate position.

Alienation and Exploitation as Forms of Evil

- Marx believed that one of the greatest evils in capitalist society is alienation. Alienation occurs when workers are separated from the products of their labor, from the process of production, from their fellow workers, and from their own humanity. In capitalism, workers do not own the products they create; instead, these are owned by the capitalist, who profits from the workers' labor. This exploitation leads to a deep sense of alienation, where individuals are estranged from their true selves and their potential as creative, fulfilled beings.

- Another form of evil for Marx is the exploitation of the working class by the bourgeoisie. In a capitalist system, workers are paid less than the value of what they produce, and the surplus value (profit) is taken by the capitalist. This exploitation is, in Marx's view, unjust and evil because it deprives workers of the full fruits of their labor and perpetuates inequality and oppression.

- For Marx, the class struggle between the bourgeoisie and the proletariat is not just an economic conflict, but also a moral one. The capitalist system, with its exploitation and alienation, is inherently unjust and leads to the oppression of the working class. Good in Marx's view is aligned with the interests of the proletariat and the abolition of class-based exploitation. Evil is embodied in the structures that uphold capitalism and perpetuate inequality, such as private property, wage labor, and the commodification of human life.

Revolution and the Communist Society as the Ultimate Good

- Marx saw the overthrow of capitalism and the establishment of a classless, communist society as the ultimate good. In a communist society, the means of production would be collectively owned, and the exploitation and alienation characteristic of capitalism would be abolished. For Marx, the good is the realization of human freedom and potential, which can only occur when class divisions are eliminated, and people are no longer enslaved by the need to sell their labor for survival.

- In a communist society, people would work not for the profit of others, but for the benefit of the community and for their own fulfillment. Work would become an expression of human creativity and individuality, rather than a means of survival or a source of alienation. Marx believed that this kind of society would allow for true human flourishing, where individuals are free to pursue their own interests and develop their full potential, unburdened by exploitation or class oppression. This vision of human flourishing represents the highest good in Marx's philosophy.

- With the abolition of capitalism and the establishment of communism, Marx envisioned an end to the ideological forms of morality that serve class interests. In a classless society, morality would no longer be shaped by the need to justify exploitation and inequality. Instead, moral concepts would reflect the needs and interests of all people, based on equality, cooperation, and mutual benefit.

Critique of Traditional Morality

- Marx rejected traditional moral systems, especially those that claimed to be universal or absolute, such as religious or idealist notions of good and evil. He argued that these moral systems were often tools used by the ruling class to maintain power and suppress revolutionary change. For example, Christian morality, with its emphasis on humility, obedience, and the sanctity of private property, was seen by Marx as a way to pacify the working class and discourage rebellion against their oppressors.

- Marx believed that moral ideas are shaped by class interests. For example, in a capitalist society, good is defined in terms of protecting private property and maintaining order, while evil is associated with rebellion or any threat to the existing social order. In contrast, for the working class, good would be the overthrow of the capitalist system and the establishment of a classless society, while evil would be the continuation of exploitation and alienation.

Marx Summary

For Karl Marx, good and evil are not abstract, eternal concepts but are shaped by the material conditions of society, particularly the economic system and the relations of production. In a capitalist society, what is defined as good or evil reflects the interests of the bourgeoisie, the ruling class that exploits the working class through alienation and surplus labor. Good in Marx's view is aligned with the abolition of capitalism, the establishment of communism, and the realization of human freedom and potential. Evil is represented by the structures that perpetuate exploitation, alienation, and inequality, and that serve the interests of the capitalist class. Marx believed that the true moral good would be achieved in a classless society, where individuals could live free from exploitation and fully realize their creative potential.

Nietzsche

Friedrich Nietzsche's perspective on good and evil challenges traditional moral frameworks. In his philosophy, he critiques conventional morality, particularly that of Christianity, and offers an alternative view that emphasizes power, individualism, and self-overcoming. Nietzsche's ideas on good and evil are most famously explored in works like *Thus Spoke Zarathustra, Beyond Good and Evil,* and *On the Genealogy of Morality.*

Rejection of Traditional Morality

- Nietzsche argues that concepts of good and evil are products of different systems of morality, which he categorizes as master morality and slave morality.

- This morality is created by the strong, powerful, and noble individuals who value qualities such as strength, power, nobility, creativity, and vitality. In master morality, what is good is associated with what is life-affirming, strong, and self-determined, while bad refers to what is weak, passive, and inferior. It is a morality of those who affirm their own power and existence without guilt or self-denial.

- Nietzsche contends that traditional Western morality, particularly Christian morality, is a form of slave morality. This morality is born from the resentment (ressentiment) of the weak against the powerful. It values qualities like humility, meekness, submission, and self-sacrifice, which Nietzsche sees as life-denying. In slave morality, evil refers to the qualities of the strong and the powerful, while good is defined as what serves the interests of the weak (e.g., humility, pity, and compassion). Nietzsche criticizes this as a morality that glorifies weakness and mediocrity.

Good and Evil in Traditional Morality

- Nietzsche argues that slave morality inverts the values of master morality. What the strong and noble consider good (strength, pride, dominance), the weak reframe as evil because they cannot achieve it. Conversely, what is considered bad or weak by the noble class (submission, humility) becomes morally elevated as good in slave morality. Nietzsche sees this as a fundamental distortion of life and human potential.

- Nietzsche's critique of Christianity is central to his discussion of good and evil. He argues that Christianity promotes slave morality, encouraging values like guilt, sin, and self-denial, which weaken individuals and prevent them from embracing life fully. Nietzsche's proclamation of the "death of God" symbolizes the collapse of the traditional, Christian-based moral order. With the decline of religious faith, Nietzsche believed that humanity must redefine good and evil on its own terms, without relying on divine authority.

The Will to Power and the Overcoming of Traditional Morality

- Nietzsche's concept of the will to power is fundamental to his understanding of good and evil. The will to power refers to the inherent drive in all living things to grow, assert themselves, and overcome obstacles. For Nietzsche, good is anything that enhances an individual's will to power, enabling them to assert their strength, creativity, and individuality. Evil is anything that weakens or diminishes this will.

- Nietzsche advocates for the idea of self-overcoming, the process of transcending traditional values and creating one's own meaning.

The ideal individual in Nietzsche's philosophy is the Übermensch (Overman), who creates their own values, rises above conventional good and evil, and lives in accordance with their will to power. The Übermensch represents the ultimate affirmation of life, power, and creativity, unburdened by guilt or moral constraints.

- The good for the Übermensch is the constant striving for greatness, the ability to create new values, and the rejection of societal norms that limit human potential.

- Evil is seen as anything that promotes mediocrity, conformity, or weakness. Nietzsche rejects the idea of inherent evil; instead, he views it as a construct designed to control and weaken individuals.

The Revaluation of Values

- Nietzsche calls for a transvaluation of all values, meaning a radical reevaluation of what is considered good and evil. He believes that the modern world needs to move beyond traditional moral systems, especially those based on religious doctrines, and adopt a morality that celebrates life, strength, and creativity.

- In his work *Beyond Good and Evil*, Nietzsche argues that rigid moral distinctions between good and evil are oversimplified and reflect a misunderstanding of human nature. He suggests that true strength lies in transcending these binary concepts and embracing the complexity of life, including both its creative and destructive forces.

Nihilism and Overcoming It

- Nietzsche recognized the danger of nihilism, the belief that life has no inherent meaning or value, which arises after the collapse of traditional morality (the "death of God"). Without external sources of morality, many may feel lost or believe that life lacks purpose. However, Nietzsche saw this as an opportunity rather than a despairing state.

- Nietzsche's solution to nihilism is to affirm life despite its lack of inherent meaning. By embracing the will to power and becoming creators of new values, individuals can rise above nihilism and redefine good and evil in a way that is life-affirming. The Übermensch is the figure who successfully overcomes nihilism by rejecting the constraints of old morality and creating their own path.

Nietzche Summary

Nietzsche's perspective on good and evil is a radical departure from traditional moral systems, particularly those rooted in Christianity. He argues that traditional morality, or slave morality, glorifies weakness and submission, and defines good and evil in ways that serve the interests of the weak. In contrast, Nietzsche champions master morality, where good is associated with strength, power, and self-assertion, and evil is seen as anything that hinders one's ability to grow and flourish. Nietzsche rejects absolute moral values and calls for a revaluation of values, encouraging individuals to create their own morality based on their will to power. Ultimately, good for Nietzsche is the affirmation of life, strength, and creativity, while evil is anything that promotes weakness, conformity, or mediocrity.

Pascal

Blaise Pascal, the French mathematician, physicist, and philosopher, is known for his contributions to probability theory, hydraulic engineering, and his work in theology and philosophy. Pascal's views on good and evil are deeply influenced by his religious beliefs, particularly his Catholic faith, and his philosophical reflections on human nature and the human condition.

Human Nature and the Paradox of Good and Evil

Pascal's reflections on human nature highlight the paradoxical aspects of good and evil.

- Pascal's famous work, *"Pensées,"* explores the complexities and contradictions of human nature. He acknowledges that humans are capable of both great good and profound evil. According to Pascal, human beings are in a state of moral and spiritual conflict, caught between their higher aspirations and their lower impulses. This duality reflects the inherent paradox of human existence, where good and evil coexist and influence one another.

- Pascal's "Wager" argument, which deals with belief in God, implicitly touches on moral decisions. He suggests that choosing to believe in God is the most rational choice because it offers the possibility of eternal reward versus the risk of eternal loss. This framework implies that moral decisions are critical and have significant consequences for one's ultimate destiny.

The Role of Faith and Grace

Pascal's understanding of good and evil is closely tied to his views on faith and divine grace.

- Pascal believed in the concept of original sin, which posits that humanity's moral shortcomings and inclination toward evil stem from the Fall of Adam and Eve. This fallibility results in a state of moral corruption and spiritual need that humans cannot overcome on their own.

- Pascal argued that redemption and the capacity for moral good come through divine grace rather than human effort alone. He believed that humans need God's grace to achieve true goodness and that this grace is given freely by God. Thus, for Pascal, good is ultimately a reflection of divine grace, while evil is a consequence of human sinfulness and separation from God.

Ethics and the Role of Reason

Pascal's views on ethics and reason reflect his broader philosophical concerns about human limitation and the role of faith.

- Pascal was skeptical of human reason's ability to fully grasp or address moral and existential questions. He saw human reason as limited and often misguided, which can lead to moral error and confusion. This limitation underscores the need for faith and divine guidance in understanding and achieving goodness.

- Despite his emphasis on divine grace, Pascal acknowledged the importance of human moral responsibility. He believed that individuals must strive to live according to moral principles and seek to align their actions with the divine will, even while recognizing their inherent weaknesses and the need for grace.

Critique of Human Pride and Vanity

Pascal's critique of human pride and vanity provides insight into his understanding of moral failings.

- Pascal was critical of human pride and vanity, which he saw as sources of moral failing and ethical distortion. He believed that the pursuit of personal glory and self-importance often leads to immoral behavior and a disregard for true goodness. For Pascal, humility and recognition of one's dependence on divine grace are crucial for achieving moral integrity.

- Pascal also critiqued the misuse of reason in justifying immoral behavior or dismissing the need for faith. He saw this as a reflection of human pride and a barrier to understanding true goodness.

Pascal Summary

Blaise Pascal's perspective on good and evil is deeply influenced by his Catholic faith and philosophical reflections on human nature. He acknowledges the paradox of human existence, where individuals are capable of both good and evil due to their fallibility and the effects of original sin. For Pascal, true goodness is ultimately rooted in divine grace, as human reason alone is insufficient to achieve moral perfection. His critique of human pride and vanity highlights the moral challenges individuals face, while his emphasis on faith underscores the importance of divine guidance in understanding and achieving goodness.

Philo

Philo of Alexandria, a Jewish philosopher from the 1st century CE, synthesized Jewish religious tradition with Greek philosophy, particularly Platonism and Stoicism. His views on good and evil are deeply influenced by his efforts to harmonize the Hebrew Scriptures with Greek philosophical concepts, especially the idea of a transcendent God and the nature of reality.

Good and Evil in Relation to God

Philo sees good as directly connected to God, whom he views as the ultimate source of all goodness. God is perfect, transcendent, and entirely good, and nothing evil can come from God.

- God is the highest good, and all that is good in the world comes from God's will. Everything created by God is good in its essence. For Philo, good is associated with closeness to God, the contemplation of divine truths, and living in accordance with divine will.

- Evil, in Philo's view, is not a direct creation of God. Instead, it arises as a consequence of distance from God. Evil is often described as a privation or absence of good, much like darkness is the absence of light. Since God is pure good, evil cannot originate from Him; it is rather the result of human error, moral weakness, or the limitations of the material world.

The Nature of Evil as a Lack or Absence of Good

Philo adopts a Platonic and Stoic understanding of evil as the absence of good rather than as an independent, substantive force. In this sense, evil does not have a real, positive existence but is instead a condition that arises when something lacks the good it ought to have.

- Good is understood as the fullness of existence and the fulfillment of purpose. In this view, everything that functions according to its intended purpose—especially humans who live in harmony with divine will and wisdom—participates in the good.

- Evil is the failure to reach this fulfillment or perfection. It is the imperfection or corruption of what is naturally good. For example, moral evil results when human beings fail to live according to the virtues or reason that God intends for them. This failure distances them from God, who is the source of all goodness.

The Role of the Logos in Good and Evil

Philo's concept of the Logos is central to his understanding of good and evil. The Logos, according to Philo, is the intermediary between the transcendent God and the material world. It is the divine reason or wisdom through which God governs the universe and which humans can access through reason and contemplation.

- The Logos is responsible for maintaining order and harmony in the universe, and it serves as a guide for human beings to live virtuous lives. Living in accordance with the Logos leads to moral goodness and brings humans closer to God. By following the divine reason inherent in the Logos, individuals align themselves with the natural order and with divine wisdom.

- Evil results from turning away from the Logos, which manifests as irrationality, ignorance, and moral disorder. When humans act against reason or fail to live according to divine wisdom, they experience moral and intellectual degradation, leading to evil behavior. Thus, evil comes from ignorance of the divine order and disconnection from the Logos.

Human Free Will and Moral Responsibility

Philo, like many Jewish and Greek thinkers, emphasizes human free will in the context of good and evil. He believes that humans have the capacity to choose between good and evil, and this freedom is a gift from God.

- Good arises when human beings use their free will to pursue wisdom, live virtuously, and follow the divine commandments. For Philo, the exercise of free will in accordance with reason and divine law leads to moral perfection and goodness. Humans are morally responsible for their choices, and choosing good brings them closer to God.

- Evil is the result of human misuse of free will. When people turn away from reason, the Logos, and divine law, they fall into ignorance and moral corruption. This turning away from God and toward base desires and passions leads to moral evil. Philo often attributes moral failure to the influence of the body and the senses, which distract humans from the higher, spiritual good.

The Body and the Soul: The Dualistic Struggle

Philo's view of good and evil is influenced by a dualistic understanding of the human being, which echoes Platonic thought. He sees a tension between the soul, which is linked to the divine and the good, and the body, which is associated with the material world and the potential for evil.

- The soul, as the divine part of the human being, naturally tends toward God and goodness. When humans follow their soul's desire for wisdom and virtue, they align themselves with the good and live in harmony with divine will.

- The body, being part of the material world, is subject to desires, passions, and physical needs that can lead people away from the pursuit of higher spiritual goods. For Philo, evil occurs when the body and its desires dominate the soul, leading individuals to focus on material pleasures and neglect their spiritual responsibilities.

Divine Providence and the Problem of Evil

Philo addresses the question of how evil exists in a world governed by a good and omnipotent God. His solution is rooted in the idea of divine providence and human free will.

- Philo believes that God's providence governs the world, and that everything ultimately serves a higher purpose, even if humans cannot always understand it. Suffering and evil may occur, but they are often a test of virtue or a means of purifying the soul. For those who live according to divine wisdom, suffering can lead to greater spiritual growth and under-standing.

- Evil, in Philo's view, is allowed by God but is not caused by Him. It exists as a consequence of human free will and the imperfection of the material world. While God does not directly cause evil, He allows it to exist as part of the broader structure of the universe, where free will is necessary for true moral choice. Evil and suffering can also be seen as part of the natural challenges that help individuals grow closer to God by testing and strengthening their virtue.

Philo Summary

Philo's perspective on good is deeply connected to God, who is the ultimate source of all goodness. Good is realized through living in accordance with divine wisdom, as manifested in the Logos, and through the proper use of human free will to pursue intellectual and moral perfection. Evil, on the other hand, is seen as a result of distance from God, ignorance, and the misuse of free will. It is not a positive force but rather the absence or corruption of good. Evil arises when humans turn away from reason, divine law, and the Logos, and instead follow base desires and the material aspects of existence.

Plato

Plato's perspective on good and evil is closely tied to his metaphysical and ethical views, particularly those expressed in his works like *The Republic*, *Phaedo*, and *Symposium*. He sees the concepts of good and evil as part of a broader cosmic order, with The Good being an ultimate, transcendent reality, and evil being the result of ignorance and a lack of harmony within the soul.

Good (The Form of the Good and Virtue)

- Central to Plato's philosophy is the idea of the Forms, eternal and perfect entities that exist beyond the physical world. The Form of the Good is the highest of all Forms, the ultimate source of truth, beauty, and morality. It is through the understanding of the Good that one can grasp all other truths. In *The Republic*, Plato describes the Form of the Good as the sun that illuminates and gives life to all other things, allowing the soul to perceive and understand reality.

- For Plato, to live a good life is to align oneself with the Form of the Good. This involves knowing and acting according to what is truly just, beautiful, and good. A person who understands the Good will naturally act virtuously because they will see that virtue leads to harmony and fulfillment, both within the soul and in society.

- Plato believed that the human soul is divided into three parts:

    1. Reason: The rational part, which seeks truth and wisdom.

2. Spirit: The part that is responsible for emotions like courage, honor, and willpower.

3. Appetite: The part that desires physical pleasures and material needs.

For a person to be good, these three parts of the soul must be in harmony, with reason governing the other two. When reason is in control, the individual acts according to knowledge of the Good, and their soul is in a state of internal justice. This harmony within the soul mirrors the harmony in a just society, where each class performs its appropriate role.

- The Cardinal Virtues, Plato identified four key virtues that align the soul with the Good:

    1. Wisdom (Sophia): The virtue of the rational part of the soul, allowing one to discern what is truly good.

    2. Courage (Andreia): The virtue of the spirited part, which enables individuals to stand by their moral convictions.

    3. Temperance (Sophrosyne): The virtue that brings balance, particularly between the appetites and reason.

    4. Justice (Dikaiosyne): The overall harmony that results when reason rules and each part of the soul performs its proper function.

Evil (Ignorance and Disorder)

- Evil as Ignorance: For Plato, evil arises not from inherent malice but from ignorance of the Good. People do evil because they do not understand what is truly good for them and are instead ruled by their baser desires (appetites) or misguided emotions (spirit). Plato believed that if people truly understood the nature of the Good, they would not choose evil because evil leads to disharmony and ultimately harms the soul.

- Disharmony in the Soul: When the three parts of the soul are out of balance, evil occurs. If the appetites or emotions rule over reason, the individual becomes enslaved to desires or passions, leading to unjust actions. This inner disorder reflects itself in unjust behavior, where a person seeks power, wealth, or pleasure without regard for justice or the well-being of others.

- The Allegory of the Cave: In *The Republic*, Plato presents the Allegory of the Cave, where prisoners are chained in a dark cave, only able to see shadows cast on the wall. These shadows represent their limited understanding of reality. Plato uses this allegory to illustrate that most people live in ignorance, mistaking appearances (shadows) for the truth. Only through philosophical education and the pursuit of wisdom can one escape the cave, come into the light, and perceive the true Form of the Good. Those who remain in ignorance are more likely to commit evil because they are unaware of the higher truth.

- The Role of Education: Plato believed that evil could be overcome through education, particularly in philosophy. The purpose of education is to turn the soul away from the shadows of ignorance and guide it toward knowledge of the Good. A philosopher, who understands the Form of the Good, is therefore best suited to lead a just life and, in Plato's view, to rule a just society.

The Relationship Between Good and Evil

- Good as the Ultimate Reality: Plato sees the Good as the ultimate reality, the source of all that is true and just. Evil, on the other hand, is not an independent force but a deficiency or absence of knowledge of the Good. When people act in ignorance, their actions deviate from the true, just path, leading to evil.

- Justice and the Ideal Society: Plato's view of good and evil extends to his vision of society. In his ideal state, as outlined in *The Republic*, each class—rulers (philosopher-kings), warriors, and producers—performs its appropriate role in harmony with the others. A just society is one in which each individual acts according to their nature and in accordance with the Good, mirroring the harmony within a virtuous soul.

Plato Summary

For Plato, good is rooted in the understanding of the Form of the Good, which represents the highest truth and moral order. Virtue comes from aligning the soul with the Good by achieving harmony between reason, spirit, and appetite. Evil arises from ignorance of the Good and a lack of balance within the soul, leading to unjust actions and a disordered life. Plato believed that through education and the pursuit of wisdom, individuals can escape ignorance, know the Good, and live a virtuous and just life.

Pythagoras

Pythagoras of Samos, the ancient Greek philosopher and mathematician best known for his contributions to geometry and number theory, also had philosophical and ethical views that intersect with his mathematical ideas. Although Pythagoras did not leave behind a systematic treatise on morality, his teachings and the Pythagorean school he founded provide some insights into his perspective on good and evil.

Harmony and Balance

Central to Pythagoras' philosophy is the concept of harmony and balance, both in the cosmos and in human life.

- Cosmic Harmony: Pythagoras believed that the universe is governed by mathematical principles and that harmony can be found in the ratios and proportions of numbers. This concept of harmony was not limited to the physical world but extended to ethical and moral dimensions. For Pythagoras, good was associated with living in accordance with the natural harmony and balance that governed the universe.

- Moral Balance: In Pythagorean ethics, good can be understood as maintaining balance and harmony in one's life and actions. This means living virtuously, practicing moderation, and aligning oneself with the cosmic order. Evil, in this context, would be seen as actions or behaviors that disrupt harmony and balance, leading to disorder and disharmony.

Numerical and Symbolic Interpretations

Pythagoras and his followers saw numbers as having symbolic and mystical significance, which extended to their understanding of morality.

- Numerical Symbolism: Pythagoras and his followers believed that numbers have inherent qualities that reflect moral and philosophical truths. For example, the number 1 represented unity and the source of all things, while numbers like 2 (duality) and 3 (harmony) had specific symbolic meanings. Good was associated with the pursuit of harmony and unity, which can be symbolically represented by certain numbers or ratios.

- Moral Symbolism: The Pythagoreans might have used numerical symbolism to represent moral concepts. For instance, living according to principles that reflect balance and harmony (such as moderation and fairness) aligns with their idea of good, whereas actions that lead to imbalance or chaos would be considered evil.

Virtue and Ethical Living

Pythagoras' teachings emphasized virtue and the importance of living a moral life.

- For Pythagoras, living a virtuous life was integral to achieving harmony and balance. Virtues such as temperance, justice, and wisdom were highly valued and considered essential for personal development and ethical behavior. Goodness was thus associated with the cultivation of virtue and adherence to moral principles that promote harmony.

- Conversely, evil would be associated with vice, which disrupts harmony and leads to moral and spiritual discord. Actions driven by excess, injustice, or ignorance were seen as contrary to the principles of harmony and balance.

Reincarnation and Moral Development

Pythagoras and his followers believed in reincarnation and the idea that the soul undergoes a cycle of rebirths.

- The belief in reincarnation suggested that individuals have the opportunity to develop morally across multiple lifetimes. Goodness involves the soul's progress toward perfection and alignment with cosmic harmony. Evil actions might be seen as contributing to the soul's entanglement in material existence and hindering its progress toward spiritual enlightenment.

Influence of Pythagorean Thought

Pythagoras' ideas influenced later philosophical and mystical traditions, including Platonism and Neoplatonism.

- Plato, a student of Pythagoras, incorporated ideas about forms and ideal states into his own philosophy. In this context, the notion of good is often associated with the pursuit of higher forms and the alignment with the ideal realm of forms, which echoes Pythagorean ideas of harmony and balance.

Pythagoras Summary

From Pythagoras' perspective, good is associated with harmony, balance, and virtue, reflecting the cosmic order and mathematical principles that govern the universe. Living in accordance with these principles involves practicing moderation, justice, and wisdom. Evil, on the other hand, is seen as disrupting harmony and balance, resulting in moral and spiritual disorder. Pythagoras' view of good and evil is intertwined with his philosophical and mathematical understanding of the world, emphasizing the importance of aligning one's life with the natural order and pursuing virtue.

Sartre

Jean-Paul Sartre, a prominent existentialist philosopher, approaches good and evil through the lens of individual freedom, responsibility, and the concept of "authenticity" versus "bad faith." His perspective is deeply rooted in his existentialist belief that humans are radically free, and it is through their choices and actions that they define themselves and the moral framework they live by.

Existence Precedes Essence

At the core of Sartre's philosophy is the idea that "existence precedes essence." This means that humans are not born with any inherent nature, essence, or moral value. Instead, individuals create their essence through their actions and choices. Good and evil are not preordained or given by any external authority (such as religion or society); they are determined by the choices each person makes in the course of their life.

- Good is defined by living authentically, meaning to act in accordance with one's own freedom and responsibility, without succumbing to external pressures.

- Evil arises when one denies their freedom or acts in "bad faith," attempting to escape the responsibility that comes with being free.

Authenticity and Bad Faith

For Sartre, the primary moral struggle is between living authentically (in good faith) and falling into bad faith.

- To live authentically is to fully embrace one's freedom and the responsibility that comes with it. An authentic person acknowledges that they alone are responsible for their choices and cannot rely on external authorities, traditions, or predetermined roles to define who they are.

Good in Sartre's view is when individuals acknowledge this freedom and make choices that reflect their true selves, without self-deception.

- Bad Faith: Bad faith is when a person lies to themselves, pretending that they do not have freedom or that they are determined by external factors. People act in bad faith when they deny their responsibility by conforming to societal roles, blaming their actions on fate, biology, or external pressures. This is a form of self-deception and is, for Sartre, a form of "moral evil."

Evil, in Sartre's terms, comes from this self-deception and refusal to embrace one's freedom. A person in bad faith gives up their individuality and autonomy, living inauthentically by conforming to external values without questioning them.

Freedom and Responsibility

Sartre's understanding of good and evil revolves around the absolute freedom of individuals to make choices. This freedom is not a luxury but a burden because with freedom comes radical responsibility. Sartre famously said, "Man is condemned to be free," meaning that humans have no choice but to be free, even though this freedom can be a source of anxiety.

- Exercising one's freedom responsibly is considered good. A "good" person, for Sartre, acknowledges the weight of their choices and takes full responsibility for the consequences of their actions. They do not try to escape or shift blame onto external forces.

- Evil arises when individuals deny their freedom and responsibility, acting as if they are passive victims of circumstance. This refusal to own one's choices leads to a life of inauthenticity, where one avoids making meaningful decisions and lives by default according to the expectations of others.

The Absurd and Meaning

Sartre, like other existentialists, believes that life has no inherent meaning or purpose. There is no divine plan or objective moral order. As a result, individuals are responsible for creating their own meaning through their actions.

- A person who faces the absurdity of life and still chooses to create meaning through their actions is seen as good, living authentically in spite of the lack of inherent meaning.

- Evil occurs when someone tries to impose a false sense of meaning on the world, for example, by blindly following societal norms or religious dogma without recognizing the fundamental absurdity of existence. This, again, is a form of bad faith.

Interpersonal Relationships and the "Look"

In Sartre's philosophy, relationships with others also shape notions of good and evil. He famously discusses how the presence of others can make us feel objectified, as we become aware of ourselves as seen through their gaze. Sartre calls this the "look" of the Other, which can lead to feelings of alienation.

- In authentic relationships, individuals respect each other's freedom and recognize the mutual responsibility that comes with freedom.

- Evil arises in relationships when one tries to dominate or objectify the other, denying their freedom. This can lead to forms of oppression or dehumanization, which Sartre would consider a moral failing.

Sartre Summary

In Jean-Paul Sartre's existentialist view, good and evil are not objective or externally defined but are tied to individual freedom and responsibility. Good is acting authentically, fully embracing one's freedom, and accepting responsibility for one's actions. Evil is living in "bad faith," where one denies their freedom, acts in self-deception, and conforms to external pressures. Sartre's moral framework revolves around the idea that humans are free to define themselves and the meaning of their lives through their choices.

Socrates

Socrates' perspective on good and evil is deeply tied to his views on knowledge, virtue, and the nature of the human soul. He believed that moral goodness is inseparable from knowledge, while evil arises from ignorance. His ethical ideas, as recorded by his student Plato, focus on the connection between wisdom and virtuous living.

Good (Virtue and Knowledge)

- Virtue is Knowledge: For Socrates, good is synonymous with virtue (arete), and virtue is essentially a form of knowledge. He argued that to know what is truly good is to do what is good, as no one willingly does wrong if they understand what is right. Socrates believed that all virtues—such as justice, courage, temperance, and wisdom—are forms of knowledge and are necessary for living a good life.

- The Good Life (Eudaimonia): Like Aristotle, Socrates believed in the concept of eudaimonia, often translated as "happiness" or "flourishing." For Socrates, the good life is one where the soul is in a state of moral and intellectual harmony, achieved through the pursuit of wisdom and virtue. The more knowledge one possesses about the nature of goodness, the closer one is to living a fulfilled and virtuous life.

- The Unexamined Life: Socrates famously stated, "The unexamined life is not worth living." This reflects his belief that the pursuit of knowledge and self-examination is central to the good life. By constantly questioning one's beliefs, values, and actions, one can uncover true knowledge and align oneself with what is good. A life without reflection and pursuit of wisdom is one that is disconnected from true goodness.

- The Role of the Soul: Socrates emphasized the importance of the soul over the body or material wealth. He believed that the soul is the true essence of a person, and that nurturing and improving the soul through the pursuit of wisdom is the highest good. Moral goodness, in Socrates' view, is directly related to the health and virtue of the soul, which is cultivated through knowledge.

Evil (Ignorance)

- Ignorance is the Root of Evil: Socrates believed that evil arises from ignorance, not from a deliberate desire to do harm. People do evil things because they do not truly know what is good. In his view, no one would willingly choose to do something harmful or wrong if they had proper knowledge of the consequences or if they fully understood what is morally right.

- Wrongdoing is Involuntary: Since Socrates equated knowledge with virtue, he argued that wrongdoing is a result of ignorance. Evil actions are involuntary in the sense that they stem from a lack of understanding. For example, someone who lies or steals does so because they falsely believe that these actions will lead to their happiness or benefit, not realizing the harm they cause to their own soul and others.

- The Harm to the Soul: Socrates believed that evil actions harm the soul more than they harm others. When a person commits an unjust act, they damage their own moral integrity and soul. Therefore, Socrates maintained that it is better to suffer injustice than to commit it because committing injustice corrupts one's soul and leads one away from true goodness.

The Relationship Between Good and Evil

- The Pursuit of Wisdom: The key to overcoming evil, according to Socrates, is the pursuit of wisdom and the continual effort to understand what is truly good. Through dialogue, self-examination, and philosophical inquiry, individuals can attain greater knowledge of virtue and, consequently, live good lives.

- Moral Education: Socrates placed great importance on education and dialogue as a means of leading people away from ignorance and toward virtue. He believed that through questioning and dialectic methods, one could help others recognize their own ignorance and begin the path toward moral improvement.

Socrates Summary

Socrates' view of good and evil centers around the idea that virtue is knowledge and that ignorance is the root of evil. For Socrates, good actions stem from understanding what is truly right, and evil arises when people act out of ignorance or a lack of knowledge. Socrates believed that no one willingly chooses to do wrong; rather, people commit evil acts because they do not fully understand what is good. The pursuit of wisdom, self-examination, and moral education are the pathways to achieving a virtuous and good life, and the greatest harm a person can do is to their own soul through unjust actions.

---

zu

Sun Tzu, the ancient Chinese military strategist and author of *The Art of War*, approaches the concepts of good and evil primarily through a practical, strategic lens rather than a philosophical or moral one. His focus is on success in warfare and leadership, so the notions of good and evil are interpreted in terms of effectiveness, advantage, and the consequences of actions in conflict.

Good and Evil in Terms of Strategy

Sun Tzu views "good" actions as those that lead to victory and success with minimal effort, loss, or damage. In contrast, "evil" would refer to actions or strategies that are wasteful, lead to unnecessary destruction, or result in defeat. The ultimate "good" in Sun Tzu's philosophy is winning a war without even having to fight, through superior strategy and intelligence.

- For example, Sun Tzu emphasizes the importance of deception in warfare: "All warfare is based on deception." Deception itself may be seen as morally questionable, but in Sun Tzu's perspective, it is "good" if it achieves the strategic goal without unnecessary conflict.

Utility over Morality

Sun Tzu does not discuss good and evil in terms of moral absolutes. His focus is on utility—what is useful, effective, and successful. An action's morality is not a consideration if it leads to victory or advantage in war. In this sense, good and evil are not determined by conventional moral standards, but by whether a particular course of action serves the end goal effectively.

- Example: Sun Tzu advises rulers and generals to avoid prolonged warfare because it depletes resources and harms both sides. Even if one wins in the end, a protracted war is considered "bad" because it weakens the nation. Victory that comes at a high cost or results in more harm than good is strategically "evil."

Balance and Harmony

Sun Tzu's strategic thinking also reflects the Taoist influence of his time, which sees balance and harmony as central to the universe. "Good" strategies align with the natural flow of events and the state of affairs (the Tao). When a leader or general acts in harmony with the circumstances, they are more likely to succeed with minimal effort. Conversely, when they act against the flow of natural forces, it is "evil" in a strategic sense, as it leads to disorder, struggle, and defeat.

- Sun Tzu's advice to know both yourself and your enemy aligns with this philosophy of balance: "If you know the enemy and know yourself, you need not fear the result of a hundred battles." Failing to align your actions with knowledge is a form of strategic evil because it invites disaster.

Leadership and the Greater Good

Sun Tzu's teachings imply that "good" leadership is one that leads to stability, prosperity, and the protection of one's state and people. Leaders who act selfishly, impulsively, or carelessly, causing unnecessary harm or putting their nation at risk, embody "evil" in Sun Tzu's framework. In war, good leadership is pragmatic, thoughtful, and seeks the best outcome for the greatest number, while evil leadership is reckless and self-serving.

- A general who wages war recklessly or with disregard for the people is considered "evil" because such actions lead to unnecessary suffering.

Minimizing Harm

While Sun Tzu is not focused on morality in the Western sense, he does emphasize minimizing harm and achieving goals through efficient and non-destructive means. For example, he advocates for winning without fighting, diplomacy over direct conflict, and quick, decisive actions that avoid prolonged suffering.

- "The greatest victory is that which requires no battle." This demonstrates that "good" in his view is achieving success with minimal bloodshed, which can be seen as an ethical or at least humane approach.

Tzu Summary

Sun Tzu's perspective on good and evil is pragmatic and based on strategic outcomes rather than moral principles. "Good" refers to strategies and actions that lead to success, efficiency, and minimal harm, while "evil" relates to those that result in waste, defeat, and unnecessary suffering. His teachings prioritize balance, knowledge, and leadership, viewing the effective pursuit of strategic goals as the ultimate measure of good.

Voltaire

François-Marie Arouet, non de plume M. de Voltaire, one of the leading figures of the French Enlightenment, had a unique perspective on good and evil, shaped by his critiques of organized religion, authoritarianism, and human suffering. His views were deeply influenced by rationalism, skepticism, and a strong belief in human progress through reason.

Good and Evil in Human Nature

Voltaire was a skeptic when it came to traditional religious explanations of good and evil, especially the idea of original sin. He rejected the notion that humans are born inherently sinful or evil and instead believed that human nature could be shaped and improved through reason, education, and social reform.

- Voltaire saw human beings as capable of reason, compassion, and progress. Goodness, for him, is found in actions that promote human welfare, happiness, and the betterment of society. It is rooted in reason and the pursuit of justice, tolerance, and knowledge.

- Evil, on the other hand, arises from ignorance, superstition, fanaticism, and the abuse of power. Voltaire believed that much of the evil in the world came from irrational beliefs and unjust institutions, particularly those that oppressed people or caused unnecessary suffering.

Critique of Religious Interpretations of Good and Evil

Voltaire was highly critical of organized religion, particularly the Catholic Church, and its explanations of good and evil. In his famous work *Candide*, he mocked the optimistic theological belief that "all is for the best in the best of all possible worlds" (associated with the philosopher Leibniz), which suggested that all evil had a divine purpose. Voltaire found this view absurd in the face of real human suffering, such as natural disasters and war.

- Voltaire argued that good is not something divinely ordained but something that humans must create through reason and compassion. He believed in the importance of religious tolerance and saw morality as something that should be based on reason and the common good, not on dogma or divine command.

- For Voltaire, evil was often the result of religious fanaticism, intolerance, and the persecution of those with different beliefs. He strongly opposed religious justifications for violence, oppression, and suffering, and saw these as man-made evils, not divine will.

Good and Evil in Society

Voltaire believed that much of what was considered "evil" in society was the product of unjust institutions, tyrannical governments, and the oppression of the weak by the powerful. He was a strong advocate for justice, freedom of speech, and individual rights. Voltaire's view of good and evil was therefore closely tied to political and social reform.

- Voltaire saw good in the pursuit of liberty, justice, and equality. He believed that societies could be improved by using reason to challenge arbitrary authority, superstition, and tradition. Good governments were those that promoted the well-being of their citizens and protected their freedoms.

- Tyranny, oppression, and inequality were seen by Voltaire as great evils. He criticized absolute monarchy, the Inquisition, and other forms of authoritarianism that suppressed human freedom and led to unnecessary suffering. Evil, in this context, was often a product of ignorance, cruelty, and the unchecked power of elites.

The Problem of Suffering and Evil

Voltaire was deeply concerned with the problem of evil in the world, particularly the suffering of innocent people. His famous poem on the *Lisbon Earthquake* (1755), which killed tens of thousands of people, was a direct attack on the idea that such disasters were part of a divine plan. Voltaire argued that natural evils like earthquakes, plagues, and famines could not be reconciled with the idea of a benevolent, omnipotent God.

- For Voltaire, the response to suffering was not passive acceptance or theological speculation, but active efforts to alleviate human misery through practical means—such as improving living conditions, advancing science, and promoting reason.

- Voltaire saw natural disasters as simply part of the indifferent workings of nature, not as a divine punishment. He believed that human beings should respond to such evils by helping one another, rather than by justifying them with religious explanations.

Voltaire's Optimism vs. Pessimism

In *Candide*, Voltaire criticizes both blind optimism and extreme pessimism. While he mocks the idea that "all is for the best," he also rejects complete despair. Voltaire advocates for a balanced, pragmatic approach to good and evil, where people recognize that the world contains both but should work toward improving it through action.

- Voltaire ultimately believed in human progress, but not through metaphysical or religious means. Instead, he championed the idea of improving the world through rational thought, scientific discovery, and social reform. The famous closing line of *Candide*, "we must cultivate our garden," suggests that individuals should focus on practical efforts to make their immediate world better.

- Voltaire believed that much evil could be reduced through education, tolerance, and reform. He was skeptical of grand, idealistic systems and instead promoted a more realistic, hands-on approach to improving society and combating ignorance and suffering.

Voltaire Summary

From Voltaire's perspective, good is associated with reason, justice, tolerance, and the pursuit of human welfare. It comes from efforts to improve society and promote happiness, freedom, and knowledge. Evil, on the other hand, arises from ignorance, superstition, religious fanaticism, and the abuse of power. Voltaire rejected traditional religious explanations for good and evil, arguing instead that human beings must use reason and compassion to alleviate suffering and build a better world. He advocated for pragmatic action to combat the evils of tyranny, inequality, and intolerance, while embracing human progress through education and reform.

Voices

Carlson

Tucker Carlson, an American television host and political commentator, frames good and evil through the lens of cultural conservatism, nationalism, and criticism of elite institutions. His perspective is influenced by his views on American politics, media, and cultural issues.

Good as Traditional Values and National Identity

For Carlson, good is closely tied to the preservation of traditional values and national identity. He emphasizes the importance of cultural conservatism and a return to what he sees as foundational American principles.

- Carlson often defines good in terms of traditional family structures, religious faith, and cultural norms that he believes have historically supported American society. He advocates for policies and societal attitudes that reinforce these traditional values, arguing that they provide stability and continuity in a rapidly changing world.

- Carlson views the protection of national identity and sovereignty as essential to the good. This includes a strong stance on immigration control, protecting American jobs, and preserving American cultural heritage from what he sees as external and internal threats.

Evil as Elite Institutions and Cultural Leftism

Carlson frequently characterizes evil as the actions and ideologies promoted by what he refers to as elite institutions and cultural leftism. He often criticizes these forces for undermining traditional values and societal cohesion.

- In Carlson's framework, evil is associated with the actions of elite institutions such as large corporations, media organizations, and government entities that he believes are working against the interests of ordinary people. He argues that these institutions promote agendas that are contrary to traditional American values and undermine national unity.

- Carlson often describes cultural leftism—which includes progressive social movements, identity politics, and political correctness—as a force of evil. He argues that these ideologies seek to erode traditional cultural norms, promote division, and impose restrictive policies on free speech and individual expression.

Good as Populism and Common Sense

Carlson champions populism and common sense as central to his concept of the good. He believes that these principles represent the interests and values of ordinary people against what he perceives as an out-of-touch elite.

- For Carlson, good is represented by populist movements and policies that reflect the will of the common people rather than the elite. He argues that populism is a way to reclaim political and cultural power from those he believes are disconnected from the everyday concerns of Americans.

- Carlson emphasizes the importance of common sense and practicality in addressing social and political issues. He criticizes what he sees as the imposition of complex, ideologically driven policies that do not align with everyday experiences and practical realities.

Good as Defending Freedom of Speech and Expression

Carlson places a strong emphasis on freedom of speech and expression as fundamental to the good. He argues that protecting these freedoms is essential for maintaining a vibrant and democratic society.

- Carlson defends the right to free speech against what he perceives as attempts to censor or suppress dissenting viewpoints. He argues that the freedom to express diverse and controversial opinions is crucial for a healthy society and for preventing the rise of authoritarianism.

- In addition to defending free speech, Carlson often focuses on the broader issue of expression, including artistic and cultural expressions that he believes are being stifled by political correctness and ideological conformity.

Good as Protection of American Institutions and Traditions

Carlson views the protection and restoration of American institutions and traditions as a key component of the good.

- Carlson advocates for the preservation of American political institutions, such as the Constitution and the Bill of Rights, which he believes provide the framework for a just and functional society. He argues that these institutions are under threat from both domestic and foreign forces and need to be defended.

- He also emphasizes the importance of cultural and social traditions that he argues have historically provided stability and continuity. Carlson believes that a return to these traditions is essential for maintaining societal cohesion and countering what he sees as harmful changes imposed by progressive ideologies.

Evil as Government Overreach and Globalism

Carlson frequently describes government overreach and globalism as forms of evil that threaten national sovereignty and individual freedoms.

- Carlson criticizes what he sees as excessive government intervention and regulation, which he believes infringes on personal freedoms and autonomy. He argues that such overreach often leads to inefficiencies and abuses of power.

- Carlson is also critical of globalism—the idea of increasing global governance and international cooperation. He argues that globalist policies undermine national sovereignty and prioritize international elites over the interests of ordinary citizens.

Carlson Summary

For Tucker Carlson, good is defined by the defense of traditional values, national identity, and freedom of speech. It involves a commitment to populism, common sense, and the preservation of American institutions and traditions. Evil, in Carlson's view, is represented by elite institutions and cultural leftism, which he believes undermine societal cohesion and traditional norms. He also sees government overreach and globalism as threats to individual freedoms and national sovereignty.

Chomsky

Noam Chomsky, an influential linguist, philosopher, and cognitive scientist, has a nuanced perspective on good and evil that is often framed within the context of political theory, human nature, and social justice. While Chomsky's primary focus is on linguistics and cognitive science, his political writings offer insights into his views on morality and ethics.

Good as Social Justice and Ethical Action

Chomsky's conception of good is closely aligned with principles of social justice and ethical action. He emphasizes the importance of fairness, equality, and the protection of human rights.

- For Chomsky, good is often associated with actions and policies that promote social justice, equality, and the protection of individual rights. This includes advocating for the rights of marginalized and oppressed groups, ensuring equitable distribution of resources, and challenging systems of power and inequality.

- Chomsky argues that ethical action involves challenging unjust systems and working towards a more just and humane society. This includes questioning and critiquing institutions that perpetuate injustice, inequality, and abuse of power.

Evil as Systems of Oppression and Injustice

Chomsky's view of evil is often framed in terms of systems of oppression, exploitation, and injustice. He focuses on the structural factors that contribute to moral wrongs.

- From Chomsky's perspective, evil is represented by systems and actions that exploit, oppress, or marginalize individuals or groups. This includes political, economic, and social structures that perpetuate inequality, war, and human rights abuses.

- Chomsky frequently critiques institutions and policies that he believes contribute to systemic injustice. This includes critiques of corporate power, militarism, and authoritarianism that he argues undermine democratic values and human dignity.

Good as Rational Inquiry and Critique

Chomsky values rational inquiry and critical thinking as essential components of understanding and addressing moral issues. He believes that intellectual rigor and skepticism are necessary for identifying and combating evil.

- For Chomsky, good involves a commitment to rational inquiry and the pursuit of truth. This means critically examining beliefs, practices, and policies to ensure they are just and equitable. He argues that informed and reasoned critique is crucial for advancing ethical standards and social justice.

- Chomsky stresses the importance of critiquing power structures and challenging those who wield power in ways that harm others. He believes that questioning authority and exposing abuses of power are key aspects of ethical action.

Human Nature and Moral Potential

Chomsky's views on human nature also inform his understanding of good and evil. He often discusses the inherent potential for both ethical behavior and moral failings within human nature.

- Chomsky posits that humans have an inherent potential for both good and evil. He emphasizes the importance of social and environmental factors in shaping moral behavior and argues that individuals and societies have the capacity to strive for ethical ideals and justice.

- Chomsky believes that moral development is influenced by social conditions, educational opportunities, and cultural values. He argues that creating just and equitable social conditions can help individuals realize their moral potential and act in ways that are consistent with ethical principles.

Good and Evil in Political Context

Chomsky's political writings often address issues related to imperialism, capitalism, and democratic governance, framing good and evil within these contexts.

- In the political sphere, good is associated with democratic governance, human rights, and social equity. Chomsky advocates for political systems and policies that promote these values and address the needs of the most vulnerable.

- Chomsky identifies evil in imperialistic policies, economic exploitation, and authoritarian regimes that he believes undermine democratic values and contribute to global injustices. He criticizes the concentration of power and resources in the hands of a few, which he argues leads to widespread suffering and inequality.

Chomsky Summary

For Noam Chomsky, good is defined by the promotion of social justice, ethical action, and rational inquiry. It involves challenging systems of power and oppression, advocating for the rights of marginalized groups, and striving for a more equitable society. Evil, in Chomsky's view, is associated with systems of oppression, injustice, and exploitation that undermine human dignity and democratic values. His perspective emphasizes the importance of critical thinking, ethical critique, and the need for structural changes to address moral wrongs.

$\mathcal{D}$avis

Angela Davis, a political activist, philosopher, and scholar, approaches the concepts of good and evil through a lens of critical theory, Marxism, feminism, and social justice. Her views are deeply informed by her experiences as a civil rights activist, her imprisonment in the early 1970s, and her critiques of systemic oppression. Davis's understanding of good and evil is not framed in traditional moral terms, but rather in terms of structures of power, oppression, and liberation.

Good as the Pursuit of Justice and Liberation

For Davis, good is defined by the struggle for justice, equality, and liberation from oppressive systems. Her worldview is grounded in the fight against racism, capitalism, patriarchy, and the prison-industrial complex, and she views these systems as the roots of evil.

- Goodness, in Davis's perspective, is the collective struggle for freedom from all forms of oppression. It involves dismantling the systemic injustices that keep marginalized people—particularly Black people, women, and the poor—in positions of subjugation. Davis advocates for radical change, including prison abolition, anti-capitalism, and the end of all forms of discrimination based on race, gender, and class. Good, therefore, is any action, ideology, or movement that works toward human emancipation and equality.

- Solidarity and Collective Action: For Davis, good is not just an individual moral quality but is inherently tied to collective action and solidarity. She believes that fighting for social justice is not only a moral imperative for oppressed groups but also for privileged individuals and communities who must stand in solidarity with those who are marginalized.

Evil as Systems of Oppression

In Angela Davis's framework, evil is not inherent in individuals but is embedded in systems of domination and structural violence. She critiques institutions like prisons, capitalism, racism, and patriarchy as embodiments of societal evil.

- Evil, according to Davis, is embodied in structural inequality and oppressive systems that exploit and dehumanize certain groups while privileging others. These systems perpetuate violence, exploitation, and inequality, and they function to maintain the status quo of power for the ruling class, often at the expense of marginalized communities. Examples of such evils include:

  Racism: Particularly the systemic racism that underpins the criminal justice system, education, housing, and employment in the United States. Davis has long critiqued how racial oppression serves to control and exploit Black people and other communities of color.

  Capitalism: For Davis, capitalism is an exploitative economic system that privileges the wealthy few while keeping the working class, especially people of color, in perpetual poverty and subjugation. She argues that capitalism's reliance on inequality and exploitation makes it fundamentally unjust.

  Patriarchy: Davis also sees patriarchy as an evil system that oppresses women, particularly women of color, by reinforcing gender inequality, violence, and economic dependency.

  The Prison-Industrial Complex: Davis is a staunch critic of mass incarceration and the prison-industrial complex, which she believes is one of the most visible forms of systemic evil in modern society. She argues that prisons are used to maintain control over marginalized populations, particularly Black and Brown people, rather than to rehabilitate or address societal problems.

Good as Resistance and Empowerment

For Angela Davis, resistance against oppression is a moral good. Resistance movements, whether through activism, education, or political struggle, are vital to confronting and dismantling systems of evil.

Goodness is found in the empowerment of oppressed people and their ability to resist exploitation and domination. This includes:

Activism and Advocacy: Davis views social activism as a key method of achieving good. She encourages people to engage in political movements that fight for the abolition of prisons, gender equality, racial justice, and economic fairness.

Education and Consciousness: Davis believes that education is a powerful tool for resistance and transformation. Raising consciousness about issues of oppression, exploitation, and inequality helps people recognize the structural causes of their suffering and empowers them to fight for change.

- Abolitionism as a Path to Good: One of the central tenets of Davis's philosophy is abolitionism, particularly the abolition of prisons. She believes that prisons are inherently dehumanizing and perpetuate the very violence and harm they claim to prevent. Abolitionism, for Davis, represents the creation of new systems that focus on restorative justice, healing, and community support, rather than punishment and retribution.

Intersectionality and the Understanding of Good and Evil

Davis's view of good and evil is deeply influenced by intersectionality—the idea that multiple forms of oppression intersect to create unique experiences of marginalization, particularly for women of color.

- Good is found in the recognition of how various systems of oppression—such as racism, sexism, classism, and ableism—intersect and compound. Davis advocates for movements that take an intersectional approach, recognizing the interconnectedness of struggles for racial justice, gender equality, and economic liberation.

- Evil, in this framework, is the failure to address the multiple, interconnected forms of oppression that affect individuals and communities. Davis argues that focusing on a single axis of oppression (such as racism alone) without understanding how it intersects with others (like gender or class) perpetuates inequality. This lack of intersectional awareness is seen as a form of complicity in maintaining systemic evil.

Good as Utopian Imagination and Radical Change

Angela Davis has often spoken about the need for a radical reimagining of society in order to confront and overcome entrenched systems of evil.

- Good is the ability to imagine a world free from the oppressions of capitalism, patriarchy, and the prison system. Davis encourages people to think beyond reformist approaches and to envision radically different futures—where communities are not policed, where people are not imprisoned, and where social and economic systems are based on equality and collective well-being.

- Evil is the acceptance of the status quo—the belief that society as it exists is the best we can do, or that the problems we face are inevitable and unsolvable. Davis challenges this mindset, arguing that accepting systemic oppression and not working toward radical change is itself a form of moral failure.

The Role of Solidarity in Good

Davis emphasizes the importance of global solidarity in the fight for justice, seeing good in the ability of different movements—such as the fight for Black liberation, feminist struggles, LGBTQ+ rights, and labor movements—to come together in pursuit of common goals.

- Goodness is found in solidarity with oppressed peoples across the world. Davis promotes internationalism and the idea that struggles for justice are interconnected globally. This includes solidarity with Palestinian liberation, anti-apartheid movements, and struggles for freedom across the globe.

- Evil arises when solidarity is denied, when struggles are fragmented, or when privileged groups fail to recognize their complicity in oppression. For Davis, failing to align oneself with global movements for justice represents a continuation of the evils of exploitation and oppression.

Davis Summary

For Angela Davis, good is defined by the pursuit of justice, equality, and liberation from systemic oppression. Goodness is found in collective action, resistance to exploitative systems, and the creation of a world based on equality and mutual respect. Evil, on the other hand, is embodied in the structural systems of oppression—such as racism, capitalism, patriarchy, and mass incarceration—that dehumanize and exploit marginalized populations. Rather than viewing good and evil as intrinsic qualities, Davis sees them as outcomes of societal structures and the actions we take to either challenge or uphold those structures.

Dawkins

Richard Dawkins, an evolutionary biologist and prominent atheist, approaches the concepts of good and evil from a scientific and secular perspective. His views are shaped by his understanding of evolution, biology, and his critique of religion.

Good and Evil as Evolutionary Constructs

Dawkins views good and evil through the lens of evolutionary biology and genetics.

- Evolutionary Ethics, Dawkins argues that moral behavior, including concepts of good and evil, can be understood through evolutionary processes. He suggests that traits such as empathy, cooperation, and altruism have evolved because they confer survival and reproductive advantages. These traits are seen as beneficial adaptations that promote social harmony and collective well-being.

- In his book *"The Selfish Gene,"* Dawkins introduces the idea that genes are the fundamental units of selection in evolution. While the theory emphasizes genetic self-interest, it also acknowledges that genes can promote behaviors that benefit others, such as altruism. These behaviors are seen as strategies that enhance the survival of the genes that promote them, thus aligning with evolutionary notions of good.

Secular Morality

Dawkins advocates for a secular morality that does not rely on religious doctrines.

- Ethics Without Religion: Dawkins believes that moral values do not need to be grounded in religious beliefs. Instead, he argues that ethical principles can be derived from reason, empathy, and a commitment to improving human well-being. He contends that secular moral frameworks can provide robust and rational foundations for understanding good and evil.

- Humanism: Dawkins supports humanism, which emphasizes the importance of human welfare, dignity, and rationality. In this view, good is associated with actions that enhance human flourishing and contribute to the common good, while evil is associated with actions that cause harm or suffering.

Critique of Religious Morality

Dawkins is critical of religious interpretations of good and evil, which he believes can be harmful or misguided.

- Dawkins argues that religious moral systems are often based on outdated or arbitrary principles and that they can perpetuate intolerance, conflict, and oppression. He challenges the notion that moral values are derived solely from religious teachings and emphasizes the need for a more rational and evidence-based approach to ethics.

- Dawkins criticizes moral absolutism—the idea that there are absolute, unchanging moral truths dictated by religious authorities. He argues that moral values are better understood as evolving social constructs that can adapt to new knowledge and ethical considerations.

Moral Progress and Reason

Dawkins emphasizes the role of reason and moral progress in understanding good and evil.

- Reason and Evidence: Dawkins advocates for the use of reason and evidence in moral deliberation. He believes that ethical decisions should be based on rational analysis, scientific understanding, and a consideration of the consequences of actions.

- Moral Progress: Dawkins acknowledges that human societies have made moral progress over time, moving towards greater inclusivity, equality, and justice. He views this progress as a result of increasing rationality, empathy, and social awareness rather than religious influence.

Dawkins Summary

Richard Dawkins' perspective on good and evil is grounded in evolutionary biology, secular morality, and rational ethics. Good is seen as behaviors and actions that enhance survival, promote human well-being, and contribute to social harmony, while evil is associated with actions that cause harm or suffering. Dawkins rejects religiously based moral frameworks in favor of secular and evidence-based approaches to ethics. He emphasizes the role of reason and moral progress in understanding and defining moral values, advocating for a rational and humanistic approach to ethics that is independent of religious doctrines.

Gandhi

Mahatma Gandhi, the leader of the Indian independence movement and a proponent of non-violent resistance, had a deeply rooted and unique perspective on good and evil. His views were shaped by his commitment to non-violence (ahimsa), truth (satya), and his philosophy of moral and spiritual development.

Non-Violence (Ahimsa) and Truth (Satya)

Gandhi's core principles of non-violence and truth are central to his understanding of good and evil.

- Non-Violence (Ahimsa): For Gandhi, good is inherently linked to the principle of ahimsa, which means non-violence in thought, word, and action. He believed that good actions are those that avoid causing harm to others and that respect for all living beings is fundamental. Non-violence is not merely the absence of physical violence but also includes the avoidance of hatred, anger, and resentment.

- Truth (Satya): Gandhi considered truth (satya) to be another foundational principle. Goodness, for him, is closely related to living in alignment with truth. This involves honesty, integrity, and the pursuit of justice. Truth, in Gandhi's view, is a universal principle that guides ethical behavior and is integral to achieving moral and spiritual purity.

Moral and Spiritual Development

Gandhi's understanding of good and evil is intertwined with his views on moral and spiritual growth.

- Gandhi believed that personal transformation is crucial for understanding and practicing good. He

265

emphasized that individuals must cultivate inner purity, self-discipline, and spiritual awareness to align themselves with ethical principles. This inner transformation leads to a life of goodness and harmony with others.

- For Gandhi, good involves self-realization and the development of one's moral character. This includes the practice of virtues such as humility, compassion, and forgiveness. Evil, conversely, is seen as stemming from moral failings, ignorance, and the inability to control one's negative impulses.

Social and Political Implications

Gandhi's perspective on good and evil also extends to social and political contexts.

- Gandhi's fight against social injustice, such as the caste system and colonial oppression, reflects his belief that good involves working towards justice, equality, and the upliftment of marginalized communities. Evil, in this context, is associated with social injustice, exploitation, and discrimination.

- Gandhi's method of non-violent resistance (satyagraha) was based on the idea that good can be achieved through peaceful means, even in the face of oppression. He believed that non-violence is a powerful and morally superior way to confront and overcome evil, as it aligns with the principles of truth and respect for all.

Unity and Harmony

Gandhi's perspective also emphasizes the importance of unity and harmony in human relationships.

- Gandhi saw all human beings as interconnected and believed that good involves fostering unity and harmony among people. He stressed that individual actions should contribute to the common good and promote mutual understanding and cooperation.

- Forgiveness and reconciliation are important aspects of Gandhi's philosophy. He believed that true goodness involves overcoming hatred and enmity through forgiveness and working towards reconciliation, even with those who have wronged us.

Gandi Summary

Mahatma Gandhi's perspective on good and evil is deeply rooted in the principles of non-violence (ahimsa) and truth (satya). Goodness, for Gandhi, is associated with living in harmony with these principles, which include not causing harm, pursuing justice, and practicing personal and moral integrity. Evil is seen as stemming from violence, dishonesty, and moral ignorance. Gandhi's ethical framework extends to social and political realms, emphasizing the importance of justice, equality, and non-violent resistance. His perspective also highlights the significance of personal transformation, unity, and reconciliation in achieving a moral and just society.

Hawking

Stephen Hawking, the renowned theoretical physicist, did not specifically develop a detailed moral philosophy on good and evil in the way that philosophers or theologians might. However, his views on these concepts can be inferred from his scientific and philosophical writings, especially in the context of his views on the universe, humanity, and ethics.

Good and Evil in a Scientific Context

Hawking's work primarily focused on the nature of the universe, cosmology, and theoretical physics. His approach to good and evil can be contextualized within his broader scientific worldview.

- From a scientific standpoint, the universe is a system governed by physical laws without inherent moral values. Hawking's perspective suggests that concepts of good and evil are not intrinsic to the cosmos but are human constructs that arise from our social and evolutionary development.

- Hawking would likely view good and evil as constructs that have evolved within human societies. These concepts are shaped by cultural, social, and evolutionary factors rather than being derived from the fundamental laws of physics.

Ethics and Human Responsibility

Although Hawking did not focus extensively on ethics, his work implies some views on human responsibility and the implications of our actions.

- In his writings, particularly in *"The Grand Design"* and *"Brief Answers to the Big Questions,"* Hawking discussed the responsibility humanity has towards itself and the planet. He emphasized the need for global cooperation and the importance of addressing issues like climate change, nuclear proliferation, and artificial intelligence.

- Hawking's concern with existential risks and the future of humanity suggests that ethical considerations are important in ensuring the survival and well-being of human civilization. While he may not provide a detailed moral framework, his emphasis on addressing global challenges implies an underlying ethical concern for the collective good.

The Role of Reason and Evidence

Hawking's approach to understanding the universe was deeply rooted in reason and empirical evidence, which can extend to his views on ethics.

- Hawking valued reason and empirical evidence as the basis for understanding the universe. Similarly, one might infer that he would support ethical decisions based on rational analysis and evidence rather than on religious or dogmatic principles.

- In line with his scientific worldview, Hawking might view moral progress as a result of increasing knowledge and rationality. Just as scientific understanding evolves, so too do ethical norms and values as societies gain more insight into the consequences of their actions.

The Impact of Technology and Knowledge

Hawking frequently addressed the implications of scientific advancements, particularly in relation to ethics.

- Hawking expressed concern about the potential dangers of advanced technologies, such as artificial intelligence and genetic engineering. He highlighted the ethical need to ensure that these technologies are used responsibly to avoid negative consequences for humanity.

- The advancement of knowledge, including scientific and technological developments, brings with it ethical responsibilities. Hawking's emphasis on the careful consideration of these advancements reflects a view that ethical decision-making is crucial for the beneficial use of technology.

Hawking Summary

Stephen Hawking's perspective on good and evil can be understood through the lens of his scientific and philosophical views. He would likely view good and evil as human constructs shaped by social, cultural, and evolutionary factors rather than intrinsic properties of the universe. His emphasis on reason, empirical evidence, and global responsibility implies that ethical decisions should be based on rational analysis and a concern for the collective well-being. Although he did not provide a specific moral philosophy, his work underscores the importance of addressing global challenges and using knowledge and technology responsibly to ensure the survival and flourishing of humanity.

Hitler

Adolf Hitler's perspective on good and evil was deeply rooted in his extreme and distorted ideology, which was shaped by his beliefs in racial supremacy, nationalism, and authoritarianism. His views were a perversion of moral and ethical concepts, and they led to some of the most heinous atrocities in history.

Racial Supremacy and Ideology

- Hitler's concept of good was closely tied to his belief in racial purity and the superiority of the "Aryan" race. He saw the Aryan race as the pinnacle of human evolution and believed that it was the duty of this "superior" race to dominate and control other races. Goodness, in Hitler's view, involved the advancement and preservation of the Aryan race and the elimination of those he deemed "inferior."

- Hitler perceived evil as anything that threatened the racial purity and superiority of the Aryan race. This included Jews, Roma, disabled individuals, Slavs, and other groups he considered "undesirable" or "degenerate." He viewed these groups as corrupting influences that needed to be removed to maintain the purity and strength of the Aryan race.

Authoritarianism and Totalitarianism

- Hitler's regime was characterized by extreme authoritarianism and totalitarian control. Goodness, from his perspective, involved absolute loyalty to the Führer and the state, and the implementation of policies that furthered his ideological goals. Evil was associated with dissent, opposition, and any form of resistance to his regime's authority and objectives.

- Hitler's notion of good also included militarism and territorial expansion. He believed that the expansion of German territory was a legitimate and necessary goal, justified by his ideology of racial superiority. Evil, in this context, was any resistance to or hindrance of Germany's militaristic and expansionist ambitions.

Manipulation of Morality

- Hitler and the Nazi regime used propaganda to manipulate and distort concepts of good and evil. They portrayed their policies and actions as virtuous and necessary for the betterment of the Aryan race and the German nation. The regime indoctrinated the public with these distorted notions, making extreme cruelty and violence appear justifiable and even righteous.

- Hitler's perspective was characterized by a form of moral relativism, where the moral framework was entirely contingent upon the goals of his ideology. Actions and policies that were universally recognized as evil, such as genocide and oppression, were redefined as morally acceptable or even necessary in the context of his racial and political goals.

Ethical Implications and Historical Consequences

- Hitler's views fundamentally rejected universal moral principles and ethical standards. His perspective on good and evil was entirely relative to his own extremist ideology and objectives, leading to the justification of horrific atrocities and crimes against humanity.

- The consequences of Hitler's perspective on good and evil were devastating. The Holocaust and other atrocities committed under his regime are stark reminders of the destructive potential of ideologies that corrupt and distort moral values. Hitler's views led to immense suffering and loss of life and remain a powerful example of the dangers of extremist ideology and moral perversion.

Hitler Summary

Adolf Hitler's perspective on good and evil was based on a deeply flawed and harmful ideology that prioritized racial supremacy, authoritarian control, and militaristic expansion. Goodness, in his view, was associated with the advancement of the Aryan race and the consolidation of his totalitarian regime, while evil was defined as anything that threatened these goals or contradicted his ideology. Hitler's manipulation of morality and rejection of universal ethical standards led to some of the most egregious human rights violations in history. His perspective illustrates the extreme consequences of distorting and weaponizing moral concepts for ideological and political ends.

King

Martin Luther King Jr., the prominent civil rights leader and advocate for social justice, approached the concepts of good and evil from a moral and ethical standpoint deeply rooted in his Christian faith, as well as his commitment to justice and equality. His perspective is shaped by his teachings on nonviolence, love, and the fight against systemic injustice.

Good as Justice, Love, and Nonviolence

King's understanding of good is grounded in the principles of justice, love, and nonviolence.

- For King, good is closely associated with the pursuit of justice and equality. He believed that justice involves recognizing the inherent dignity and worth of every individual and working to dismantle systems of oppression and inequality. This pursuit of justice is a central theme in his speeches and writings, including his famous "I Have a Dream" speech.

- King emphasized the importance of agape love—a selfless, unconditional love that seeks the well-being of others. This form of love is not merely an emotional feeling but a proactive force for good that drives individuals to act with compassion and fairness towards others. King's concept of love is a powerful moral force that transcends personal grievances and seeks to uplift and reconcile communities.

- King advocated for nonviolent resistance as a means to achieve social change and address injustices. He believed that nonviolence was not only a practical strategy for achieving civil rights but also a moral imperative that aligns with the teachings of Jesus and the principles of justice and love.

Evil as Injustice, Oppression, and Violence

King's concept of evil is closely linked to injustice, oppression, and violence.

- Evil, in King's view, is manifest in systems and actions that perpetuate injustice and inequality. This includes practices and policies that discriminate against individuals based on race, socioeconomic status, or other characteristics. King's activism was dedicated to exposing and addressing these injustices, advocating for civil rights and equality.

- King saw oppression as a form of evil that dehumanizes individuals and perpetuates suffering. He fought against institutional racism, segregation, and discrimination, believing that these forms of oppression were deeply immoral and contrary to the principles of human dignity and equality.

- King condemned violence as a destructive force that undermines the pursuit of justice and reconciliation. He argued that violence degrades both the perpetrator and the victim, and that true progress can only be achieved through peaceful means. His philosophy of nonviolence was inspired by figures such as Mahatma Gandhi and rooted in his Christian beliefs.

Moral Responsibility and the Beloved Community

King's perspective on good and evil includes a vision of a "Beloved Community" and the moral responsibility of individuals and society.

- King envisioned a Beloved Community as a society where justice, equality, and love prevail, and where individuals work together to create a just and compassionate world. This vision reflects his belief in the possibility of social transformation through collective action and moral commitment.

- King emphasized the moral responsibility of individuals to act against evil and work for the common good. He believed that individuals have a duty to stand up against injustice, support the oppressed, and contribute to building a more equitable and just society.

Theological and Ethical Foundations

King's views on good and evil are deeply influenced by his Christian theology and ethical beliefs.

- King's perspective is rooted in his Christian faith, which teaches that love, justice, and compassion are central to the moral life. He drew on biblical teachings to advocate for social justice and to frame his understanding of good and evil.

- Ethically, King's views are grounded in the principles of moral courage and integrity. He believed that individuals should act according to their highest moral values, even in the face of adversity, and should seek to create a just and compassionate world.

King Summary

Martin Luther King Jr.'s perspective on good and evil is centered on the principles of justice, love, and nonviolence. Good is defined by the pursuit of justice, the practice of agape love, and the commitment to nonviolent resistance. Evil is associated with injustice, oppression, and violence. King's vision includes the creation of a Beloved Community and the moral responsibility of individuals to act against evil and promote the common good. His views are deeply influenced by his Christian faith and ethical beliefs, emphasizing the transformative power of love and nonviolence in achieving social justice.

$\mathcal{La\,Vey}$

Anton LaVey, the founder of the Church of Satan and author of "The Satanic Bible," offers a unique and controversial perspective on good and evil that diverges significantly from traditional religious and moral frameworks. LaVey's views are rooted in Satanism, which he defined as a form of individualism and personal empowerment.

Good and Evil as Constructs of Human Nature

LaVey's perspective on good and evil is grounded in a pragmatic and human-centered view of morality.

- LaVey argued that concepts of good and evil are largely based on human nature and desires. He rejected the notion of absolute moral truths dictated by an external deity and instead posited that moral values are subjective and shaped by individual and societal interests.

- According to LaVey, what is considered good or evil can vary depending on cultural, personal, and situational factors. He believed that traditional moral codes, especially those derived from religious doctrines, are artificial constructs that often serve to suppress natural human instincts.

Satanism as a Philosophy of Self-Interest

LaVey's brand of Satanism emphasizes self-interest and personal empowerment, and this philosophy significantly influences his view of good and evil.

- In LaVeyan Satanism, good is often equated with actions that serve one's own interests, desires, and personal goals. The pursuit of self-fulfillment and gratification is seen as a natural and acceptable aspect of human life.

- LaVey championed individualism and personal responsibility. Good actions are those that advance the individual's own well-being and success, while evil is often seen as behavior that hinders or opposes personal advancement.

Rejection of Traditional Moral Codes

LaVey was a vocal critic of traditional religious and moral codes, particularly those from Christianity.

- LaVey rejected religiously based moral frameworks that he saw as oppressive and hypocritical. He argued that such systems often promote self-denial and guilt while glorifying self-sacrifice and submission.

- For LaVey, good is associated with the exercise of personal power, autonomy, and freedom. He encouraged people to embrace their desires and instincts, viewing these as natural and valid expressions of human nature.

Ethical Pragmatism and Consequentialism

LaVey's ethical views are pragmatic and consequentialist, focusing on the outcomes of actions rather than adherence to fixed moral principles.

- LaVey's approach to ethics is pragmatic, meaning that actions are evaluated based on their practical outcomes and effectiveness in achieving personal goals. What is considered good or evil is determined by the results of one's actions and their impact on the self and others.

- Actions are judged by their consequences. Good actions lead to beneficial outcomes for the individual, while evil actions result in harm or negative consequences. This perspective prioritizes the practical effectiveness of actions over adherence to abstract moral ideals.

Symbolism and Ritual

In LaVeyan Satanism, rituals and symbols play a significant role in expressing and reinforcing personal values and beliefs.

- LaVey utilized rituals not necessarily to invoke supernatural forces but as a means of psychological and symbolic reinforcement. Rituals are seen as a way to focus one's will and achieve personal desires.

- The use of symbols, such as the Sigil of Baphomet, serves to express and embody the principles of Satanism, including the embrace of individualism, personal power, and rebellion against conventional moral norms.

LaVey Summary

Anton LaVey's perspective on good and evil is characterized by a focus on self-interest, individual empowerment, and pragmatism. Good is defined as actions that align with personal desires and goals, while evil is seen as behavior that obstructs personal advancement or causes harm. LaVey rejected traditional moral codes and religious doctrines, advocating instead for a philosophy that values personal freedom and pragmatic evaluation of actions. His views reflect a broader critique of conventional morality and an embrace of individualism and self-fulfillment.

Montessori

Maria Montessori, the founder of the Montessori method of education, didn't approach the concepts of good and evil in a traditional moral or philosophical framework. Instead, her perspective on good and evil is largely framed within her educational philosophy and her understanding of human development, focusing on the natural tendencies of children and how they grow into moral, autonomous individuals. Montessori's approach to moral development emphasizes the innate goodness of the child and the role of education in nurturing that goodness through independence, respect, and self-discipline.

The Innate Goodness of the Child

Montessori believed that children are born with an intrinsic sense of good and a natural desire to contribute positively to their environment. In her view, children are inherently good, curious, and capable of developing moral behavior when given the right conditions to grow.

- According to Montessori, good is rooted in the natural development of the child's personality and character. Children have an innate desire to learn, explore, and engage with the world around them. When children are given the freedom to act independently in a prepared environment that respects their developmental needs, they naturally express positive behaviors such as cooperation, empathy, and responsibility. Montessori saw this as a manifestation of their intrinsic goodness.

- Montessori did not believe that children are born evil. Instead, she viewed "evil" or negative behaviors as a result of frustration, unmet developmental needs, or external constraints that suppress the child's natural growth. When children are hindered by rigid or authoritarian environments, or when they lack opportunities to explore and develop their abilities, they may exhibit destructive behaviors. These behaviors, however, are not innate but are reactions to unfavorable circumstances.

Moral Development and Autonomy

Montessori's philosophy emphasizes the importance of independence and autonomy in the moral development of the child. She believed that children learn moral concepts like good and evil through real-life experiences, self-directed activity, and social interactions in an environment where they are respected and given freedom within clear limits.

- Goodness arises when children develop self-discipline and moral awareness through independent action. Montessori argued that when children are allowed to make choices and take responsibility for their actions, they develop a sense of inner discipline and morality. A child who is free to choose, within the boundaries of respect for others and their environment, learns to act out of their own sense of what is right, rather than from external rewards or punishments.

- Evil, in Montessori's perspective, can be understood as behavior that disrupts harmony, either in the classroom environment or in social relationships. This could be selfishness, violence, or disobedience, but Montessori saw these behaviors as symptoms of an underlying issue—typically an environment that does not meet the child's developmental needs. In her view, children exhibiting such behaviors need guidance and a supportive environment to re-channel their energies toward positive ends, rather than punishment or harsh discipline.

Freedom and Responsibility

Central to Montessori's philosophy is the balance between freedom and responsibility. She believed that children should be given freedom to make their own choices, but with that freedom comes the responsibility to respect others and their environment. Montessori viewed this balance as essential to the development of moral reasoning.

- Goodness is linked to the ability to exercise freedom responsibly. When children are given choices, they learn to evaluate the consequences of their actions and develop a sense of accountability. Montessori classrooms are structured so that children learn to respect the rights of others, care for their environment, and contribute to the well-being of the community. In doing so, they cultivate moral virtues like fairness, kindness, and cooperation.

- "Evil" occurs when freedom is used without responsibility. Montessori believed that when children misuse their freedom—such as by acting selfishly, destructively, or without regard for others—it reflects a lack of understanding about how to balance their own needs with the needs of those around them. However, rather than labeling these actions as inherently evil, Montessori saw them as learning opportunities where the child can be guided to make better choices.

The Role of the Environment in Shaping Good and Evil

Montessori placed great importance on the prepared environment in shaping a child's moral development. In her view, the environment plays a key role in fostering or hindering a child's natural inclination toward good.

- A well-prepared environment encourages goodness by promoting independence, concentration, and respect for others. Montessori classrooms are designed to be orderly, calm, and rich with materials that engage the child's curiosity and intellect. In such an environment, children naturally develop positive behaviors because they are given the tools to succeed, feel respected, and are able to engage in meaningful, purposeful work. The structured freedom within this environment helps children internalize concepts of order, respect, and community.

- In contrast, Montessori believed that chaotic or overly restrictive environments can lead to what might be considered "evil" behaviors—such as disobedience, aggression, or apathy. When children's needs for movement, exploration, and independence are stifled, they may become frustrated and act out. Montessori saw this not as inherent evil, but as a sign that the environment is not supporting the child's natural development. Correcting the environment, rather than punishing the child, is the solution to these behaviors.

Work and the Development of Moral Character

Montessori viewed work—in the sense of purposeful, self-directed activity—as essential to the development of moral character. She believed that engaging in meaningful work fosters a sense of purpose, discipline, and respect for oneself and others.

- Goodness, for Montessori, is closely tied to the development of concentration, self-discipline, and love of learning, all of which are cultivated through engaging in meaningful work. When children are given opportunities to work on tasks that interest them and challenge their abilities, they develop patience, persistence, and respect for the process of learning. This, in turn, fosters a sense of personal responsibility and an understanding of their role in contributing to the community.

- Montessori saw laziness, disorder, or destructive behaviors as symptoms of a lack of meaningful engagement. When children are not given opportunities to engage in purposeful work, they may act out of boredom, frustration, or a lack of direction. In her view, the absence of constructive work leads to negative behavior, which she saw as preventable through proper guidance and environment.

Education as a Path to Moral Goodness

For Montessori, education is not just about intellectual development, but also about moral and spiritual growth. She believed that through education, children learn not only academic skills but also how to be good, ethical, and responsible members of society.

- The goal of Montessori education is to help children realize their full potential as independent, moral beings. By providing an environment that fosters independence, respect, and responsibility, education becomes a process of self-construction where children learn to be good by actively engaging with their world and understanding their role in it.

- "Evil," in Montessori's view, is largely a failure of education or environment, rather than something inherent in the child. When education is rigid, authoritarian, or fails to meet the developmental needs of children, it stifles their natural goodness and leads to frustration, rebellion, or apathy. Montessori saw the educator's role as helping to guide children back to positive behaviors through understanding, patience, and respect.

Montessori Summary

For Montessori, good is the natural expression of a child's development when they are provided with an environment that fosters independence, respect, and purposeful work. Children are born with the potential for good, and education plays a vital role in nurturing that goodness. Evil, on the other hand, is not innate but arises from frustration, unmet developmental needs, or inappropriate environments that prevent children from developing their full potential. Montessori's approach to good and evil emphasizes the importance of freedom, responsibility, and respect, and she saw moral education as a process of guiding children toward self-discipline and inner harmony.

Murray

Douglas Murray is a British author and commentator known for his writings on political and cultural issues. His perspective on good and evil is influenced by his views on modern politics, cultural conflicts, and social issues. Murray often addresses these concepts within the context of cultural and moral decline, identity politics, and the challenges facing Western civilization.

Good as Defense of Western Values and Rational Discourse

Murray often defines good in terms of defending and preserving Western values, such as freedom of speech, individual liberty, and rational discourse. He believes that these values are foundational to a just and prosperous society.

- For Murray, the good involves upholding the principles that have traditionally supported Western democracies, including respect for individual rights, freedom of expression, and a commitment to rational debate. He argues that these values are under threat from various ideological movements that he perceives as undermining these principles.

- Murray emphasizes the importance of rational debate and the free exchange of ideas. He argues that open discussion and the ability to critique prevailing ideologies are essential for a healthy society. In his view, suppressing controversial or dissenting opinions, whether through political correctness or other means, is a threat to societal progress and moral integrity.

Evil as Ideological Extremism and Cultural Decay

Murray often frames evil as the manifestation of ideological extremism and what he sees as the decline of cultural and moral standards.

- In Murray's perspective, evil is found in the rise of ideological extremism and identity politics that he believes undermine social cohesion and rational discourse. He criticizes movements and ideologies that, in his view, seek to silence dissent, enforce ideological conformity, or disrupt societal norms. This includes critiques of political correctness, identity politics, and social justice movements which he argues contribute to societal fragmentation and conflict.

- Murray sees the erosion of traditional cultural norms and values as a form of moral and societal decline. He argues that a loss of shared values and a breakdown in societal cohesion lead to greater division and conflict, which he views as a form of cultural evil.

Good as the Preservation of Social Order and Civilizational Values

Murray frequently discusses the need to preserve and restore what he considers to be the core values of Western civilization, which he believes are essential for social order and progress.

- For Murray, the good is found in efforts to preserve and restore traditional social and cultural norms that he believes have historically underpinned stable and prosperous societies. This includes a commitment to individual rights, personal responsibility, and social order.

- Murray argues that societal norms and values that promote individual achievement, responsibility, and social stability are crucial for maintaining a functioning society. He often critiques the erosion of these norms as contributing to social fragmentation and moral decay.

Good and Evil in the Context of Modern Political Issues

Murray's views on good and evil are also influenced by his analysis of contemporary political issues, including the debates over immigration, national identity, and cultural integration.

- In this context, Murray often portrays the good as policies and attitudes that he believes support national cohesion, law and order, and cultural integration. He argues that effective immigration policies and a commitment to social integration are essential for maintaining societal stability.

- Murray views certain political ideologies and policies that he believes undermine national cohesion or promote division as forms of evil. This includes what he perceives as the negative consequences of uncontrolled immigration or multiculturalism that he argues can lead to social fragmentation and conflict.

Good as a Commitment to Objective Truth and Moral Integrity

Murray emphasizes the importance of objective truth and moral integrity in defining good.

- He argues that a commitment to objective truth and moral integrity is essential for addressing societal problems and maintaining a just society. This involves resisting ideological dogma and focusing on evidence-based arguments and honest dialogue.

- For Murray, moral integrity involves adhering to principles of truthfulness and rationality, and resisting the pressures of ideological conformity or political correctness. He believes that maintaining moral integrity is crucial for addressing the challenges facing modern societies and for promoting a just and functional social order.

Murray Summary

For Douglas Murray, good is defined by the defense of Western values, rational discourse, and social order. It involves upholding individual rights, personal responsibility, and the principles that have historically supported stable societies. Evil, in Murray's view, is represented by ideological extremism, identity politics, and the perceived decay of cultural and moral standards. He sees these as threats to societal cohesion and progress, arguing that preserving traditional values and promoting objective truth are essential for maintaining a just and functional society.

Peterson

Jordan Peterson, a Canadian psychologist and cultural critic, approaches the concepts of good and evil through a blend of psychology, philosophy, and religious traditions, particularly influenced by Jungian psychology, Christianity, and existentialist thought. His views are shaped by his interest in how individuals navigate the tension between order and chaos, responsibility and meaning, and how society constructs morality. Peterson's perspective on good and evil is deeply rooted in the idea that humans are capable of both, and it is through individual responsibility and confronting one's own darkness that people can strive toward the good.

Good as the Pursuit of Meaning and Responsibility

For Peterson, good is fundamentally tied to living a life of meaning, which is achieved through the acceptance of personal responsibility. He argues that life is inherently full of suffering, and the highest form of good is to confront this suffering directly, take on responsibility, and strive toward order and meaning.

- Goodness, according to Peterson, is found in taking responsibility for oneself and for others. This involves confronting the chaos and suffering of life, making order out of chaos, and contributing to the well-being of society. He often refers to this as carrying your "cross" or "burden," borrowing from Christian symbolism. To be good is to act morally and ethically in a way that reduces suffering for oneself and others, while also promoting order and structure in a chaotic world.

- For Peterson, living in accordance with truth is central to doing good. He argues that telling the truth—especially difficult truths—is essential for psychological health and societal well-being. Lying, or avoiding hard truths, leads to personal chaos and societal collapse, which he views as a form of moral failure.

- Goodness comes from accepting the burden of responsibility—whether it's responsibility toward family, society, or one's own potential. Peterson often talks about the importance of aiming for the highest possible good, and that this is achieved through the individual taking on as much responsibility as they can bear, rather than seeking comfort or avoiding hardship.

Evil as Resentment, Malevolence, and Nihilism

Peterson's conception of evil is deeply tied to the psychological states of resentment, malevolence, and the rejection of meaning. He believes that individuals can fall into evil when they allow these dark impulses to take over, leading them to inflict unnecessary suffering on others.

- Peterson identifies evil with the willful infliction of suffering, especially when that suffering is unnecessary or stems from a desire to hurt others. He often cites historical atrocities like the Holocaust and the Soviet Gulags as examples of what happens when ideologies that promote resentment and division take hold of society. Evil is not just the existence of chaos or suffering, but the deliberate magnification of it for the sake of power, control, or personal vengeance.

- One of the primary sources of evil, according to Peterson, is resentment. When people feel wronged by life, society, or others, they can become resentful. Instead of taking responsibility for their own lives, they blame external forces and may seek revenge. This mindset leads to malevolent behavior—where people consciously or unconsciously aim to harm others as a way of dealing with their own pain. This is a form of nihilism, where life's meaning is rejected, and destruction becomes the goal.

- Nihilism and Ideological Possession: Peterson is a strong critic of nihilism, which he views as the belief that life has no inherent meaning or value. Nihilism can lead to despair, and in its worst form, can result in the pursuit of evil as a form of revenge against existence itself. He also criticizes ideological possession, where people adopt rigid belief systems (such as extreme forms of Marxism or totalitarianism) and lose their ability to think critically, which he sees as a pathway to evil. He argues that ideologies that emphasize resentment and division can lead to societal collapse and atrocities.

Order, Chaos, and the Balance of Good and Evil

Peterson often discusses the symbolic interplay between order and chaos, which he associates with the potential for good and evil. In his view, both order and chaos are necessary elements of existence, but balance between the two is crucial for a morally upright life.

- Order represents stability, structure, tradition, and the known. It is associated with rules, social hierarchies, and cultural norms. Order is necessary for society to function, and for individuals to live meaningful lives. However, too much order can lead to rigidity and oppression—a state where freedom and creativity are stifled.

- Chaos represents the unknown, potential, change, and creativity. It is the realm of new ideas, exploration, and personal growth, but also of fear, uncertainty, and destruction. Too much chaos leads to disorder, confusion, and violence. Peterson believes that individuals must confront chaos (often symbolized by the hero's journey), integrate it into their lives, and transform it into productive order.

- Good and Evil as Balance: In Peterson's framework, good is achieved when individuals can balance order and chaos in their lives. Too much order leads to tyranny, while too much chaos leads to anarchy. People who avoid the challenges of chaos may become overly rigid, while those who reject order can fall into destructive behaviors. The ideal state is one where individuals engage with both order and chaos responsibly, striving to make meaning out of the challenges they face.

The Jungian Shadow and Confronting Inner Evil

Peterson frequently discusses the Jungian concept of the shadow, which refers to the darker, unconscious aspects of the self. He believes that everyone has the capacity for evil within them and that recognizing and confronting this capacity is essential for moral growth.

- Peterson argues that part of being good is acknowledging one's own potential for evil. He often cites historical examples (such as Nazi Germany) to illustrate how ordinary people can become complicit in atrocities. To be truly good, individuals must confront their own capacity for evil, integrate it, and channel it in constructive ways. Ignoring the shadow or denying its existence can lead to moral blindness, where people fail to recognize the evil within themselves and project it onto others.

- Evil arises when individuals fail to integrate their darker impulses and allow those impulses to dominate. This can lead to violence, cruelty, and the destruction of others. For Peterson, moral maturity involves coming to terms with one's own potential for malevolence and choosing instead to act in ways that promote life and reduce suffering.

Good as Upholding Traditional Values and Individual Responsibility

Peterson often defends traditional values, such as family, religion, and social hierarchies, as frameworks that help individuals live moral lives.

He believes that these structures are essential for maintaining order and preventing the spread of chaos.

- For Peterson, good is tied to upholding traditional values, which have been shaped by centuries of human experience. These values help people find meaning, responsibility, and stability in life. He argues that abandoning these structures—whether it's through radical political movements or the rejection of personal responsibility—leads to social decay and the proliferation of evil.

- Another key tenet of Peterson's idea of good is the focus on individual responsibility over rights or entitlements. He argues that people should strive to take responsibility for their lives and the lives of others, rather than demanding more rights without corresponding duties. In his view, this focus on responsibility helps individuals find meaning and contribute to the common good.

Religion and the Archetype of Good and Evil

Peterson draws heavily on religious and mythological archetypes to explain his view of good and evil, particularly the Judeo-Christian tradition.

- Peterson often refers to the Christian idea of Christ as an archetype of the ultimate good: someone who takes on the sins and suffering of the world, voluntarily accepts responsibility, and strives for redemption. He views this archetype as a powerful symbol of the highest form of moral good.

- Peterson views evil through the lens of archetypes like Satan or Cain—figures that represent resentment, pride, and the rejection of responsibility. These figures symbolize the individual's descent into malevolence when they refuse to confront their own suffering and blame others for their misfortune.

Peterson Summary

For Jordan Peterson, good is the pursuit of meaning, truth, and responsibility, achieved by confronting the inherent suffering and chaos of life and striving to create order and reduce suffering for oneself and others. Evil, on the other hand, is characterized by resentment, nihilism, and malevolence—the willful infliction of suffering and rejection of meaning. Peterson emphasizes the importance of personal responsibility, the balance between order and chaos, and confronting one's own capacity for darkness as crucial to living a moral life.

Rand

Ayn Rand, a 20th-century philosopher and novelist, developed a distinctive perspective on good and evil rooted in her philosophy of Objectivism. Her views challenge traditional religious and altruistic moralities by emphasizing rational self-interest, individualism, and the pursuit of one's own happiness as the highest moral purpose. Rand's ethical framework sharply contrasts with both collectivist ideologies and moral systems based on self-sacrifice.

Good as Rational Self-Interest

At the core of Rand's ethics is the idea that good is defined by what furthers one's life and well-being through rational thought and actions. According to her, the highest moral aim is to live a life guided by reason, which leads to personal flourishing and happiness.

- For Rand, good is acting in one's rational self-interest. This means making choices that are based on reason, long-term thinking, and the goal of achieving personal happiness and fulfillment. She rejects the notion that self-interest means exploiting others, as rational self-interest requires individuals to respect the rights and autonomy of others while pursuing their own goals.

- Happiness as the Ultimate Goal: Rand argues that an individual's happiness is the moral purpose of life. Happiness, in her view, is achieved by pursuing one's values, which should be selected rationally. Living in accordance with reality, using one's mind to understand the world, and acting to sustain one's own life are the hallmarks of a moral existence.

Evil as Altruism and Self-Sacrifice

Rand's view of evil is strongly opposed to the traditional morality of altruism, which she defines as the belief that individuals should live for others and place others' needs above their own. In her view, altruism and self-sacrifice are morally destructive because they undermine the individual's right to pursue their own happiness and value their own life.

- Rand considers altruism evil because it demands the sacrifice of an individual's self-interest for the sake of others. She believes that by prioritizing others over oneself, altruism denies the moral worth of the individual and leads to self-destruction and resentment.

- For Rand, the concept of self-sacrifice is inherently immoral. She rejects the idea that virtue lies in sacrificing one's interests, goals, or happiness for others. Instead, she promotes rational self-interest as the moral alternative to self-sacrifice, arguing that it leads to healthier, more fulfilling relationships and societies.

The Virtue of Selfishness

Rand's use of the term "selfishness" is central to her philosophy, but she redefines it to mean acting in one's rational self-interest rather than behaving in a short-sighted or destructive manner.

- Rand argues that selfishness, properly understood, is a virtue. She believes that individuals should act in ways that serve their own lives and well-being, as long as they do so rationally and without violating the rights of others. Rational selfishness involves creating value for oneself through productive work, voluntary exchange, and maintaining self-esteem.

- Selflessness, on the other hand, is considered evil by Rand. To her, selflessness means abandoning one's own values, goals, and happiness for the sake of others. She sees this as a denial of life and a rejection of the individual's right to exist for their own sake.

Reason as the Primary Virtue

Reason is the highest virtue in Rand's ethical system, and all moral choices must be grounded in reality and rational thought. She rejects emotionalism, mysticism, and any form of faith-based or collectivist thinking as destructive to the individual.

- Good is using reason to understand the world, to choose one's values, and to act in ways that support one's life and long-term happiness. For Rand, reason is the only means of gaining knowledge and the only guide to living a successful, moral life.

- Irrationality is evil because it leads to self-destructive choices. Rand believes that acting based on emotions, whims, or the demands of others without rational justification is a betrayal of one's mind and values. Any philosophy or worldview that rejects reason, such as religious faith or collectivism, is viewed by Rand as fundamentally evil because it undermines the individual's ability to live a fulfilling life.

Individualism vs. Collectivism

Rand's philosophy is deeply individualistic, and she sees collectivism as one of the greatest evils in human society. Collectivism, for Rand, is the idea that the group or society is more important than the individual, and that individuals exist to serve the collective.

- Individualism, for Rand, is the essence of moral goodness. She believes that every individual has the right to live for their own sake, without being coerced to serve others. A good society is one that respects individual rights, including property rights, and allows people to freely pursue their own happiness.

- Collectivism is evil because it denies the rights of the individual and demands that people sacrifice their values and interests for the sake of the group. Rand saw collectivist ideologies—such as socialism, communism, and fascism—as morally bankrupt because they prioritize the collective over the individual, leading to oppression and the destruction of human potential.

Productiveness and Achievement

In Rand's view, productive work is central to the moral life. Creating value in the world through work is an expression of the individual's rational mind and the way people achieve self-esteem and happiness.

- Productiveness is a key virtue because it allows individuals to sustain their lives, achieve independence, and create wealth. In *Atlas Shrugged*, Rand celebrates the creators, inventors, and entrepreneurs as the moral heroes who drive human progress through their achievements.

- Rand condemns parasitism, laziness, and those who seek to live off the efforts of others without contributing value themselves. In her view, individuals who exploit or rely on others for their survival, without engaging in productive work, embody evil because they betray the principle of self-reliance and independence.

Rights and Freedom

Rand's ethical system also emphasizes the importance of individual rights, particularly the right to life, liberty, and property. She believes that a proper political system is one that protects these rights and allows individuals to live freely without interference from others or the state.

- A just society is one that upholds individual rights and ensures that each person is free to pursue their own life and happiness without coercion. Rand advocates for capitalism as the only moral social system because it respects individual rights and allows people to engage in voluntary exchanges for mutual benefit.

- Any form of coercion—whether by the state or by individuals—is evil in Rand's view. She opposes government intervention in the economy, redistribution of wealth, and any form of collectivism that infringes on personal freedom. Rand believes that such systems rob individuals of their ability to act in their own self-interest and achieve their own happiness.

Rand Summary

For Ayn Rand, good is the pursuit of rational self-interest, where individuals use reason to guide their actions and seek personal happiness through productive work and moral independence. She sees evil as anything that undermines the individual's ability to live freely and pursue their own happiness, especially systems of altruism, collectivism, and irrationality. In Rand's philosophy, the moral life is one of self-responsibility, where each person is the creator of their own destiny, and the greatest virtue is to live for one's own sake.

Somerville

Margaret Somerville, a Canadian professor of bioethics and law, offers a unique perspective on good and evil that is informed by her expertise in bioethics, law, and philosophy. Her views are often centered around the implications of ethical decision-making in the context of modern science and medicine, and she draws on both secular and religious ethical traditions.

Good as Promoting Human Dignity and Well-Being

Somerville's understanding of good is closely tied to the concepts of human dignity, well-being, and the moral significance of human life. She emphasizes the importance of respecting the inherent value of individuals and the ethical implications of decisions that affect their lives.

- From Somerville's perspective, good involves actions and policies that promote human dignity and well-being. This includes ensuring that ethical considerations are central to decisions in medicine, law, and society, and that these decisions uphold the inherent value and worth of individuals.

- Somerville places a strong emphasis on the principle of human dignity, which she argues should be a foundational consideration in ethical decision-making. She believes that recognizing and respecting the intrinsic worth of every person is essential for determining what is good.

Evil as Actions that Undermine Human Dignity and Moral Integrity

In contrast, Somerville defines evil in terms of actions or policies that undermine human dignity, moral integrity, and ethical principles. She is concerned with how modern practices and technological advancements can challenge traditional moral values.

According to Somerville, evil is associated with actions that compromise human dignity, exploit or degrade individuals, and violate ethical principles. This includes practices that she believes erode the moral fabric of society or fail to respect the intrinsic worth of individuals.

- Somerville often critiques contemporary practices and technologies that she believes pose ethical challenges, such as euthanasia, genetic engineering, and reproductive technologies. She argues that these practices can sometimes undermine human dignity and moral integrity if not carefully regulated and ethically considered.

Good as Adherence to Ethical Principles and Moral Traditions

Somerville's views are influenced by both ethical principles and moral traditions, which she believes provide guidance in navigating complex ethical dilemmas.

- Somerville argues that adherence to established ethical principles, such as respect for life, justice, and compassion, is crucial for determining what is good. She believes that these principles help guide decision-making in areas like bioethics and law.

- She also draws on moral traditions, including religious and philosophical traditions, to inform her understanding of good and evil. Somerville believes that these traditions offer valuable insights into the moral dimensions of human actions and the nature of ethical decision-making.

Good and Evil in the Context of Modern Science and Medicine

Somerville frequently addresses ethical issues arising from modern science and medicine, examining how technological advancements intersect with moral values.

- In this context, good is defined by how well modern scientific and medical practices align with ethical principles and contribute to the well-being of individuals and society. This includes ensuring that advancements are used in ways that respect human dignity and promote ethical integrity.

- Conversely, evil involves scientific and medical practices that, in Somerville's view, pose significant ethical risks or undermine fundamental moral values. She raises concerns about how certain technologies and practices might challenge traditional ethical frameworks and the implications for human dignity and integrity.

Ethical Decision-Making and Moral Challenges

Somerville's work emphasizes the importance of ethical decision-making and the need to address moral challenges posed by new technologies and social changes.

- For Somerville, making ethical decisions involves careful consideration of how actions affect human dignity and well-being. This requires balancing competing values and addressing the moral implications of new developments.

- She highlights the need to engage with moral challenges posed by contemporary issues, such as advances in biotechnology, and to navigate these challenges in a way that upholds ethical standards and respects human dignity.

Somerville Summary

Margaret Somerville's perspective on good and evil is centered around the principles of human dignity, well-being, and ethical decision-making. Good is defined by actions and policies that respect human dignity and promote moral integrity, while evil is associated with actions that undermine these values. Her views are influenced by ethical principles, moral traditions, and the ethical implications of modern scientific and medical practices. Somerville advocates for careful consideration of the moral dimensions of contemporary issues and the importance of adhering to ethical standards in decision-making.

Zedong

Mao Zedong, the founding father of the People's Republic of China, had a distinctive and politically charged perspective on good and evil that was deeply influenced by his revolutionary ideology, Marxism-Leninism, and his vision for the transformation of Chinese society.

Ideological and Political Framework

- For Mao, good was closely tied to the success of the Communist revolution and the implementation of socialist policies. Actions that advanced the goals of the revolution, such as land redistribution, the establishment of collective farming, and the consolidation of Communist power, were considered good. Mao's perspective on good was heavily aligned with his commitment to Marxist-Leninist ideology and his vision for a classless society.

- Evil, in Mao's view, was associated with anything that opposed or undermined the revolutionary goals of the Communist Party. This included those who were perceived as counter-revolutionaries, class enemies, or imperialist forces. Individuals and groups that resisted or opposed Mao's policies, such as landlords, capitalists, and political rivals, were labeled as enemies of the revolution and thus as embodiments of evil.

Class Struggle and Moral Judgment

- Mao's perspective on morality was deeply intertwined with his concept of class struggle. Good was defined in terms of supporting the working class and peasantry in their struggle against the bourgeoisie and feudal elements. Evil was identified with the interests of the exploiting classes and their attempts to preserve their privilege and power.

- Mao promoted the idea of moral purity in relation to revolutionary ideals. This included the expectation that individuals would demonstrate unwavering loyalty to the Communist Party and adhere to its ideological principles. Deviations from these principles, including dissent or perceived disloyalty, were considered morally wrong and were often met with severe consequences.

Cultural Revolution and Ideological Purity

- During the Cultural Revolution (1966-1976), Mao's perspective on good and evil was manifest in the campaign to purge Chinese society of "bourgeois" and "counter-revolutionary" elements. Good was associated with the radical transformation of society and the promotion of Maoist thought, while evil was linked to perceived enemies of the revolution, including intellectuals, traditionalists, and political opponents. The campaign led to widespread persecution, violence, and social upheaval.

- Mao's emphasis on ideological purity meant that moral judgments were often based on conformity to his vision of socialism. Actions and policies that advanced the revolutionary cause were seen as good, while those that contradicted or challenged his ideology were deemed evil.

Utilitarian Perspective

- Mao's approach to morality was often pragmatic, focusing on the outcomes of policies and actions rather than adhering to abstract moral principles. The ends were seen to justify the means if they served the goals of the revolution. This utilitarian perspective led to policies and actions that could be harsh and ruthless, justified by the belief that they were necessary for achieving the greater good of revolutionary transformation.

- Mao's view of good and evil also involved the willingness to make significant sacrifices for the sake of the revolution. The immense human suffering and loss during the Great Leap Forward and the Cultural Revolution were rationalized as necessary for achieving the goals of building socialism and purifying Chinese society.

Historical Materialism

- Mao's understanding of good and evil was influenced by historical materialism, a Marxist concept that views history as a process driven by material conditions and class struggle. Good was associated with actions that advanced the material conditions and revolutionary objectives of the working class, while evil was related to actions that preserved or perpetuated existing class structures and inequalities.

Zedong Summary

Mao Zedong's perspective on good and evil was grounded in his revolutionary ideology and commitment to Marxist-Leninist principles. Good was defined by its alignment with the goals of the Communist revolution and the transformation of Chinese society, while evil was associated with opposition to these goals and resistance from class enemies. Mao's views were shaped by class struggle, the pursuit of ideological purity, and a utilitarian approach that justified harsh measures for the sake of revolutionary objectives. His perspective led to significant social and political upheavals, including widespread persecution and violence during the Cultural Revolution.

Epilogue

I am confident that you have encountered and considered many different perspectives on the nature of good and evil. My hope is that you take some time to reflect and see where these ideas resonate within your mind and heart, allowing you to form your own theories that bring you peace and understanding. Remember, this is a deeply personal journey, and only you can determine what feels true for you—there are no right or wrong answers.

As for my own thoughts on good and evil, I must admit that I don't hold a single, definitive belief on the matter. Instead, I have several theories that shift depending on the circumstances. It's important to note that good and evil manifest in various degrees of morality and depravity.

One aspect that is often overlooked when rushing to label something as good or evil is the importance of pausing and making an honest effort to consider the situation from different perspectives. Too often, people take things personally when they should try to understand who or what is truly impacted by the situation. When you take a step back and view it from various angles, you may be surprised by what you discover—things you hadn't previously considered that could shift your perception depending on the circumstances.

Let me dive right into my perspective on the concept of evil. Do I believe that evil truly exists? While I don't subscribe to the idea of a literal devil, I do believe in God, who, at times, can be seen as less than benevolent. God, in my view, has a way of balancing the scales and imparting lessons to those who need them. However, this process can sometimes catch innocent people in its path. Large groups may become casualties of evil acts—not because they have done anything wrong or have lessons to learn, but because their suffering serves as a sacrifice to teach broader, more profound lessons to others. These individuals who endure such suffering may have chosen this path, possibly in a previous life or through an agreement with God, to undergo hardship for the greater good of others.

When considering figures such as Hitler, Stalin, Mao Zedong, Pol Pot, and Saddam Hussein, it becomes clear that these were leaders consumed by power, with a degree of psychopathy that drove them to commit unimaginable atrocities. Their actions embody evil on multiple levels. Yet, a crucial question arises: Why were these individuals not stopped sooner? It's a question worth reflecting on.

Another question to ponder is: What good, if any, has come from their actions? Even after all this time, can we see any positive outcomes now, or do you think more time is needed for that clarity? For me, it isn't about balancing the scales, where the negative must be matched by an equal positive. It's more about understanding the greater good. Perhaps it's a greater good that we cannot yet see, but we need to trust and have faith that God knows what He is doing. If nothing else, I firmly believe there is always a reason behind everything. We all have lessons to learn, often ones we may not immediately recognize or comprehend. Yet, over time, these lessons guide us toward what some might describe as an enlightened state of being. God's purpose is always at work, even if it isn't always clear to us.

For deeply personal reasons, I consider Hitler to be the most horrific perpetrator of evil in history. It took me numerous attempts before I was finally able to watch *Schindler's List* in its entirety. As haunting as it was, the atrocities were not solely the actions of one man; by 1945, the Nazi Party had swelled to 8 million members. Were all 8 million individuals inherently evil? Were they manipulated and brainwashed? Should they all be judged with the same severity as their leader?

What good could possibly emerge from such a horrific period marked by countless deaths? These questions can lead us down an endless path of reflection. Many of us search for a version of the truth that brings some measure of peace, or we may choose to label it all as pure evil and leave it at that. For most, Hitler, the death of millions of Jews, and absolute evil are inseparable concepts—packaged together and set aside. Yet, there is much more to what happened, far more to understand, and even ways to see glimpses of good amid the darkness. The "never forget" and "never again" movements are profoundly significant and very real. The bonds within the Jewish community are unparalleled, fostering a sense of unity and resilience that is unmatched by any other group. To me, this has God's name written all over it. However, I am not sure we have seen the end game yet.

Suggested Reading

Religion

Amish

"The Amish Way: Patient Faith in a Perilous World" by Donald B. Kraybill, Steven M. Nolt, and David L. Weaver-Zercher. This book dives deeply into the religious life of the Amish, exploring their values, rituals, and spiritual beliefs. It highlights how their faith shapes their daily lives and communities.

"An Amish Paradox: Diversity and Change in the World's Largest Amish Community" by Charles E. Hurst and David L. McConnell. While this book examines the diversity and changes within Amish communities, it also provides a thorough look at how religious beliefs are maintained and adapted, particularly in the face of modern challenges.

"Amish Society" by John A. Hostetler. A classic and foundational text on Amish life, this book includes significant information on their religious practices and theological underpinnings. Hostetler, himself raised in an Amish community, offers a nuanced perspective on their spirituality.

Atheism

"The God Delusion" by Richard Dawkins – A foundational modern book on atheism, Dawkins critiques religion from a scientific perspective, offering arguments about why belief in God is irrational. It's a passionate, often provocative, examination of atheism and secular humanism.

"God is Not Great: How Religion Poisons Everything" by Christopher Hitchens – Hitchens argues against organized religion, providing historical and moral critiques. His sharp wit and eloquent style make complex arguments accessible and memorable.

"Breaking the Spell: Religion as a Natural Phenomenon" by Daniel Dennett – Dennett, a philosopher, explores why religion exists and how it evolved as a natural phenomenon. He offers a more scientific and philosophical approach to understanding atheism.

"Letter to a Christian Nation" by Sam Harris – This book is concise and straightforward, providing a powerful critique of Christian beliefs and a defense of secularism, making it ideal for those who want a quick but impactful read.

"Atheism: The Case Against God" by George H. Smith – A classic text, this book examines religious faith and offers logical arguments for atheism. It's especially helpful for those interested in philosophical debates about God's existence.

"Why I Am Not a Christian" by Bertrand Russell – This collection of essays by philosopher Bertrand Russell critiques Christianity and theistic beliefs from an ethical, rational, and philosophical standpoint.

Baha'i

"The Kitáb-i-Íqán (The Book of Certitude)" by Bahá'u'lláh – This is one of the core theological texts of the Bahá'í Faith, written by its founder, Bahá'u'lláh. It explores essential principles, the nature of God, and the concept of progressive revelation in a unique religious philosophy.

"Gleanings from the Writings of Bahá'u'lláh" – This collection includes selected writings of Bahá'u'lláh, covering topics such as spirituality, justice, unity, and peace. It's approachable for readers looking for an overview of Bahá'í teachings and beliefs.

"The Hidden Words" by Bahá'u'lláh – A poetic, spiritual text that condenses the essence of ethical and spiritual teachings in the Bahá'í Faith. Each passage is intended as a source of guidance and meditation.

"The Promise of World Peace" by The Universal House of Justice – This is a formal statement issued by the Bahá'í governing body, addressing global peace and unity. It gives readers a sense of the Bahá'í approach to global issues and their emphasis on unity.

"God Speaks Again: An Introduction to the Bahá'í Faith" by Kenneth E. Bowers – This book is an accessible introduction to Bahá'í beliefs and history, making it a great starting point for newcomers.

"A Short History of the Bahá'í Faith" by Peter Smith – A concise overview of the origins and development of the Bahá'í Faith, covering key historical events and figures, including Bahá'u'lláh and the early Bahá'ís.

Buddhism

"What the Buddha Taught" by Walpola Rahula – A classic introduction to core Buddhist teachings directly from the Pali Canon, the earliest Buddhist scriptures. This book is accessible, concise, and respected for its straightforward explanations.

"The Heart of the Buddha's Teaching" by Thich Nhat Hanh – Vietnamese Zen master Thich Nhat Hanh presents a compassionate, clear exploration of the key teachings of Buddhism, including the Four Noble Truths, the Eightfold Path, and more, all with practical guidance for everyday life.

"In the Buddha's Words: An Anthology of Discourses from the Pali Canon" edited by Bhikkhu Bodhi – This anthology offers a deeper dive into the Buddha's original teachings, organized by themes such as ethics, meditation, and wisdom. It's ideal for those interested in exploring early Buddhist scripture directly.

"The Art of Happiness" by the Dalai Lama and Howard Cutler – This best-selling book offers a practical approach to Buddhism through the lens of happiness and inner peace, blending Western psychology with Buddhist teachings.

"Buddhism Without Beliefs" by Stephen Batchelor – An approachable book for secular readers, Batchelor presents a non-dogmatic approach to Buddhism, focusing on its practical and philosophical aspects without requiring religious belief.

"The Tibetan Book of Living and Dying" by Sogyal Rinpoche – This book presents Tibetan Buddhist views on life, death, and rebirth, offering guidance on meditation, mindfulness, and compassionate living.

Caodaism

"Caodaism: A Vietnamese Syncretic Religion" by Sergei Blagov – This is a comprehensive introduction to Caodaism, its origins, beliefs, and rituals. Blagov examines its unique blend of Eastern and Western spiritual elements, including Buddhism, Taoism, Confucianism, Christianity, and spiritism.

"Caodai Spiritism: A Study of Religion in Vietnamese Society" by Sergei Blagov – Another work by Blagov, this book dives into Caodaism's spiritual practices and mediumship, including how the religion's followers connect with spirits and spiritual leaders. It provides insight into the religion's role in Vietnamese culture and history.

"The Religions of South Vietnam in Faith and Fact: Section I, Cao Dai" by United States Department of the Army – This report provides an overview of Caodaism's history, beliefs, and practices as understood during the Vietnam War era. Though dated, it offers an informative and historical perspective on Caodaism within Vietnam.

"Caodaism: Vietnamese Traditionalism and Its Leap into Modernity" by Victor L. Oliver – Oliver's book explores how Caodaism navigates the balance between traditional Vietnamese spiritual beliefs and modernity, offering a sociological perspective on the religion's development and adaptation.

"Divine Path to Eternal Life" by Phạm Công Tắc – This book, written by a former leader of the Caodai faith, explores the religion's doctrines and philosophical outlook from an insider's perspective. It gives readers insight into the practices and spiritual goals of Caodai followers.

Christianity

"Mere Christianity" by C.S. Lewis – This classic book is an accessible and thoughtful introduction to core Christian beliefs, including morality, faith, and the concept of God. Written for a broad audience, Lewis's style is both philosophical and practical.

"The Case for Christ" by Lee Strobel – A former journalist, Strobel investigates the evidence for Jesus's life, death, and resurrection from a legal and historical perspective. This book is accessible for beginners and is particularly useful for those interested in an evidential approach to Christianity.

"Simply Christian: Why Christianity Makes Sense" by N.T. Wright – Wright, a respected biblical scholar, provides a modern, reasoned defense of Christianity, covering topics like justice, spirituality, and the resurrection of Jesus. His approach is both intellectual and approachable.

"The Story of Christianity" by Justo L. González – This two-volume work provides an in-depth history of Christianity from its origins through modern times. González's writing is clear and comprehensive, making this a great choice for those interested in the historical development of the faith.

"The Cost of Discipleship" by Dietrich Bonhoeffer – A powerful exploration of what it means to truly follow Jesus, written by the German theologian who resisted Nazi rule. Bonhoeffer's focus on the ethics and demands of Christianity is both challenging and inspiring.

"Christianity: The First Three Thousand Years" by Diarmaid MacCulloch – A comprehensive, scholarly history of Christianity, covering its ancient roots, development, and influence in the modern world. Though detailed, MacCulloch's writing makes complex topics understandable.

"Knowing God" by J.I. Packer – A classic in Christian theology, Packer explores the nature of God and how Christians can build a relationship with Him. It's a devotional and theological text that delves deep into Christian beliefs about God and salvation.

"The Reason for God: Belief in an Age of Skepticism" by Timothy Keller – Keller addresses common questions and doubts about Christianity in a way that is both philosophical and pastoral, making it ideal for skeptics and believers alike.

Confucianism

"The Analects of Confucius" translated by Arthur Waley or D.C. Lau – The Analects is the foundational text of Confucianism, a collection of Confucius's teachings compiled by his disciples. Both translations are well-regarded, making the core teachings accessible and relevant.

"Confucianism: A Very Short Introduction" by Daniel K. Gardner – This concise book provides a clear and engaging overview of Confucianism, covering its historical development, key texts, ethical teachings, and influence on Chinese society and culture.

"Confucianism and Chinese Civilization" by Arthur F. Wright – Wright's book delves into how Confucianism has influenced Chinese history, politics, and culture over centuries. It's a solid introduction for those interested in the societal impact of Confucianism.

"Confucianism: Origins, Beliefs, Practices, Holy Texts, Sacred Places" by Peter Morgan – This book provides an accessible introduction to Confucianism's basic principles, historical roots, and practices, with sections dedicated to the main texts and the way Confucianism manifests in daily life and social organization.

"The World of Thought in Ancient China" by Benjamin I. Schwartz – This comprehensive work examines Confucianism in the context of ancient Chinese philosophy, comparing it to other schools of thought like Daoism and Legalism. Schwartz's work is highly regarded for its depth and scholarly approach.

"Confucianism and Modern China" by Xinzhong Yao – Yao's book explores how Confucian values and ideas have adapted to modernity and globalization. This book is great for understanding how Confucianism remains relevant in contemporary East Asian societies.

"The Four Books: The Basic Teachings of the Later Confucian Tradition" translated by Daniel K. Gardner – Gardner's translation and commentary on the Four Books (including The Analects and Mencius) provides insight into Confucian teachings that influenced East Asia for centuries, emphasizing ethics, governance, and personal cultivation.

316

Druze

"The Druze Faith" by Sami Nasib Makarem – This book is one of the most comprehensive resources on Druze theology, philosophy, and rituals. Makarem, a Lebanese scholar and Druze himself, offers a detailed and accessible introduction to the core beliefs of the Druze faith.

"The Druzes in a Changing World" by Robert Brenton Betts – Betts provides a historical and sociopolitical overview of the Druze, covering their origins, beliefs, and the challenges they face in modern society. This is a great resource for understanding the Druze community within the larger Middle Eastern context.

"The Druze: A New Cultural Perspective" by Yusri Hazran – This book provides a fresh perspective on Druze identity, culture, and the complexities of their integration in the modern nation-states where they reside, particularly Lebanon and Israel.

"Between Heaven and Earth: The Druze People" by Mordechai Nisan – Nisan explores the history and beliefs of the Druze and provides insights into their role in the Middle East. He examines their political alliances, military involvement, and the impact of modernization on their religious traditions.

"The Origins of the Druze People and Religion" by Philip K. Hitti – This classic work delves into the historical roots of the Druze faith and people, tracing the origins of their beliefs to Ismaili Islam and exploring their development into a unique religious community.

"Secrets of Mount Hermon: The Occult Tradition of the Druze" by Talal H. Fandi – This book explores some of the mystical elements associated with the Druze faith, though it remains respectful of the esoteric nature of Druze doctrine.

Eastern Christianity

"The Orthodox Church" by Timothy Ware (Bishop Kallistos Ware) – This classic introduction is accessible yet comprehensive, covering the history, beliefs, and practices of the Eastern Orthodox Church, with insights on its sacraments, theology, and spirituality.

"The Eastern Church" by Henry Chadwick – Chadwick offers a concise history of the Eastern Orthodox Church, focusing on its theological development and key historical events. His writing is clear and insightful, making it suitable for beginners.

"The Mystical Theology of the Eastern Church" by Vladimir Lossky – Lossky's work is a deeper theological exploration of Eastern Christian mysticism and spirituality, covering key concepts such as the Trinity, the Incarnation, and divine energies. This book is ideal for those seeking a philosophical and mystical perspective.

"The Orthodox Way" by Kallistos Ware – Another book by Bishop Kallistos Ware, this one delves into the spiritual life and practices of Eastern Orthodox Christians, presenting a deeper exploration of prayer, sacraments, and spiritual formation within Orthodoxy.

"The Blackwell Companion to Eastern Christianity" edited by Ken Parry – This comprehensive academic guide covers the history, theology, and liturgical practices of various Eastern Christian traditions, including the Oriental Orthodox, Eastern Orthodox, and Eastern Catholic churches. It's an excellent resource for deeper study.

"For the Life of the World: Sacraments and Orthodoxy" by Alexander Schmemann – Schmemann discusses the sacramental worldview of Eastern Christianity, focusing on how the sacraments are viewed as a means of encountering God and understanding the world through a sacred lens.

"The Coptic Orthodox Church: A Brief Introduction to Its History and Spirituality" by Christine Chaillot – This book offers a clear and accessible introduction to the Coptic Orthodox Church, one of the major branches of Oriental Orthodoxy, covering its history, theology, and unique cultural elements.

Folk

"The Sacred and the Profane: The Nature of Religion" by Mircea Eliade – Though not strictly focused on folk religion, this classic text by Eliade explores the essence of religious belief, ritual, and myth in a way that provides insight into the symbolic elements often present in folk religions.

"Folk Religion: An Overview of Beliefs and Practices" by Stephen Sharot – This book provides a scholarly exploration of folk religion, looking at its core elements, such as ancestor worship, shamanism, and magic, and how these interact with institutional religions worldwide.

"The World of Shamanism: New Views of an Ancient Tradition" by Roger Walsh – Walsh provides a more modern approach to understanding shamanism, explaining how these practices are still relevant in contemporary contexts and offering insights into folk beliefs that transcend cultural boundaries.

"Folk Religion: An Introduction" by John Lynch – This introductory text explores folk religion globally, addressing common themes like sacred spaces, local deities, and the interplay between folk beliefs and formal religions.

God

"The Idea of the Holy" by Rudolf Otto – This classic work explores the concept of the "numinous," a sense of the divine that is both mysterious and awe-inspiring. Otto's philosophical approach is essential for understanding the experiential side of the concept of God.

"The Case for God" by Karen Armstrong – Armstrong provides a historical perspective on how the idea of God has evolved over time in different cultures and religions, covering concepts from ancient polytheism to modern monotheism and mystical understandings.

"God: A Biography" by Jack Miles – This Pulitzer Prize-winning book treats God as a character in the Hebrew Bible, analyzing God's development and personality throughout the texts. It's a unique literary approach to the concept of God in scripture.

"Mere Christianity" by C.S. Lewis – Lewis presents a classic Christian view of God, arguing for the rationality of faith and exploring Christian beliefs about God, morality, and the meaning of life. His accessible writing has made this a favorite among those exploring Christian theology.

"The Experience of God: Being, Consciousness, Bliss" by David Bentley Hart – Hart examines the philosophical and mystical dimensions of God across multiple religious traditions, including Christianity, Hinduism, and Buddhism. It's a deep, contemplative approach to understanding the nature of God.

"The Power of Now: A Guide to Spiritual Enlightenment" by Eckhart Tolle – Although not strictly about "God," Tolle's spiritual philosophy delves into ideas of presence, consciousness, and a divine reality beyond the individual self, resonating with the mystical concept of God.

"A History of God: The 4,000-Year Quest of Judaism, Christianity, and Islam" by Karen Armstrong – Armstrong traces the development of monotheism through Jewish, Christian, and Islamic traditions, examining how each has conceived of and interacted with the idea of God.

"God: A Human History" by Reza Aslan – Aslan examines the anthropological and psychological roots of the concept of God, suggesting that human beings have shaped God in their own image. It's a unique look at how belief in God reflects human consciousness.

"The Varieties of Religious Experience" by William James – This seminal work examines religious experiences from a psychological perspective, shedding light on how different people experience the divine and perceive God in varied ways.

Hinduism

"The Bhagavad Gita" translated by Eknath Easwaran or Swami Sivananda – The Bhagavad Gita is one of Hinduism's most important sacred texts, presenting the teachings of Krishna to Arjuna on duty, devotion, and the nature of reality. Eknath Easwaran's and Swami Sivananda's translations are both accessible and faithful to the text.

"Hinduism: A Very Short Introduction" by Kim Knott – This concise book offers a clear overview of Hinduism's core beliefs, practices, history, and cultural influences. It's ideal for beginners and those looking for a quick yet thorough introduction.

"The Upanishads" translated by Eknath Easwaran – The Upanishads are philosophical texts that explore the nature of reality, self, and the divine. Easwaran's translation is accessible and includes commentary, making it a good entry point into Hindu philosophy.

"A Sourcebook in Indian Philosophy" by Sarvepalli Radhakrishnan and Charles A. Moore – This comprehensive anthology includes selections from the Vedas, Upanishads, Bhagavad Gita, and classical Hindu philosophical systems like Vedanta and Samkhya, making it essential for understanding Hindu thought.

"The Essentials of Hinduism" by Swami Bhaskarananda – This book covers the key principles and practices of Hinduism, including concepts like karma, dharma, and moksha. It's a straightforward, clear guide for those new to Hinduism or those wanting a concise reference.

"Hinduism: Beliefs and Practices" by Vasudha Narayanan – Narayanan provides a comprehensive look at Hinduism's rituals, festivals, and ethical teachings, with a particular focus on how Hinduism is practiced in everyday life. It's an insightful resource on the lived aspects of Hinduism.

Islam

"The Qur'an" translated by M.A.S. Abdel Haleem or Muhammad Asad – The Qur'an is the central religious text of Islam, and a good translation with commentary can provide essential insights into its teachings. Abdel Haleem's and Asad's translations are accessible for readers new to the text.

"No god but God: The Origins, Evolution, and Future of Islam" by Reza Aslan – This popular introduction covers the historical development of Islam, from the Prophet Muhammad's life to modern-day issues, offering a nuanced view of Islamic beliefs and practices.

"Islam: A Short History" by Karen Armstrong – Armstrong provides a concise, insightful overview of Islam's history, covering its origins, growth, and cultural impact. Her writing is accessible and provides a balanced introduction to the religion's complex history.

"The Study Quran" edited by Seyyed Hossein Nasr – This annotated Quran includes extensive commentary and explanations by respected scholars, making it ideal for those seeking a deeper understanding of the text's meanings and interpretations.

"Muhammad: His Life Based on the Earliest Sources" by Martin Lings – Lings's biography of the Prophet Muhammad is widely respected for its storytelling and accuracy, using classical Islamic sources. It's accessible and engaging, providing a sense of the Prophet's life and teachings.

"What Everyone Needs to Know About Islam" by John L. Esposito – Esposito answers common questions about Islam, covering topics such as beliefs, practices, the role of women, and contemporary issues. It's an excellent introductory book for those looking to dispel misconceptions.

Jainism

"The Jains" by Paul Dundas – This is a widely respected introduction to Jainism, covering its history, beliefs, and practices. Dundas provides an accessible yet comprehensive overview, making it ideal for both beginners and those seeking a deeper understanding.

"Jainism: A Very Short Introduction" by Jeffery D. Long – This brief but thorough introduction covers the essential aspects of Jain philosophy, ethics, and spirituality. Long's writing is approachable, and he provides a balanced view of Jainism's core teachings and values.

"The Book of Compassion: A Jain Handbook for Compassionate Living" by Kirit Daftary and Kurt Titze – This book offers practical guidance on living in alignment with Jain principles, especially ahimsa (non-violence). It's a great resource for those interested in applying Jain ethical principles in everyday life.

"Jainism and Ecology: Nonviolence in the Web of Life" edited by Christopher Key Chapple – This collection of essays examines Jain beliefs from an ecological perspective, showing how its principles align with environmental consciousness. It's ideal for readers interested in the intersection of religion and ecology.

"The Jain Path: Ancient Wisdom for the West" by Manish Modi – Modi provides an introduction to Jain philosophy and lifestyle, presenting Jain ethics, spirituality, and values in a way that resonates with Western readers, particularly those interested in spiritual growth.

"An Introduction to Jainism" by Bharat S. Shah – This is a straightforward guide to Jainism's foundational beliefs and practices, covering concepts like karma, cosmology, and the soul. It's suitable for beginners looking for a concise, introductory overview.

"Tattvartha Sutra: That Which Is" by Umasvati, translated by Nathmal Tatia – This is a core text in Jain philosophy that lays out Jain cosmology, metaphysics, and ethics. This translation includes commentary, making it accessible for readers new to Jain thought.

Jehovah's Witnesses

"Apocalypse Delayed: The Story of Jehovah's Witnesses" by M. James Penton. Written by a former Jehovah's Witness and historian, this book provides a comprehensive look at the origins, beliefs, and evolution of the religion. It offers an objective analysis of its teachings and organizational structure.

"Jehovah's Witnesses: Portrait of a Contemporary Religious Movement" by Andrew Holden. This sociological study explores the lives of Jehovah's Witnesses, focusing on their beliefs, practices, and interactions with society. It provides a balanced perspective on how their faith shapes their daily lives.

"Crisis of Conscience" by Raymond Franz. Authored by a former member of the Jehovah's Witnesses Governing Body, this book offers a personal account of the inner workings of the organization. It's particularly insightful for those interested in the governance and decision-making processes of the religion.

Judaism

"The Torah: The Five Books of Moses" translated by Robert Alter or the Jewish Publication Society (JPS) – The Torah is the foundational text of Judaism, and these translations make it accessible with modern English and commentary that enrich understanding of its narratives and laws.

"Jewish Literacy: The Most Important Things to Know About the Jewish Religion, Its People, and Its History" by Rabbi Joseph Telushkin – This comprehensive yet accessible book covers over 3,000 years of Jewish thought, history, and practices. Organized in short, readable sections, it's perfect for both beginners and those seeking a well-rounded introduction.

"A History of the Jews" by Paul Johnson – This historical account provides a sweeping overview of the Jewish people from biblical times to modern-day Israel. Johnson's storytelling style makes complex history accessible and engaging.

"The Essential Talmud" by Adin Steinsaltz – This book is an introduction to the Talmud, a central text in Judaism. Steinsaltz explains the structure, content, and purpose of the Talmud in a way that is accessible to those unfamiliar with it.

"To Life!: A Celebration of Jewish Being and Thinking" by Rabbi Harold Kushner – Kushner provides a thoughtful overview of Jewish beliefs, values, and customs, making it ideal for those interested in the philosophical and ethical aspects of Judaism.

"Living a Jewish Life: Jewish Traditions, Customs, and Values for Today's Families" by Anita Diamant – This practical guide covers Jewish holidays, rituals, and everyday customs, making it ideal for those interested in how Judaism is practiced and lived.

"Judaism: A Very Short Introduction" by Norman Solomon – Part of the "Very Short Introduction" series, this book is a concise overview of Jewish history, beliefs, and practices, suitable for readers new to Judaism.

"The Jewish Bible: A Translation with Commentary" by Robert Alter – Alter's translation of the Hebrew Bible (Tanakh) is highly regarded for its literary style and scholarship. His accompanying commentary offers valuable insights into the text.

"The Book of Jewish Belief" by Louis Jacobs – Jacobs provides an introduction to Jewish theology, covering topics like God, the Torah, and ethics. It's suitable for those interested in the philosophical and theological side of Judaism.

"As a Driven Leaf" by Milton Steinberg – A novel based on the life of Elisha ben Abuyah, a rabbi who questions his faith, this book offers an imaginative look into early Rabbinic Judaism and the struggle between faith and reason.

"The Sabbath" by Abraham Joshua Heschel – A classic exploration of the spiritual significance of the Sabbath in Jewish life. Heschel's writing is both poetic and philosophical, highlighting the beauty of Jewish spirituality.

"God in Search of Man: A Philosophy of Judaism" by Abraham Joshua Heschel – This book is a profound philosophical and theological exploration of Judaism, dealing with the nature of faith, the relationship between God and humanity, and the essence of Jewish spirituality.

Mu-ism

"Korean Shamanism: The Cultural Paradox" by Chongho Kim – This book provides an accessible introduction to Korean shamanism, discussing its paradoxical place in modern society. Kim explores how Muism has survived and adapted in South Korea amid modernization and globalization.

"The Life and Hard Times of a Korean Shaman: Of Tales and the Telling of Tales" by Laurel Kendall – Kendall's work is an engaging ethnographic account of a Korean shaman and her experiences. The book explores the personal life of a shaman, revealing the challenges and changes Muism faces in modern Korea.

"Shamans, Housewives, and Other Restless Spirits: Women in Korean Ritual Life" by Laurel Kendall – Kendall examines the role of women in Korean shamanistic practices, offering insights into the rituals, spirit possession, and the shaman's role in addressing family and community issues.

"Korean Shamanistic Rituals" by Jung Young Lee – This book takes an academic approach to understanding the rituals and religious significance of Muism. Lee covers the cosmology, spirits, and ritual practices central to Korean shamanism.

"Kut: Happiness Through Reciprocity" by Hyun-key Kim Hogarth – The author explores the kut rituals, central ceremonies in Korean shamanism, where shamans communicate with spirits for blessings, healing, and guidance. Hogarth's insights offer an in-depth view of the ritual's cultural and spiritual significance.

"Voices from the Straw Mat: Toward an Ethnography of Korean Story Singing" by Chan E. Park – Although not exclusively about shamanism, this book discusses p'ansori (Korean narrative singing) and its connections with shamanistic elements. It's useful for understanding the interplay between Korean folklore and Muism.

"Korean Shamanism: Muism" by Kim Tae-kon and Chang Soo-kyung – This book provides a foundational overview of Muism, discussing its history, beliefs, and rituals. It's a great introductory resource for readers new to Korean shamanism.

Paganism

"The Triumph of the Moon: A History of Modern Pagan Witchcraft" by Ronald Hutton – This scholarly yet accessible book is widely considered the definitive history of modern Paganism and Wicca. Hutton traces the origins and development of Pagan practices in the Western world, particularly focusing on the British Isles.

"Paganism: An Introduction to Earth-Centered Religions" by Joyce and River Higginbotham – This introductory book covers the basics of Pagan beliefs, traditions, and rituals. It's a great choice for beginners looking for an approachable guide to the philosophy and values of Pagan spirituality.

"Drawing Down the Moon: Witches, Druids, Goddess-Worshippers, and Other Pagans in America" by Margot Adler – Adler, a journalist and Pagan herself, explores the diversity of modern Paganism in America. Her book includes interviews, historical context, and insights into the practices and lives of contemporary Pagans.

"The Spiral Dance: A Rebirth of the Ancient Religion of the Great Goddess" by Starhawk – This classic work on Wicca and Goddess spirituality is both a practical guide to rituals and an inspiring manifesto on feminist spirituality within Paganism. Starhawk's writing is influential in the Pagan community, especially for those interested in witchcraft and nature-based worship.

"Pagan Theology: Paganism as a World Religion" by Michael York – York provides a more academic perspective, analyzing Paganism as a cohesive and legitimate world religion. He examines its theology, beliefs, and commonalities with other religions, making it suitable for readers interested in a scholarly approach.

"The Elements of Ritual: Air, Fire, Water & Earth in the Wiccan Circle" by Deborah Lipp – Focusing on ritual practice, this book offers a thorough look at how modern Pagans and Wiccans use rituals to connect with natural elements. It's an excellent resource for those interested in the practical aspects of Pagan spirituality.

"A Book of Pagan Prayer" by Ceisiwr Serith – This collection offers prayers and devotions tailored to Pagan beliefs, addressing deities, nature, and personal intentions. It's a unique resource for those interested in deepening their spiritual practice with written devotionals.

"Witchcraft Today" by Gerald Gardner – Gardner, considered the founder of modern Wicca, shares his views on Paganism, witchcraft, and ritual practices. Although dated, it provides valuable historical insight into the roots of modern Paganism and Wicca.

Panentheism

"Panentheism: The Other God of the Philosophers" by John W. Cooper. This book provides a thorough historical and theological analysis of Panentheism, tracing its development and exploring its relationship to traditional theism and pantheism. Cooper critically examines the philosophical and theological implications of this worldview.

"The Emergent Self" by William Hasker. While not exclusively about Panentheism, this book explores related themes in philosophy of mind and metaphysics, offering insights into the concept of an interconnected and divine universe. It's an excellent resource for understanding Panentheism within the broader context of metaphysical inquiry.

"Spirit and Nature: The Study of Panentheism in Indian Philosophy and Christianity" by Y. Masih. This book explores the parallels between Panentheistic views in Indian philosophies and Christianity. It provides a comparative analysis of how the divine is perceived as immanent and transcendent across different cultural and religious frameworks.

Quaker

"A Light that Is Shining: An Introduction to the Quakers" by Harvey Gillman. This accessible book serves as an introduction to Quaker beliefs, practices, and spirituality. Gillman explains the Quaker emphasis on inner light, simplicity, and peace, making it a great starting point for understanding the tradition.

"The Quakers: A Very Short Introduction" by Pink Dandelion. Part of Oxford University Press's "Very Short Introduction" series, this book offers a concise yet comprehensive overview of Quaker history, theology, and cultural impact. Pink Dandelion is a respected scholar in Quaker studies, making this a reliable and insightful read.

"Silence and Witness: The Quaker Tradition" by Michael L. Birkel. This book explores the spiritual practices and theological foundations of Quakerism, emphasizing the importance of silence, simplicity, and the inner experience of the divine. It also addresses the Quaker commitment to social justice and peace.

Rastafari

"Rastafari: Roots and Ideology" by Barry Chevannes – This well-researched book provides a comprehensive history of the Rastafari movement, tracing its origins in Jamaica and exploring its development as a social and religious movement. Chevannes's work is considered foundational for understanding Rastafari.

"The Rastafarians" by Leonard E. Barrett – Barrett's classic book is one of the earliest and most comprehensive studies of the Rastafari movement. It covers Rastafari beliefs, symbolism, and the movement's social and cultural impact in Jamaica and beyond.

"Dread Talk: The Language of Rastafari" by Velma Pollard – This book explores the unique language, or Dread Talk, that has developed within

Rastafari culture, including its phrases, symbols, and significance. Pollard's work is essential for understanding the linguistic aspect of Rastafarian identity.

"Rasta and Resistance: From Marcus Garvey to Walter Rodney" by Horace Campbell – Campbell examines Rastafari as part of a larger resistance movement against colonialism and oppression, linking it with the pan-African movements of Marcus Garvey and others. It's an insightful resource for those interested in the political side of Rastafari.

"Reggae Wisdom: Proverbs in Jamaican Music" by Anand Prahlad – While not exclusively about Rastafari, this book explores the proverbs and teachings found in reggae music, an essential cultural expression within Rastafari. Prahlad provides insight into the movement's values, spirituality, and worldview through music.

"Rastafari: A Very Short Introduction" by Ennis B. Edmonds – This concise book provides a solid overview of Rastafari beliefs, practices, and cultural significance. It's a great introductory resource for those new to the subject.

"The First Rasta: Leonard Howell and the Rise of Rastafarianism" by Hélène Lee – Lee's biography of Leonard Howell, one of the founders of Rastafari, provides a fascinating look at the early days of the movement and Howell's influence on its core beliefs, including the divinity of Haile Selassie and anti-colonialism.

"Chanting Down Babylon: The Rastafari Reader" edited by Nathaniel Samuel Murrell, William David Spencer, and Adrian Anthony McFarlane – This anthology is a collection of essays by various scholars and practitioners, offering diverse perspectives on Rastafari theology, culture, and influence. It's a great resource for those looking for a broader view.

"Rastafari: From Outcasts to Culture Bearers" by Ennis B. Edmonds and Michelle A. Gonzalez – This book discusses the transformation of Rastafari from a marginalized group in Jamaica to a global cultural influence. It explores Rastafari symbols, lifestyle, and its impact on global culture and identity.

"Black Roots: A Beginner's Guide to Rastafari" by Ras Albert W. Gilmore – This accessible introduction covers basic Rastafari beliefs, symbols, and practices. It's a good starting point for those new to the movement or seeking a clear, concise overview.

Seventh-day Adventist

"Seeking a Sanctuary: Seventh-day Adventism and the American Dream" by Malcolm Bull and Keith Lockhart. This critically acclaimed book offers a comprehensive history and analysis of the Seventh-day Adventist Church, exploring its development, theology, and cultural context. It provides an objective look at how Adventism interacts with broader societal trends.

"The Adventists" by George R. Knight. George Knight is a leading scholar on Adventist history and theology. This book offers an accessible and engaging overview of the church's origins, key beliefs, and the people who shaped its development. It's an excellent introduction for those new to Adventism.

"Questions on Doctrine" (Annotated Edition, edited by George R. Knight). Originally published in 1957, this book outlines the core theological beliefs of Seventh-day Adventism, with particular focus on how Adventism aligns with and diverges from other Christian denominations. The annotated edition adds historical context and commentary.

Shinto

"Shinto: The Way Home" by Thomas P. Kasulis – This book is an excellent introduction to Shinto, explaining its core principles, such as harmony with nature, purity, and reverence for the kami (spirits or gods). Kasulis provides insights into the philosophy and worldview of Shinto.

"A Year in the Life of a Shinto Shrine" by John K. Nelson – Nelson provides a close look at the daily practices and annual rituals of a Shinto shrine in Japan. This ethnographic study is great for understanding how Shinto is practiced today and how it blends with Japanese culture.

"Shinto: The Kami Way" by Sokyo Ono – This accessible guide covers the basics of Shinto, including its origins, rituals, festivals, and the role of the kami. Ono's writing is clear and straightforward, making it ideal for beginners.

"Shinto in History: Ways of the Kami" edited by John Breen and Mark Teeuwen – This scholarly collection of essays traces the development of Shinto from ancient Japan to the modern era. It's excellent for readers interested in the historical evolution of Shinto beliefs and practices.

"The Essence of Shinto: Japan's Spiritual Heart" by Motohisa Yamakage – Written by a Shinto priest, this book explores the spiritual heart of Shinto and the ways in which it connects with nature, Japanese culture, and the inner self. Yamakage's perspective offers a deeply spiritual approach to understanding Shinto.

"Shinto: A History" by Helen Hardacre – Hardacre's book is a comprehensive, scholarly examination of Shinto, covering its development from early Japan to contemporary society. It includes historical analysis, discussions of political influences, and modern adaptations.

"Kami no Michi: The Way of the Kami" by Yukitaka Yamamoto – Yamamoto, a respected Shinto priest, discusses the philosophical and spiritual dimensions of Shinto. His reflections offer insight into the beliefs and values that underpin Shinto practice.

"The Sacred Power of Shinto: A Look at Nature, Rituals, and Symbols" by Akira Yusa – This book examines the symbolic world of Shinto, particularly its connection to nature and the way shrines and rituals reflect the Japanese view of the sacred.

Sikhism

"The Guru Granth Sahib: Canon, Meaning, and Authority" by Pashaura Singh – This book provides an in-depth study of the Guru Granth Sahib, the central scripture of Sikhism. Singh examines its history, compilation, and the theological significance of the hymns and teachings it contains.

"Sikhism: A Very Short Introduction" by Eleanor Nesbitt – Part of Oxford's "Very Short Introduction" series, this concise book offers a quick overview of Sikh beliefs, history, practices, and the Sikh diaspora. It's great for readers seeking an accessible entry point.

"Sikhism: A Guide for the Perplexed" by Arvind-Pal Singh Mandair – Mandair provides a clear and insightful guide to Sikh philosophy, ethics, and religious practices, making it an ideal resource for those wanting a deeper but accessible understanding of Sikhism.

"The Sikhs" by Khushwant Singh – This historical account traces the history of the Sikhs from their origins to modern times, covering major events, religious developments, and cultural contributions. Singh's storytelling style makes it a compelling read.

"The Sikh Religion, Its Gurus, Sacred Writings and Authors" by Max Arthur Macauliffe – Originally published in the early 20th century, this classic work is still one of the most respected resources on Sikhism. Macauliffe provides translations of key Sikh texts and extensive commentary on the lives and teachings of the Gurus.

"The Book of Nanak" by Navtej Sarna – This biography of Guru Nanak, the founder of Sikhism, offers insight into his life, teachings, and spiritual vision. It's a great book for understanding the origins of Sikh beliefs and values.

"The Oxford Handbook of Sikh Studies" edited by Pashaura Singh and Louis E. Fenech – This comprehensive volume is a collection of scholarly essays on various aspects of Sikhism, including its history, theology, politics, and diaspora. It's suitable for readers interested in an academic perspective on Sikh studies.

"Sikhism: An Introduction" by Nikky-Guninder Kaur Singh – Singh provides an overview of Sikh theology, ethics, and cultural practices, with a focus on how Sikhism promotes equality, social justice, and spirituality. Her approach is insightful, particularly on the topic of gender in Sikhism.

Spiritualism

"The Spiritualists: The Passion for the Occult in the Nineteenth and Twentieth Centuries" by Ruth Brandon – This historical exploration examines the rise of Spiritualism in the 19th century and its cultural impact, covering key figures, séances, and the connection between Spiritualism and societal changes.

"Talking to the Dead: Kate and Maggie Fox and the Rise of Spiritualism" by Barbara Weisberg – Focusing on the Fox sisters, who are credited with sparking the American Spiritualist movement, Weisberg provides a compelling narrative of how Spiritualism began and evolved in America.

"A History of Modern Spiritualism and the Occult" by Frank Podmore – A classic work by an early investigator of Spiritualism, this book covers the development of Spiritualism, including investigations into mediums, psychic phenomena, and key figures within the movement.

"The Afterlife Experiments: Breakthrough Scientific Evidence of Life After Death" by Gary E. Schwartz – Schwartz, a psychologist, presents scientific studies conducted on mediums and spiritual communication, making it an intriguing read for those interested in the scientific approach to Spiritualism.

"The Medium and the Message: The Rise of Spiritualism" by John Warne Monroe – Monroe offers an academic exploration of Spiritualism, its influence on Western culture, and how it intersected with science, religion, and gender dynamics, especially during the Victorian era.

"Spirit Communication: A Comprehensive Guide to the Extraordinary World of Mediums, Psychics, and the Afterlife" by Roy Stemman – Stemman provides a modern overview of Spiritualism, covering mediums, psychic phenomena, and stories of spirit communication. It's an approachable guide for beginners.

"Modern Spiritualism: The Science of Life and Death" by Emma Hardinge Britten – A Spiritualist and medium herself, Britten's classic work offers insights into Spiritualist beliefs, practices, and the philosophy behind them, especially focusing on life after death.

"Survival of the Soul: A Modern Guide to the Afterlife" by Lisa Williams – Medium Lisa Williams provides insights into what she believes about the afterlife, drawn from her experiences as a practicing medium. This book is more focused on contemporary Spiritualist beliefs and practices.

Sufism

"The Essential Rumi" translated by Coleman Barks – This popular collection of Rumi's poetry, one of the most beloved Sufi poets, is an accessible introduction to the mysticism, love, and devotion at the heart of Sufism. Barks' translation captures the beauty and wisdom of Rumi's spiritual insights.

"The Sufis" by Idries Shah – A classic introduction to Sufism, Shah's book covers Sufi teachings, stories, and practices, weaving together spiritual insights with cultural and historical perspectives. It's highly regarded for its depth and readability.

"Sufism: A Beginner's Guide" by William C. Chittick – Chittick provides a clear and comprehensive overview of Sufism's core beliefs, practices, and history, making it an excellent starting point for beginners interested in understanding Sufi philosophy and spirituality.

"The Heart of Sufism: Essential Writings of Hazrat Inayat Khan" by Hazrat Inayat Khan – A renowned Sufi teacher who introduced Sufism to the West, Inayat Khan's teachings emphasize love, harmony, and the unity of all religions. This collection offers insights into Sufi practices and concepts in a relatable way.

"The Garden of Truth: The Vision and Promise of Sufism, Islam's Mystical Tradition" by Seyyed Hossein Nasr – Nasr explores Sufism's core teachings on the nature of God, the soul, and the path to spiritual enlightenment. His scholarly approach is accessible and provides a deep understanding of Sufi beliefs within the context of Islam.

"The Conference of the Birds" by Farid ud-Din Attar, translated by Sholeh Wolpé or Dick Davis – This Sufi allegorical poem is a masterpiece of Persian literature, detailing the journey of the soul in search of spiritual truth. Its symbolic stories convey profound Sufi teachings on love, ego, and divine unity.

"Sufism: Love and Wisdom" edited by Jean-Louis Michon and Roger Gaetani – This anthology contains essays by various scholars on Sufi philosophy, practices, and poets. It covers a wide range of topics and offers both spiritual and academic perspectives on Sufism.

"Mystical Dimensions of Islam" by Annemarie Schimmel – Schimmel, a leading scholar on Islamic mysticism, provides a thorough and engaging overview of Sufi beliefs, practices, and poetry. Her work is highly regarded for its depth and insight into the mystical dimensions of Islam.

Sunni

"In the Footsteps of the Prophet: Lessons from the Life of Muhammad" by Tariq Ramadan – This biography of the Prophet Muhammad is written from a Sunni perspective, highlighting lessons from his life and character that are central to Sunni values and beliefs. Ramadan's accessible style makes this a great introductory book.

"An Introduction to Islamic Law" by Wael B. Hallaq – This book provides a detailed overview of Islamic law, or sharia, with an emphasis on its development within Sunni Islam. Hallaq is a respected scholar, and his work offers insight into how Sunni jurisprudence has shaped Islamic societies.

"The Four Imams: Their Lives, Works and Their Schools of Thought" by Muhammad Abu Zahra – This book covers the lives and teachings of the four major Sunni Imams (Abu Hanifa, Malik, Shafi'i, and Ahmad ibn Hanbal), whose schools of thought (madhabs) form the basis of Sunni jurisprudence. It's a must-read for those interested in Sunni legal traditions.

"The Creed of Imam al-Tahawi" translated by Hamza Yusuf – The Aqidah al-Tahawiyyah is a classical Sunni text summarizing Sunni theology. Hamza Yusuf's translation and commentary make this foundational text accessible to modern readers, exploring core Sunni beliefs about God, prophecy, and the afterlife.

"The Sunni Path: A Handbook of Islamic Belief" by Abdurrahman al-Sheha – This concise guide provides an overview of Sunni beliefs, worship, and practice, including chapters on the five pillars, morality, and key theological concepts. It's a helpful resource for beginners or anyone seeking a clear overview.

"A History of Islamic Societies" by Ira M. Lapidus – Though it covers Islamic societies broadly, this book provides in-depth coverage of the development of Sunni Islam, its institutions, and its spread across the world. It's a valuable resource for understanding Sunni Islam in its historical context.

"Principles of Islamic Jurisprudence" by Mohammad Hashim Kamali – This comprehensive work examines the sources and methods of Sunni jurisprudence (fiqh), such as the Qur'an, Hadith, consensus (ijma), and analogy (qiyas). Kamali's book is scholarly yet accessible, ideal for those interested in Sunni legal theory.

"Revival of the Religious Sciences" by Abu Hamid al-Ghazali, translated by various scholars – Known as Ihya' Ulum al-Din, this classic work by the famous Sunni scholar al-Ghazali covers topics of faith, ethics, and spirituality, aiming to revive Islamic values. It is essential reading for those interested in Sunni spirituality and ethics.

Taoism

"Tao Te Ching" by Lao Tzu, translated by D.C. Lau or Stephen Mitchell – The Tao Te Ching is the foundational text of Taoism, attributed to Lao Tzu. Both Lau and Mitchell provide accessible translations, capturing the essence of Taoist philosophy—emphasizing harmony, balance, and the "Way" (Tao).

"Chuang Tzu: Basic Writings" translated by Burton Watson – This classic collection of writings by Zhuangzi (Chuang Tzu) offers a unique perspective on Taoist philosophy, focusing on spontaneity, freedom, and the nature of reality. Watson's translation is highly regarded for its readability and insight.

"The Book of Lieh-Tzu" translated by A.C. Graham – Lieh Tzu is one of the lesser-known but essential Taoist texts, filled with parables and stories that illustrate Taoist ideas about nature, simplicity, and cosmic harmony. Graham's translation is thorough and provides helpful context.

"The Tao of Pooh" by Benjamin Hoff – This modern classic uses characters from Winnie-the-Pooh to explain Taoist principles in an accessible, enjoyable way. Hoff's book is ideal for beginners, introducing Taoism through storytelling and relatable examples.

"Understanding the Chinese Mind: The Philosophical Roots" by Robert E. Allinson – Allinson provides an overview of Chinese philosophy, focusing on Taoism's role and influence. This book is helpful for understanding Taoism in relation to other Chinese philosophies, like Confucianism and Buddhism.

"The Secret of the Golden Flower: A Chinese Book of Life" translated by Thomas Cleary – This ancient Taoist text focuses on meditation and inner alchemy, exploring Taoist practices for spiritual and personal development. Cleary's translation includes insights into Taoist mysticism and meditation techniques.

"Taoism: An Essential Guide" by Eva Wong – Wong offers a comprehensive introduction to Taoism, covering its philosophy, religious practices, and historical development. She provides an overview of both philosophical Taoism and religious Taoism, making it a well-rounded resource.

"Lao Tzu and the Tao Te Ching" by Livia Kohn – This scholarly work explores the historical background and philosophical themes of the Tao Te Ching. Kohn also discusses how Taoism evolved over time, making this book a good choice for readers interested in both the text and its broader impact.

Unitarian Universalist

"A Chosen Faith: An Introduction to Unitarian Universalism" by John A. Buehrens and Forrest Church. Written by two prominent UU ministers, this book serves as a foundational introduction to Unitarian Universalism. It explores the faith's core principles, its historical development, and the diverse beliefs held within the community.

"The Unitarian Universalist Pocket Guide" (Edited by Susan Frederick-Gray). This concise guide is perfect for those looking for an overview of Unitarian Universalist beliefs, history, and practices. It includes essays from various UU thinkers and leaders, making it an accessible and informative resource.

"A House for Hope: The Promise of Progressive Religion for the Twenty-First Century" by John A. Buehrens and Rebecca Ann Parker. This book offers a theological perspective on Unitarian Universalism, emphasizing its progressive values and relevance in today's world. It explores themes like justice, community, and spirituality, making it an inspiring read for those interested in the UU approach to faith.

Voodoo

"Mama Lola: A Vodou Priestess in Brooklyn" by Karen McCarthy Brown – This well-regarded ethnographic work tells the story of Mama Lola, a Haitian Vodou priestess living in Brooklyn, New York. Brown's book offers a personal look into Vodou practices, beliefs, and the community around Mama Lola, making it accessible and insightful.

"Vodou Visions: An Encounter with Divine Mystery" by Sallie Ann Glassman – A respected New Orleans Voodoo practitioner, Glassman provides a practical guide to Vodou, covering rituals, spirituality, and the pantheon of Vodou spirits (lwa). This book is a good introduction to the mystical aspects of Voodoo.

"The Spirits and the Law: Vodou and Power in Haiti" by Kate Ramsey – This historical and legal study explores how Haitian Vodou has been shaped by and resisted colonial and state authorities. Ramsey provides a well-researched look at Vodou's resilience and its significance in Haitian culture and politics.

"Divine Horsemen: The Living Gods of Haiti" by Maya Deren – Filmmaker and anthropologist Maya Deren's work is a classic exploration of Haitian Vodou. Based on Deren's own experiences in Haiti, the book covers the spiritual and ritual life in Vodou, including the role of spirit possession.

"Haitian Vodou: An Introduction to Haiti's Indigenous Spiritual Tradition" by Mambo Chita Tann – This accessible introduction to Haitian Vodou covers beliefs, spirits, and the structure of Vodou ceremonies, written by a Haitian Vodou priestess. It's a great starting point for those new to Vodou.

"The Voodoo Hoodoo Spellbook" by Denise Alvarado – Focusing on New Orleans Voodoo, Alvarado's book explores the intersection of Voodoo with Hoodoo folk magic, including spells, recipes, and traditional practices. This book provides insights into the folk magic side of New Orleans Voodoo culture.

"Serving the Spirits: The Religion of Haitian Vodou" by Hector Salva – Written by a Vodou priest, this book covers the basics of Vodou practice, the role of the lwa (spirits), and how practitioners serve the spirits. Salva's work provides a practical and respectful introduction to Haitian Vodou.

"Secrets of Voodoo" by Milo Rigaud – Rigaud provides an in-depth look at the religious philosophy and symbols of Vodou, offering insights into its African roots and the spiritual and ethical principles at its core. This book is more academic, suitable for readers looking for a deeper, philosophical approach.

Yingyangjia

"The Book of Changes (I Ching): A Guide to Life's Turning Points" translated by Richard Wilhelm – The I Ching is one of the foundational texts that incorporates Yin-Yang theory in its divinatory system. Wilhelm's translation includes commentary that explains the principles of Yin and Yang as they relate to change and harmony in life.

"The Dao of Chinese Medicine: Understanding an Ancient Healing Art" by Donald E. Kendall – This book explores how Yin-Yang and Five Elements theory are integrated into Chinese medicine, detailing their use in diagnosing and treating health conditions. Kendall's work is ideal for those interested in the practical application of Yin-Yang in medicine.

"Yin-Yang and Five Elements: A Guide to Understanding Traditional Chinese Medicine" by Zhu Wenjun – Zhu provides an accessible introduction to Yin-Yang theory and the Five Elements, focusing on their roles in Chinese medicine and holistic health. This is an excellent book for beginners looking to understand the foundational principles.

"The Tao of Symbols: How to Understand and Use the Five Elements and Yin-Yang" by Chung-yuan Chang – This book offers a deep dive into the symbolic and philosophical aspects of Yin-Yang and the Five Elements. Chang explores their applications across various aspects of life, including art, culture, and personal development.

"Yin-Yang: The Philosophy of Opposites and the Natural Order" by Evelyn Lip – Lip's book provides a historical overview of Yin-Yang philosophy and how it influenced Chinese thought, art, architecture, and everyday life. It's accessible and well-suited for readers new to the concept.

"The Complete I Ching: The Definitive Translation" by Taoist Master Alfred Huang – Huang's translation of the I Ching includes commentary that emphasizes the role of Yin-Yang in understanding life's cyclical changes. It's a useful resource for understanding how Yin-Yang concepts were woven into early Chinese philosophy.

"The Five Elements: Understand Yourself and Enhance Your Relationships with the Wisdom of the World's Oldest Personality Type System" by Dondi Dahlin – While not exclusively about the Yin-Yang school, this book explores how the Five Elements system, closely tied to Yin-Yang theory, can help in understanding personality and improving relationships.

"Heavenly Stems and Earthly Branches: TianGan DiZhi" by Zhongxian Wu – This book provides an in-depth look at the Heavenly Stems and Earthly Branches system, which incorporates Yin-Yang theory and the Five Elements. It's particularly valuable for those interested in the astrological and cosmological aspects of Yin-Yang thought.

Zoroastrianism

"Zoroastrians: Their Religious Beliefs and Practices" by Mary Boyce – This is one of the most comprehensive and respected books on Zoroastrianism. Boyce covers the history, theology, and practices of Zoroastrianism, providing insight into how it has developed from ancient Persia to the modern era.

"The Zend-Avesta: The Sacred Books of the East, Volume 4" translated by James Darmesteter – The Avesta is the primary collection of sacred texts in Zoroastrianism. Darmesteter's translation provides access to Zoroastrian prayers, hymns, and teachings, making it essential for understanding Zoroastrian beliefs.

"The Teachings of Zoroaster and the Philosophy of the Parsi Religion" by S. A. Kapadia – This classic work is an accessible overview of the core teachings of Zoroaster (Zarathustra) and the beliefs of the Parsi community, one of the main groups practicing Zoroastrianism today.

"A History of Zoroastrianism" (3-volume series) by Mary Boyce and Frantz Grenet – This scholarly series traces Zoroastrianism's development from its origins to its later influence on other religions. It's ideal for readers looking for a deep, academic approach to Zoroastrian history and evolution.

"In Search of Zoroaster" by Paul Kriwaczek – Kriwaczek explores Zoroastrianism's history from ancient Persia to its influence on Western religions, offering a narrative approach that makes the book accessible and engaging for general readers.

"Zoroastrianism: An Introduction" by Jenny Rose – Rose provides a beginner-friendly introduction to Zoroastrian beliefs, rituals, and cultural practices. This book is concise yet thorough, making it ideal for those new to the subject.

"The Zoroastrian Faith: Tradition and Modern Research" by Solomon A. Nigosian – Nigosian's book explores Zoroastrianism from both a historical and modern perspective, covering key beliefs, sacred texts, and Zoroastrianism's influence on other religions.

"Zarathustra: A God That Can Dance" by Osho – Although not a traditional historical or religious text, Osho's book offers an interpretation of Zoroaster's teachings with a focus on spirituality and self-awareness. It's more philosophical and aimed at readers interested in applying Zoroastrian principles to personal growth.

Philosopher

Aristotle

"Aristotle: The Nicomachean Ethics" translated by Terence Irwin – This is one of Aristotle's most influential works, focusing on ethics, virtue, and the good life. Irwin's translation is clear and provides helpful commentary, making Aristotle's thoughts on human nature and happiness accessible to modern readers.

"Aristotle's 'Politics': A New Translation" by C.D.C. Reeve – Aristotle's Politics explores the nature of society, government, and citizenship, ideas that continue to be foundational in political theory. Reeve's translation includes an introduction and notes that provide valuable context for understanding Aristotle's views on politics and governance.

"Aristotle: A Very Short Introduction" by Jonathan Barnes – For a concise overview, Barnes's book offers an accessible introduction to Aristotle's life, major works, and key philosophical contributions across topics like metaphysics, ethics, and logic. This book is ideal for those new to Aristotle and serves as a guide to his thought and influence.

Augustine

"Confessions" by Saint Augustine, translated by Henry Chadwick –
Confessions is Augustine's spiritual autobiography and one of his most
famous works, exploring his journey from a life of sin to faith. Chadwick's
translation is both accessible and accurate, making this a foundational text
for understanding Augustine's views on God, human nature, and conversion.

"The City of God" by Saint Augustine, translated by Marcus Dods – This
monumental work addresses the role of Christianity in society and history,
contrasting the "City of God" with the "City of Man." Dods' translation
captures Augustine's arguments on theology, politics, and philosophy,
making it essential reading for those interested in Augustine's vision of a
Christian society.

"Augustine of Hippo: A Biography" by Peter Brown – Brown's biography is
widely regarded as the definitive work on Augustine's life, offering an in-
depth exploration of his writings, ideas, and the historical context that
shaped his thought. This book is ideal for readers who want a
comprehensive view of Augustine's intellectual and spiritual journey.

Buber

"I and Thou" by Martin Buber – This is Buber's most famous work, in which
he introduces his philosophy of dialogue, exploring the nature of human
relationships and the distinction between "I-Thou" (genuine, reciprocal
relationships) and "I-It" (objectified interactions). This book is foundational
for understanding Buber's ideas on human connection, God, and existence.

"The Way of Man: According to the Teachings of Hasidism" by Martin Buber
– In this short but profound book, Buber draws on Hasidic teachings to
explore themes of self-discovery, spirituality, and the journey to a
meaningful life. It's a wonderful introduction to his integration of Hasidic
wisdom with his existentialist approach, and it's accessible for readers new
to Buber.

"Martin Buber: A Life of Faith and Dissent" by Paul Mendes-Flohr – This
biography provides a detailed look at Buber's life, intellectual journey, and
contributions to philosophy, theology, and politics. Mendes-Flohr places
Buber's work in the context of 20th-century history, making it ideal for
readers interested in understanding the man behind the ideas and his
impact on modern thought.

Descartes

"Meditations on First Philosophy" by René Descartes, translated by Donald
A. Cress – This foundational text is where Descartes introduces his method

of doubt, the famous phrase "I think, therefore I am" (Cogito, ergo sum), and his arguments for the existence of God and the nature of reality. Cress's translation is accessible and includes helpful notes, making it an excellent choice for understanding Descartes' core ideas.

"Descartes: An Intellectual Biography" by Stephen Gaukroger – Gaukroger's biography provides a comprehensive look at Descartes' life, intellectual development, and the historical context of his work. It's particularly insightful for those interested in how Descartes' scientific and philosophical ideas evolved and influenced each other.

"Descartes: A Very Short Introduction" by Tom Sorell – Sorell's concise book is an accessible introduction to Descartes' philosophy, covering his major works, philosophical contributions, and lasting impact on modern thought. It's ideal for beginners seeking a quick but thorough overview of Descartes' key ideas and legacy.

Dewey

"Democracy and Education" by John Dewey – This is Dewey's most influential work on education, where he argues that education should be a democratic process focused on experiential learning and personal growth. The book outlines his ideas on how education and democracy are interconnected, making it essential reading for understanding Dewey's educational philosophy.

"Experience and Nature" by John Dewey – In this major philosophical work, Dewey explores the concept of experience as foundational to human understanding, bridging naturalism and pragmatism. This book provides a deep dive into Dewey's views on how experience shapes perception, thought, and the relationship between humans and nature.

"The Later Works of John Dewey, Volume 1: 1925–1953, Experience and Education" edited by Jo Ann Boydston – This volume in the collected works series includes Experience and Education, a concise summary of Dewey's ideas on education and experience. Written later in his career, it clarifies and refines his views, making it accessible for readers new to Dewey's educational philosophy.

Hume

"An Enquiry Concerning Human Understanding" by David Hume – This is one of Hume's most influential works, where he presents his ideas on empiricism, causation, and skepticism about human knowledge. It's accessible and offers a clear introduction to Hume's core arguments, including his famous "problem of induction."

"A Treatise of Human Nature" by David Hume – In this comprehensive work, Hume develops his philosophy of human psychology, emotions, and moral theory. Although more challenging, it's essential for understanding the depth of Hume's thoughts on reason, passion, and human nature. This is foundational for anyone seeking to dive deeply into his philosophy.

"Hume: A Very Short Introduction" by A.J. Ayer – This concise book by Ayer provides a quick and accessible overview of Hume's life, major works, and key ideas. Ayer, a philosopher influenced by Hume, explains Hume's contributions in a clear and engaging way, making it ideal for readers new to Hume's thought.

Jung

"Man and His Symbols" by Carl Jung and others – This accessible book was written for the general reader and provides an introduction to Jung's key ideas on symbolism, the collective unconscious, and archetypes. It includes contributions from Jung and his followers, making it a great entry point into his theories.

"The Archetypes and The Collective Unconscious" by Carl Jung – Part of Jung's Collected Works, this book delves into his concepts of archetypes (such as the Self, the Shadow, and the Anima/Animus) and the collective unconscious. It's fundamental for understanding Jung's theories on how universal symbols shape human psychology.

"Memories, Dreams, Reflections" by Carl Jung, recorded and edited by Aniela Jaffé – This autobiographical work offers personal insights into Jung's life, spiritual experiences, and the development of his psychological theories. It's a unique combination of autobiography and philosophy, giving readers a deeper understanding of Jung's inner world and intellectual journey.

Kant

"Critique of Pure Reason" by Immanuel Kant, translated by Paul Guyer and Allen W. Wood – This foundational text introduces Kant's groundbreaking ideas on epistemology and metaphysics, including his concepts of a priori knowledge and the "categories of understanding." Guyer and Wood's translation is highly regarded and includes helpful notes for readers tackling this challenging work.

"Groundwork for the Metaphysics of Morals" by Immanuel Kant, translated by Mary Gregor and Jens Timmermann – This is Kant's key work on ethics, where he introduces the concept of the "categorical imperative" and his ideas on moral duty and autonomy. It's a more accessible text than the Critique of Pure Reason and essential for understanding Kant's ethical philosophy.

"Kant: A Very Short Introduction" by Roger Scruton – This concise book by philosopher Roger Scruton provides an accessible overview of Kant's life, ideas, and major works. Scruton explains Kant's contributions to epistemology, ethics, and aesthetics in clear terms, making it ideal for beginners.

Leonardo

"Leonardo da Vinci" by Walter Isaacson – This comprehensive biography draws from Leonardo's extensive notebooks and provides a rich portrayal of his life, art, and scientific pursuits. Isaacson's engaging storytelling makes this a highly accessible and informative read, perfect for those looking for a well-rounded view of Leonardo's genius.

"Leonardo da Vinci: The Complete Paintings and Drawings" by Frank Zöllner and Johannes Nathan – This beautifully illustrated volume is ideal for art lovers, offering high-quality reproductions and detailed analyses of Leonardo's artworks and sketches. Zöllner and Nathan provide context for each piece, giving readers a deep appreciation of Leonardo's artistic process and innovations.

"Leonardo da Vinci Notebooks" selected and translated by Irma A. Richter, edited by Martin Kemp – This book presents a selection of Leonardo's personal writings and sketches, covering a range of subjects, from anatomy and engineering to philosophy and art. It offers a unique window into his mind, showing his diverse interests and methodical approach to understanding the world.

Locke

"An Essay Concerning Human Understanding" by John Locke – This is Locke's most influential philosophical work, where he develops his theory of knowledge and ideas, arguing against innate knowledge and laying the foundation for empiricism. It's essential for understanding Locke's views on the nature of the human mind, perception, and knowledge.

"Two Treatises of Government" by John Locke – In this seminal political work, Locke presents his arguments on natural rights, the social contract, and government legitimacy, laying the groundwork for modern democratic theory. It's particularly famous for its influence on political thought, especially in the development of liberalism and concepts like life, liberty, and property.

"Locke: A Very Short Introduction" by John Dunn – For those seeking an accessible overview, this book by renowned Locke scholar John Dunn provides a concise introduction to Locke's life, major works, and philosophical contributions. Dunn covers Locke's theories on knowledge, personal identity, politics, and religion in a straightforward manner, making it ideal for beginners.

Luther

"Here I Stand: A Life of Martin Luther" by Roland H. Bainton – This classic biography is one of the most accessible and engaging accounts of Luther's life. Bainton combines historical context with Luther's personal struggles and theological battles, making it an excellent starting point for understanding Luther's role in the Reformation.

"The Bondage of the Will" by Martin Luther, translated by J.I. Packer and O.R. Johnston – This work is one of Luther's most important theological writings, in which he argues against free will in matters of salvation and defends the doctrine of predestination. It's essential reading for those interested in Luther's theological ideas and his debates with Erasmus, a prominent Catholic scholar.

"Martin Luther: Visionary Reformer" by Scott H. Hendrix – This biography provides a well-rounded and modern perspective on Luther, exploring his life, beliefs, and the social and political environment of his time. Hendrix's work is accessible and offers fresh insights into how Luther's reforms reshaped religious and cultural landscapes.

Maimonides

"The Guide for the Perplexed" by Moses Maimonides, translated by Shlomo Pines – This is Maimonides' most famous work, addressing the relationship between philosophy and religion, the nature of God, and the purpose of the Torah. Pines' translation includes an extensive introduction that provides helpful context, making it ideal for understanding Maimonides' complex ideas.

"Maimonides: Life and Thought" by Moshe Halbertal – This accessible biography provides a thorough overview of Maimonides' life, intellectual influences, and lasting impact on Jewish thought. Halbertal explores Maimonides' contributions to philosophy, Jewish law, and ethics, offering readers a well-rounded understanding of his legacy.

"Maimonides" by Herbert A. Davidson – Davidson's book is a comprehensive academic study that delves into Maimonides' philosophy, theology, and interpretation of Jewish law. It's a well-researched work that covers Maimonides' intellectual development and provides insight into his ideas on reason, faith, and the nature of the divine.

Marx

"Capital: Volume 1" by Karl Marx – This is Marx's seminal work on political economy, where he critiques capitalism, explores labor theory, and introduces concepts like surplus value and commodity fetishism. It's foundational for understanding Marx's economic theories and the workings of capitalist society.

"The Communist Manifesto" by Karl Marx and Friedrich Engels – This short, accessible text is one of the most influential political documents in history. It outlines Marx and Engels' vision of class struggle, the role of the proletariat, and the call for revolutionary change, making it essential reading for those new to Marxist thought.

"Karl Marx: A Nineteenth-Century Life" by Jonathan Sperber – Sperber's biography provides a comprehensive look at Marx's life and intellectual development within the context of 19th-century Europe. It's an insightful exploration of Marx's influences and personal experiences, offering a nuanced view of the man behind the ideas.

Nietzsche

"Thus Spoke Zarathustra" by Friedrich Nietzsche – This is one of Nietzsche's most famous and influential works, written in a poetic, allegorical style. It introduces key concepts such as the Übermensch (Overman), the eternal recurrence, and the will to power, making it essential for understanding Nietzsche's vision of human potential and self-overcoming.

"Beyond Good and Evil" by Friedrich Nietzsche – In this work, Nietzsche critiques traditional morality, explores the nature of truth, and introduces his ideas on perspectivism and the psychology of philosophers. It's one of Nietzsche's more accessible works and provides a solid foundation in his critiques of conventional morality and societal norms.

"Nietzsche: A Very Short Introduction" by Michael Tanner – This concise introduction to Nietzsche's life and philosophy is accessible and well-suited for beginners. Tanner provides an overview of Nietzsche's major ideas, including his views on morality, religion, and culture, making it an excellent starting point for those new to Nietzsche's thought.

Pascal

"Pensées" by Blaise Pascal – Pensées is Pascal's most famous work, a collection of philosophical and theological fragments that explore human nature, faith, and reason. This unfinished masterpiece addresses the limits of human knowledge, the "wager" on God's existence, and the tension between reason and faith. Many translations exist, but Peter Kreeft's version includes helpful commentary and is widely appreciated for its accessibility.

"The Mystery of Pascal" by Henri de Lubac – This influential book by Catholic theologian Henri de Lubac explores Pascal's religious thought, particularly his critiques of rationalism and defense of Christian faith. De Lubac provides context for Pascal's intense spirituality and highlights the depth of his philosophical reflections on faith, doubt, and the human condition.

"Blaise Pascal: Reasons of the Heart" by Marvin R. O'Connell – O'Connell's biography gives a comprehensive view of Pascal's life, intellectual achievements, and religious conversion, placing his thoughts within the context of 17th-century France. It's an accessible and engaging introduction to both Pascal's scientific accomplishments and his spiritual journey.

Philo

"The Works of Philo" translated by C.D. Yonge – This comprehensive collection includes most of Philo's surviving works, covering his interpretations of Jewish scripture through the lens of Greek philosophy, especially Platonism and Stoicism. Yonge's translation is accessible, making it an excellent resource for those wanting to engage directly with Philo's writings.

"Philo of Alexandria: An Introduction to the Jewish Exegesis and Philosophical Thought of Philo" by Samuel Sandmel – Sandmel's book provides an accessible overview of Philo's life, thought, and influence on both Jewish and early Christian thought. It's a great introduction for readers new to Philo, presenting his ideas within the context of both Jewish tradition and Hellenistic philosophy.

"Philo of Alexandria and the Construction of Jewish and Christian Identity" by Maren R. Niehoff – Niehoff explores Philo's influence on both Jewish and early Christian identity formation, showing how his work bridged Jewish theology and Greek philosophy. This scholarly book is ideal for readers interested in understanding Philo's long-lasting impact on both traditions.

Plato

"The Republic" by Plato, translated by Allan Bloom or Benjamin Jowett – The Republic is Plato's most famous and influential work, where he discusses justice, the ideal society, and the philosopher-king. This foundational text introduces key concepts like the Theory of Forms, the Allegory of the Cave, and the nature of knowledge and reality. Bloom's translation is widely respected for its clarity and faithfulness to the original.

"Plato: A Very Short Introduction" by Julia Annas – Annas provides a concise and accessible overview of Plato's life, major ideas, and philosophical contributions. This introduction covers Plato's metaphysics, ethics, political philosophy, and his lasting influence, making it ideal for beginners.

"Plato Complete Works," edited by John M. Cooper and D.S. Hutchinson – This comprehensive collection includes all of Plato's dialogues and letters, with translations by various respected scholars. It's an invaluable resource for readers who want to explore the full range of Plato's thought, from early dialogues to more complex works like The Laws and The Timaeus.

Pythagoras

"Pythagoras: His Life, Teaching, and Influence" by Christoph Riedweg – This accessible biography provides a comprehensive overview of what we know about Pythagoras, his teachings, and his influence on mathematics, philosophy, and spirituality. Riedweg sifts through historical sources to present a balanced view of Pythagoras' life and the origins of his ideas.

"The Pythagorean Sourcebook and Library: An Anthology of Ancient Writings" translated and compiled by Kenneth Sylvan Guthrie – This anthology includes primary texts on Pythagorean thought, including writings attributed to Pythagoras and his followers. It covers themes in mathematics, mysticism, and philosophy, making it an excellent resource for readers wanting direct access to Pythagorean teachings and later interpretations.

"The Pythagorean Theory of Music and Color" by Joscelyn Godwin – This book explores the mystical and philosophical aspects of Pythagoras' work, particularly his theories on the harmony of music and color, and their connection to mathematical principles. Godwin's analysis highlights how Pythagoras' influence extended into fields beyond mathematics, offering a unique perspective on his holistic approach to knowledge.

Sartre

"Being and Nothingness" by Jean-Paul Sartre – This is Sartre's magnum opus and a foundational text of existentialist philosophy. In it, Sartre explores concepts such as freedom, bad faith, consciousness, and human existence. While dense, it's essential for understanding Sartre's ideas on freedom, selfhood, and the nature of existence.

"Existentialism Is a Humanism" by Jean-Paul Sartre – Originally a lecture given by Sartre, this short book provides an accessible overview of existentialism and defends its core principles. Sartre addresses common criticisms and explains key concepts like freedom, responsibility, and the idea that "existence precedes essence," making it a great starting point for newcomers.

"Sartre: A Very Short Introduction" by Christina Howells – Howells provides a concise and approachable introduction to Sartre's life, philosophical works, and literary contributions. Covering his ideas in philosophy, literature, and politics, this book is perfect for readers new to Sartre and those seeking a broad overview of his influence.

Socrates

"The Trial and Death of Socrates" by Plato – This collection includes four of Plato's most famous dialogues: Euthyphro, Apology, Crito, and Phaedo, which recount Socrates' trial, his defense, his views on justice, and his final moments. These dialogues offer a powerful portrait of Socrates' ideas on morality, virtue, and the examined life, as well as his willingness to die for his beliefs.

"Socrates: A Very Short Introduction" by C.C.W. Taylor – Taylor's concise introduction provides an accessible overview of Socrates' life, philosophy, and influence. Covering what we know from sources like Plato, Xenophon, and Aristotle, this book is ideal for readers seeking a quick yet thorough introduction to Socratic thought and his unique approach to questioning.

"Socrates: A Man for Our Times" by Paul Johnson – Johnson's biography combines historical context with philosophical analysis to bring Socrates to life as a person and thinker. This engaging and accessible book explores Socrates' impact on Western thought and the timeless nature of his philosophical questions, making it suitable for both beginners and those familiar with his philosophy.

Tzu

"The Art of War" by Sun Tzu, translated by Thomas Cleary – This is the foundational text itself, providing Sun Tzu's timeless principles on strategy, conflict resolution, and leadership. Cleary's translation is accessible and includes insightful commentary, making it ideal for readers who want a clear understanding of Sun Tzu's strategies.

"The Art of War: A New Translation" by Michael Nylan – This recent translation by sinologist Michael Nylan offers a fresh perspective on The Art of War, with updated language and historical context that illuminate the philosophical underpinnings of Sun Tzu's work. Nylan provides commentary that connects Sun Tzu's ideas to broader Chinese philosophy, making it a great choice for readers interested in the cultural context.

"The Mind of War: John Boyd and American Security" by Grant T. Hammond – While not exclusively about Sun Tzu, this book examines how Sun Tzu's strategies have influenced modern military thinkers, particularly American strategist John Boyd. Hammond's analysis demonstrates the relevance of Sun Tzu's ideas in contemporary military strategy and international relations.

Voltaire

"Candide, or Optimism" by Voltaire – Candide is Voltaire's most famous work, a satirical novella that critiques blind optimism, religious hypocrisy, and societal injustice. It's essential reading for understanding Voltaire's wit, his criticisms of philosophical optimism (especially that of Leibniz), and his advocacy for reason and tolerance.

"Voltaire: A Life" by Ian Davidson – Davidson's biography provides an in-depth look at Voltaire's life, intellectual journey, and the social and political contexts in which he wrote. This comprehensive and engaging account gives readers insight into Voltaire's struggles, his influence on the Enlightenment, and his contributions to literature and philosophy.

"Voltaire in Exile: The Last Years, 1753-1778" by Ian Davidson – This book focuses on Voltaire's later years, a period when he lived in exile and was particularly active in his critiques of intolerance and injustice. Davidson explores how Voltaire's later works, letters, and activism solidified his reputation as a fierce advocate for civil liberties, making this book ideal for understanding Voltaire's legacy as a social critic.

Voices

Carlson

"Ship of Fools: How a Selfish Ruling Class Is Bringing America to the Brink of Revolution" by Tucker Carlson – In this book, Carlson offers a critique of America's political and cultural elite, arguing that their policies have harmed ordinary Americans. Carlson examines issues like economic inequality, immigration, and media bias, providing insight into his political perspective and criticisms of both major parties.

"The Long Slide: Thirty Years in American Journalism" by Tucker Carlson – This collection of Carlson's essays, written over three decades, covers a wide range of topics from his career in journalism. It provides a unique look into his evolving views, including his commentary on media, politics, and culture, giving readers insight into how his thinking and public persona have developed.

"Tucker" by Chadwick Moore (Upcoming Biography) – Set to be published soon, this biography by journalist Chadwick Moore promises an in-depth look at Carlson's life and career, exploring his rise to fame, his influence on

American conservative media, and his personal and professional experiences. This book is expected to offer a comprehensive view of Carlson's background and impact.

Chomsky

"Syntactic Structures" by Noam Chomsky – This groundbreaking 1957 book revolutionized linguistics by introducing Chomsky's theory of transformational grammar, which explores the deep structure of language and the human capacity for language acquisition. It's foundational for understanding Chomsky's impact on linguistics and his theory of a "universal grammar."

"Manufacturing Consent: The Political Economy of the Mass Media" by Edward S. Herman and Noam Chomsky – Co-authored with economist Edward Herman, this influential work critiques mainstream media's role in shaping public perception to serve elite interests. Chomsky's analysis of media as a "propaganda model" is essential for understanding his views on media, politics, and power.

"Who Rules the World?" by Noam Chomsky – This collection of essays provides Chomsky's insights into global politics, U.S. foreign policy, economic inequality, and the impact of corporate power. It's an accessible entry into his political philosophy and critiques of state and corporate power on a global scale.

Davis

"An Autobiography" by Angela Y. Davis – In this powerful autobiography, Davis reflects on her life as a political activist, scholar, and revolutionary. She provides a firsthand account of her experiences with racial injustice, imprisonment, and the fight for civil rights, offering readers an intimate look at her journey and the events that shaped her beliefs.

"Are Prisons Obsolete?" by Angela Y. Davis – This seminal work is one of Davis's most influential books on the prison-industrial complex. She critiques the prison system in the United States, explores alternatives to incarceration, and argues for prison abolition. It's essential for understanding her views on justice, reform, and the impact of mass incarceration on marginalized communities.

"Freedom Is a Constant Struggle: Ferguson, Palestine, and the Foundations of a Movement" by Angela Y. Davis – This collection of essays and speeches connects struggles for freedom and justice across the globe. Davis discusses the interconnectedness of issues like police violence, racism, and occupation, making it an important read for understanding her internationalist approach to social justice.

Dawkins

"The Selfish Gene" by Richard Dawkins – This groundbreaking book introduces Dawkins's concept of the "selfish gene," which suggests that natural selection operates at the level of genes rather than individuals or species. It's a foundational text for understanding evolutionary biology and Dawkins's perspective on natural selection and altruism.

"The God Delusion" by Richard Dawkins – One of Dawkins's most well-known works, The God Delusion presents a passionate critique of religion and a defense of atheism. Dawkins explores arguments against the existence of God, critiques religious belief, and advocates for a secular, scientific worldview. It's a key text in contemporary atheism.

"The Greatest Show on Earth: The Evidence for Evolution" by Richard Dawkins – In this book, Dawkins provides an accessible and comprehensive explanation of the evidence supporting evolution. He presents examples from the fossil record, genetics, and other fields, making it ideal for readers interested in understanding evolution and Dawkins's arguments for its scientific validity.

Gandhi

"The Story of My Experiments with Truth" by Mahatma Gandhi – This autobiography provides an intimate look at Gandhi's life, including his personal challenges, spiritual development, and experiments with truth and nonviolence. It's foundational for understanding his philosophy of satyagraha (truth-force) and his commitment to social and political change through nonviolence.

"Gandhi: An Autobiography - The Story of My Experiments with Truth" edited by Mahadev Desai – Edited by Mahadev Desai, one of Gandhi's closest associates, this version of Gandhi's autobiography includes additional context and commentary, helping readers understand Gandhi's journey, from his early years in India to his activism in South Africa and leadership in India's struggle for independence.

"Gandhi and Churchill: The Epic Rivalry that Destroyed an Empire and Forged Our Age" by Arthur Herman – This dual biography provides a broader historical perspective, examining the contrasting lives and philosophies of Gandhi and Winston Churchill. Herman's work captures the larger geopolitical context of Gandhi's life, showing how his ideas on nonviolence and independence shaped, and were shaped by, the global political landscape.

Hawking

"A Brief History of Time" by Stephen Hawking – This classic book is one of the most popular science books of all time, where Hawking explores fundamental questions about the universe, such as the nature of time, black holes, and the Big Bang. Written for a general audience, it's essential for understanding Hawking's contributions to cosmology and his talent for explaining complex ideas in accessible terms.

"The Universe in a Nutshell" by Stephen Hawking – In this visually rich sequel to A Brief History of Time, Hawking delves deeper into theoretical physics topics, including string theory, supergravity, and the nature of space-time. The book combines detailed illustrations with Hawking's insights, making it ideal for readers interested in advanced concepts in cosmology.

"Stephen Hawking: A Memoir of Friendship and Physics" by Leonard Mlodinow – Written by physicist Leonard Mlodinow, who co-authored The Grand Design with Hawking, this memoir offers a personal look at Hawking's life, work, and personality. Mlodinow provides insights into Hawking's scientific contributions as well as his perseverance and sense of humor, making it a compelling read for those interested in the person behind the theories.

Hitler

"Hitler" by Ian Kershaw – This two-volume biography (Hubris and Nemesis) by historian Ian Kershaw is widely regarded as one of the most comprehensive studies of Hitler. Kershaw provides an in-depth analysis of Hitler's personality, political ascent, and the factors that allowed his ideology to take root in Germany. It's an essential resource for understanding the full scope of Hitler's life and impact.

"Hitler: Ascent 1889-1939" and "Hitler: Downfall 1939-1945" by Volker Ullrich – Ullrich's two-part biography offers a detailed account of Hitler's life, focusing on his political manipulation, charisma, and strategic ruthlessness. Ullrich examines Hitler's rise, his role in shaping Nazi Germany, and the road to World War II and the Holocaust, making these books essential for understanding his complex personality and influence.

"The Rise and Fall of the Third Reich" by William L. Shirer – This classic work, written by journalist William Shirer, provides a comprehensive history of Nazi Germany, with detailed insights into Hitler's rule and the structure of the Third Reich. Based on Shirer's experiences as a foreign correspondent in Germany and extensive access to German documents after the war, this book is considered one of the definitive accounts of the Nazi regime.

King

"Martin Luther King Jr.: A Life" by Marshall Frady – This concise biography offers an insightful overview of King's life, from his early years and rise as a civil rights leader to his assassination. Frady captures King's passion, challenges, and achievements, making this an accessible introduction to his life and legacy.

"Parting the Waters: America in the King Years 1954-1963" by Taylor Branch – This Pulitzer Prize-winning book is the first volume of Taylor Branch's trilogy on the civil rights movement, focusing on King's early activism and leadership. Branch's work provides a detailed look at King's role in major events like the Montgomery Bus Boycott and the Birmingham Campaign, placing them within the broader context of the civil rights movement.

"A Testament of Hope: The Essential Writings and Speeches of Martin Luther King Jr." edited by James M. Washington – This comprehensive collection includes King's most important speeches, sermons, and writings, such as "I Have a Dream," "Letter from Birmingham Jail," and his Nobel Prize acceptance speech. It's an invaluable resource for understanding King's philosophy, faith, and vision for social justice.

LaVey

"The Satanic Bible" by Anton Szandor LaVey – Published in 1969, this foundational text outlines LaVey's philosophy of modern Satanism, emphasizing individualism, self-empowerment, and skepticism of traditional religious values. It's essential for understanding LaVey's redefinition of Satanism as a secular, philosophical worldview rather than a belief in the supernatural.

"The Secret Life of a Satanist: The Authorized Biography of Anton LaVey" by Blanche Barton – Written by LaVey's longtime partner and high priestess of the Church of Satan, Blanche Barton, this biography provides an inside look at LaVey's life, beliefs, and the formation of the Church of Satan. Barton explores both his public persona and private life, offering insights into the man behind the philosophy.

"The Church of Satan: A History of the World's Most Notorious Religion" by Blanche Barton – This comprehensive history, also by Barton, traces the development of the Church of Satan from its founding in 1966 to its influence on popular culture and alternative spirituality. The book covers the organization's key figures, rituals, and philosophical evolution, making it ideal for those interested in the movement's impact.

Montessori

"The Montessori Method" by Maria Montessori – This foundational book introduces Montessori's revolutionary approach to education, emphasizing child-centered learning, independence, and the importance of a prepared environment. It's essential reading for understanding her core principles and the origins of the Montessori method.

"The Absorbent Mind" by Maria Montessori – In this book, Montessori explains her insights into early childhood development, including her concept of the "absorbent mind," which describes how young children naturally absorb knowledge from their environment. It's a valuable resource for parents and educators interested in the developmental science behind the Montessori approach.

"Montessori: The Science Behind the Genius" by Angeline Stoll Lillard – This modern analysis examines Montessori's methods in light of current scientific research on child development and learning. Lillard provides evidence-based insights into why the Montessori approach is effective, making this book ideal for those looking to understand Montessori's relevance in contemporary education.

Murray

"The Strange Death of Europe: Immigration, Identity, Islam" by Douglas Murray – This book examines the cultural and political challenges Europe faces, particularly around issues of immigration, national identity, and the influence of Islam. Murray explores themes of multiculturalism, demographic shifts, and the perceived decline of European values, making it a central work for understanding his views on European society.

"The Madness of Crowds: Gender, Race, and Identity" by Douglas Murray – In this book, Murray critiques what he sees as the excesses of identity politics, focusing on issues related to gender, race, and sexual orientation. He argues that identity politics and "social justice" movements have polarized society and fostered divisiveness, making this work essential for understanding his critique of contemporary social trends.

"The War on the West" by Douglas Murray – This more recent book addresses what Murray describes as the cultural self-criticism and attacks on Western values and history, particularly in the realms of academia, media, and politics. He explores topics like colonialism, race, and the perceived devaluation of Western cultural achievements, aiming to provide a defense of Western values.

Peterson

"12 Rules for Life: An Antidote to Chaos" by Jordan B. Peterson – This best-selling book combines psychology, philosophy, and practical advice, presenting twelve rules for living a meaningful and disciplined life. Peterson covers themes like personal responsibility, order, and the importance of truth, making it a foundational text for understanding his philosophy on self-improvement.

"Beyond Order: 12 More Rules for Life" by Jordan B. Peterson – A follow-up to 12 Rules for Life, this book offers twelve additional rules and expands on his ideas around resilience, creativity, and navigating life's complexities. It explores the balance between chaos and order, encouraging readers to seek meaning and growth even in uncertain times.

"Maps of Meaning: The Architecture of Belief" by Jordan B. Peterson – This more academic work explores the structure of beliefs and myths, examining how humans find meaning through stories, symbols, and archetypes. Drawing on psychology, mythology, and philosophy, this book provides the intellectual foundation for many of Peterson's later ideas and is ideal for readers interested in a deeper exploration of his theories.

Rand

"Atlas Shrugged" by Ayn Rand – This epic novel is Rand's magnum opus, encapsulating her philosophy of Objectivism through a story of industrialists and creators who rebel against a society that demands their sacrifice. Themes of individualism, rational self-interest, and capitalism are central, making this an essential read for understanding her worldview.

"The Fountainhead" by Ayn Rand – This earlier novel explores similar themes through the character of Howard Roark, an innovative architect who refuses to compromise his artistic vision. The Fountainhead focuses on individualism, integrity, and the struggle against societal expectations, offering a powerful introduction to Rand's beliefs about personal independence and creativity.

"Philosophy: Who Needs It" by Ayn Rand – This collection of essays, published posthumously, lays out Rand's views on the importance of philosophy in everyday life. She addresses topics such as ethics, metaphysics, and reason, making it a great resource for readers seeking a direct, non-fictional exploration of her Objectivist philosophy.

Somerville

"The Ethical Imagination: Journeys of the Human Spirit" by Margaret Somerville – This book explores the role of imagination in ethical decision-making, particularly in bioethics. Somerville discusses the importance of respect for life, human dignity, and the environment. It's a great introduction to her approach to ethics and the complexities of moral issues in modern society.

"Death Talk: The Case Against Euthanasia and Physician-Assisted Suicide" by Margaret Somerville – In this book, Somerville argues against euthanasia and physician-assisted suicide, examining the impact these practices could have on society's values and our understanding of life and death. This work is essential for understanding Somerville's perspective on end-of-life ethics and her commitment to the sanctity of life.

"Bird on an Ethics Wire: Battles about Values in the Culture Wars" by Margaret Somerville – This book addresses controversial ethical issues across various fields, including medicine, law, and society. Somerville tackles topics such as euthanasia, genetic engineering, and freedom of speech, offering her reflections on the cultural "values wars" shaping modern society.

Zedong

"Mao: The Unknown Story" by Jung Chang and Jon Halliday – This comprehensive biography offers a critical examination of Mao's life, his rise to power, and the impact of his policies on China. Based on extensive research and interviews, the book paints a detailed, often controversial, portrait of Mao, providing insights into his leadership style and the consequences of his rule.

"On Guerrilla Warfare" by Mao Zedong – Written by Mao himself, this classic text outlines his theories on guerrilla warfare and revolutionary strategy. It provides an understanding of Mao's military tactics and the principles that guided the Communist revolution in China. This work is essential for readers interested in Mao's influence on revolutionary and guerrilla movements worldwide.

"The Private Life of Chairman Mao" by Dr. Li Zhisui – Written by Mao's personal physician, Dr. Li Zhisui, this memoir offers a unique insider's perspective on Mao's private life, personality, and decision-making processes. The book provides an intimate look at Mao's character and the inner workings of his leadership, making it a compelling read for those interested in the man behind the political persona.

Made in United States
Orlando, FL
27 November 2024

54139049R00221